Bringing Down the Mountains

"*Bringing Down the Mountains* is one of the finest books yet regarding mountaintop removal mining and the destruction of the Appalachian culture and environment. Shirley Stewart Burns has written the most comprehensive account of the struggle that has been taking place in the coalfields of southern West Virginia and the long-term ecological and social consequences of mountaintop removal mining. It is a thoroughly researched and eloquent book that brings alive the true voices and great dignity of a courageous people."

JACK SPADARO, FORMER SUPERINTENDENT
OF THE NATIONAL MINE HEALTH AND SAFETY ACADEMY

"Everyone in America should read this important book. Shirley Stewart Burns understands this complex issue intimately, and she eloquently explains it from all the various angles, exposing the horrors of mountaintop removal and the way it is not only destroying the heart of a place and its people, but also affecting everyone. This is the perfect book for anyone who wants to educate themselves on this disturbing, irresponsible, and disrespectful form of Big Business gone awry."

SILAS HOUSE, AUTHOR OF *Clay's Quilt* AND *The Coal Tattoo*

"Written with passion and a sense of urgency, *Bringing Down the Mountains* is one of the most important resources available on the causes and consequences of mountaintop removal. It is historically grounded and well-documented but also remarkably current and accessible. It is always informative and alternately infuriating and inspiring as the author recounts the incestuous power relationships between the coal industry and local and national politicians, and the courage and determination of local people fighting to save their land and heritage. This should be required reading in every high school civics classroom in West Virginia and for all who care about the future of the Appalachian coalfields."

STEPHEN FISHER, EDITOR OF *Fighting Back in Appalachia:*
Traditions of Resistance and Change

"*Bringing Down the Mountains* provides a powerful, fact-filled analysis of controversial mountaintop removal coal mining in the context of more than a century of social, economic and environmental injustice experienced by coalfield communities. Shirley Burns shines a bright light on King Coal and its handmaidens who have exploited the vast mineral wealth of the region, reaping huge profits while coal mining communities continue to experience poverty, high unemployment, and economic distress."

PATRICK McGINLEY,
WEST VIRGINIA UNIVERSITY COLLEGE OF LAW

"*Bringing Down the Mountains* is a clear and impassioned account of the devastation being visited upon the mountains of southern West Virginia by the coal industry. Read it and weep."

DENISE GIARDINA

"The common ground on mountaintop removal is as narrow as the Appalachian hollows being filled in by MTR. Those on both sides of this deep divide, however, will learn something from this highly readable study which analyzes the issue within its political, economic, environmental, and human context. Written from the community perspective, it gives voice to the powerless who are most dramatically affected by this destructive practice."

RONALD L. LEWIS, WEST VIRGINIA UNIVERSITY

"*Bringing Down the Mountains* not only tells the story of coalfield residents' fight against mountaintop removal, but it puts this tale into the important historical context of the continuing fight between West Virginians and outside coal interests over the use—and sometimes abuse—of the state's natural resources. Shirley Stewart Burns reminds readers that West Virginia's history is a long series of fights over who benefits and who is damaged by coal extraction, how the riches created by the coal-based economy are divided, and over who decides the outcome of these vital issues."

KEN WARD JR., *The Charleston Gazette*

"*Bringing Down the Mountains* examines one of the most significant challenges facing the Appalachian region: mountaintop removal coal mining (MTR). Shirley

Burns's timely and comprehensive study provides important analyses of the impact of MTR on the environment, people, and communities of southern West Virginia, including economic costs and benefits. While the analyses of community and environmental impacts represent the core of the book, chapters on the United Mine Workers' role in promoting MTR; the history of legal challenges by citizens; and the relationship between the coal lobby, West Virginia's political leaders, and campaign finances are also indispensable sources of insight and information for scholars, activists, and students. This book is a must-read for anyone who loves the Appalachian Mountains or is concerned about the American environment."

DWIGHT B. BILLINGS, UNIVERSITY OF KENTUCKY

"Too often, critics of mountaintop removal mining in southern West Virginia are thought of as outsiders. Shirley Stewart Burns is a native of the West Virginia coalfields, from a mining family, and in Bringing Down the Mountains she speaks with passion and detailed knowledge. She knows these hills; she knows these people. To this she adds a depth of historical research and the persistence of a journalist. She tells stories that should indeed make us weep, for our mountains and for our own appetites that drive this quest for cheap energy, at any cost. This is truly a case in which history can and should change the future we are currently making."

GREGORY A. GOOD, WEST VIRGINIA UNIVERSITY

"This book is a wake-up call not only for southern West Virginians, but for anyone who uses electricity generated from coal. Bringing Down the Mountains is a must-have for students and scholars of energy policy, the environment, economics, politics, organized labor, and Appalachian studies."

KATIE FALLON, VIRGINIA TECH

"Bringing Down the Mountains is an invaluable study of mountaintop removal, the most devastating coal mining practice in the United States. Burns brings together history, politics, economics, sociology, ecology, biology, and interviews with coalfield residents with an efficacy and efficiency I've seen in no other book about the subject. Comprehensive and thoroughly documented, Bringing Down the Mountains is a work we've needed for a decade and a must-have for anyone concerned about the future of the Appalachian region."

ANN PANCAKE, AUTHOR OF Strange as This Weather Has Been

West Virginia and Appalachia
A series edited by Ronald L. Lewis

Volume 5

Bringing Down the Mountains

BRINGING DOWN THE
MOUNTAINS

THE IMPACT OF MOUNTAINTOP REMOVAL SURFACE COAL MINING
ON SOUTHERN WEST VIRGINIA COMMUNITIES, 1970–2004

SHIRLEY STEWART BURNS

MORGANTOWN 2007

West Virginia University Press, Morgantown 26506
© 2007 by West Virginia University Press

First edition published 2007 by West Virginia University Press
Printed in the United States of America

15 14 13 12 11 10 09 08 07   9 8 7 6 5 4 3 2 1

ISBN-10 1-933202-17-3
ISBN-13 978-1-933202-17-4
(alk. paper)

Library of Congress Cataloguing-in-Publication Data

Bringing down the mountains. The impact of mountaintop removal surface coal
    mining on southern West Virginia communities. / by Shirley Stewart Burns.
    (West Virginia and Appalachia ; 5)

p.   cm.
1.Coal mines and mining. 2 Coal mines and mining—West Virginia. 3. Coal mines
    and mining—Environmental aspect—West Virginia. 4. Mountaintop removal
    mining—Environmental aspect—West Virginia. 5. Mountaintop removal
    mining—Economic aspect—West Virginia. I. Title. II. Burns, Shirley Stewart.
    III. Series.
IN PROCESS

Library of Congress Control Number: 2007936477

Book and Cover Design by Than Saffel
Printed in USA by BookMobile

Dedicated to the people of southern West Virginia,
the most resilient people I know

CONTENTS

ACKNOWLEDGMENTS

This work is the culmination of years of research, both personally and professionally. There are a number of people to thank. My dissertation members at West Virginia University provided valuable input on the earliest draft of this work, which appeared as my doctoral dissertation. A continuing thanks is offered to all of them: Elizabeth Fones-Wolf, Roger Lohmann, Greg Good (who gave me the idea for the title to chapter 6), and John Hennen. I especially want to acknowledge Ronald Lewis who gave so much input to my dissertation and always provided good advice. In addition to these educators, I also want to thank the following excellent teachers, in the order they appeared in my life, all of whom had an important influence on me through their encouragement and professionalism. Thanks to Rebecca Lubonia, Linda Boggs, Edna Jo Bailey, John Harris, Paul Blankenship, Jeanette Toler, Betty Cook, Camy Crouse, and Dr. Robert Ours. I also would like to thank Sara Pritchard, Stacey Elza, Than Saffel, Rachel Rosolina, and Patrick Conner with the West Virginia University Press for their professionalism and enthusiasm in the production of this book.

While researching this book, I met a number of people struggling on a daily basis with the realities of mountaintop removal (MTR). The persistent courage and dedication of these individuals, who face unimaginable circumstances with a passion for and a devotion to their homes and communities, is an inspiration. I was first inspired by the forthright eloquence of Carlos Gore who stated simply and with passion what MTR had cost him and his community. He remains one of the best speakers I have ever heard on the devastation of MTR. Later, it was my extreme privilege to talk with some of the women battling MTR in their own backyards, including Judy Bonds, Patty Sebok, and Frieda Williams. I was immensely impressed with Mary Miller and Pauline Canterberry. Even while battling the MTR in their communities, they remain joyful and hopeful, and they somehow maintain wonderful senses of humor. They continue battling MTR devastation at a time in life when most people have retired and are set to relax. May we all grow to be as dedicated and feisty as these two, "the dustbusters."

Matthew Burns, my husband, has been selfless and completely supportive as I have changed this work from a dissertation to a book. He has read all versions of this work from beginning to end, including this final version, providing valuable feedback along the way. A better research assistant and more understanding partner is not to be found. He not only kept me moving forward with this project, but also assured my sanity by making me focus on other things when I needed it most.

I would like to give special thanks to Vivian Stockman of the Ohio Valley Environmental Coalition for the use of numerous photographs. I also would like to thank Mark Schmerling of Schmerling Photography for the use of his stark, beautiful photographs of southern West Virginia. I am honored to include their works in this book.

Thanks to all of my friends and family who have listened over the years to numerous stories of mountaintop removal, coal, more coal, and home, especially Christina Bailey and Connie Park Rice who patiently listened to numerous ideas over the course of this writing. In addition, I would like to thank my in-laws, Jake, Linda, and Jason Burns and my friends Copper Stewart, Lonnie Williams, Denise Ferguson, Amy and Tim Daniels, Tammy Brown, Kim Harrison, Teresa Stone, Carletta Bush, Lou Orslene, Greg Wimer, Kim Cordingly, George Demanelis, and Tom Freeman whose friendship and patience with my coal stories has always been greatly appreciated.

I come from a long line of underground coal miners, and I have always been proud of my family and its coal mining roots. Coming of age in Wyoming County, West Virginia, at a time when the mines were first booming there, both of my grandfathers, Gillis Stewart and Dave McKinney, toiled underground to support their families. I never met my grandpaw Gillis, who died at forty-two of black lung disease, but he cast a long shadow of decency and humility on his family. Grandpaw Dave had large, work-calloused hands, typical of a man who had worked decades in the mines. He had a love of horses and was better suited for farming, but mining paid the bills. My own father, Neely Stewart, was one of the brightest, most courageous people I have ever met. He died at fifty-one from black lung and heart disease, the result of thirty years working as an underground coal miner so that his family could live among the mountains of home, among our family and lifelong friends. His shortened life at the hands of the coal mining that sustained us has left an indelible mark on me and shaped not only my personal but also my academic interests.

My grandmothers knew firsthand the often-hard life of mining coal. Minnie Walker Stewart was left a young widow with eight children. To her credit, all became fine, decent men and women, and her proudest achievement was that all had obtained a high school diploma or GED. Maxine Lusk McKinney endured the strikes and lean times with a jovial outlook and smile in spite of it all. My own mother, Cora Stewart, has been the most inspirational of all. I never knew what strength was until I watched my mother endure after my father's death. She has always supported my dreams and goals, has never judged, and has been a rock in my life. I owe more than a debt of gratitude to my mom and dad who provided excellent examples of loyalty and love of home, and gave me a strong foundation.

I also want to thank my brothers, Rick and Allen Stewart, for all of their encouragement throughout the years. They have always believed in me. Allen represents the third generation of underground, union coal miners in my family. He is the last of our family to make his living underground. It is a proud heritage, but it can be a heartbreaking one as well. Still, I am thankful that I was born to this family, in this place. It has shaped me into the person I am, and informed my interests and academic pursuits in a way that only being from there can.

Most of all, thanks to God from whom all my blessings flow.

List of Abbreviations

AOC	appropriate original contour
ACTF	Affiliated Construction Trades Foundation
CEDAR	Coal Education Development and Resource of Southern West Virginia Inc.
CORA	Commission on Religion in Appalachia
CRMW	Coal River Mountain Watch
DEIS	Draft Environmental Impact Statement
DEP	Department of Environmental Protection
EPA	Environmental Protection Agency
EPT	Ephemeroptera, Plecoptera, and Trichoptera insects
FEMA	Federal Emergency Management Agency
FPEIS	Final Programmatic Environmental Impact Statement
MSHA	Mine Safety and Health Administration
MTR	mountaintop removal coal mining
OVEC	Ohio Valley Environmental Coalition
SMCRA	Surface Mining Control and Reclamation Act
SSI	Supplemental Security Income
TANF	Temporary Assistance for Needy Families
UMWA	United Mine Workers of America
WVHC	West Virginia Highlands Conservancy

Introduction

"OPEN FOR BUSINESS"

The Shameful Legacy of Natural Resource Extraction

West Virginia policymakers have a history of favoring big business over other citizens. This was not always the case: the use of legislative tax favors to develop the backcounties of West Virginia during the 1870s and 1880s was hindered by a legal system rooted in common law that protected the rights of individuals over those of the emerging industrial corporations. But if the new state were to take its place among its prosperous industrial neighbors, as the leaders of West Virginia had imagined it would do, there would have to be a tangible change in the judicial branch of the state. That critical transition occurred in 1889 and 1890, with the election of judges to the Supreme Court of Appeals who tossed aside the traditional agrarian bias and replaced it with one that favored industrial uses of land. Now the indirect state subsidies to coal and timber provided by the construction of railroads and business-friendly initiatives were complemented by a court that not only upheld these initiatives but also gave preferential treatment to industry on grounds of serving the public good. In privileging the corporations, the new court established a new legal approach and a new power paradigm.[1]

West Virginia's central location between midwestern cities and the eastern seaboard, its temperate climate, and its rich natural resources failed to generate the economic growth that state leaders had desired—and expected—during the years following the Civil War. The West Virginia

Tax Commission's 1884 Report on State Development acknowledged that the state had not experienced the prosperity that it should have, given its particular advantages. The report observed that the vast majority of West Virginia's natural-resource wealth was being devoured by outside interests by any means necessary.[2] Misguided by the belief that rich natural resources would lead to wealth, the new state leaders created a single-industry, resource-dependent economy that would ensure the state's status as a bit player in the national economy. Little attention was given to the idea of economic diversification. Natural-resource industries were in essence given free rein to provide economic development in the state, but the state's leaders soon learned that once the industries had received such power, it was impossible to take it back from them.

More than 120 years after the 1884 report, that is still the case. Because of the power structure created and solidified by the state's political system, any prosperity derived by mountaintop removal coal mining (MTR) is assured to only benefit the mine operators, and conversely, any chance of long-term, sustainable prosperity will continue to elude the state.

West Virginia, particularly southern West Virginia, exists as a peripheral region within the American and global market system. Peripheral regions typically are in larger spatial areas with comparatively smaller populations, smaller cities, and smaller amounts of power in the larger economic and political systems. Core regions, as opposed to peripheral regions, have small land areas with larger populations and a concentration of the economic and political power. It is to these areas that the periphery supplies its natural resources. Power resides in the core, and resources from the periphery flow in that direction. Like a colony, the periphery supplies raw materials cheaply so that the core can benefit from the production of goods and services for the national and global market. Any attempt to alter this relationship leads to mobilization by the powerful core against the weaker periphery as the core seeks to maintain its control.

Sociologist David Walls was one of the first scholars to examine Appalachia as a periphery within the context of advanced capitalist society. He found that Appalachia acts as a supplier of natural resources to the nation, thus functioning as a periphery on the fringe of the dominant, core society controlled by a power elite.[3] In *Who Rules America: Power and Politics,* sociologist G. William Domhoff defines the power elite as those groups "that exercise power on behalf of the owners of all large income-producing properties."[4] This power elite constitutes a national ruling class comprising members of an identifiable American upper class as well as members of the corporate community that shape policies directly affecting the entire country.[5] In the southern West Virginia coalfields, this power elite is composed of the massive coal corporations, organizations with coal-centered agendas (such as the West Virginia Coal Association and Friends of Coal), other large industries with vested economic interests in coal (such as machine manufacturers and distributors), and politicians who support ideas and legislation that benefit the coal industry. Throughout this book, this group is referred to as the "coal interests."

For more than a century, West Virginia's southern counties have been ruled by a coal-centered power. The beginning of the twentieth century witnessed the construction of company towns throughout the coal-rich valleys of southern West Virginia. Coal companies funded, built, and governed company towns, and maintained control in all aspects of community life. In southern West Virginia, where larger towns were scarce and where workers were frequently brought into the area for the explicit purpose of mining coal, the number of miners living in these communities made up more than 70 percent of the total population. On the surface, coal operators pointed to the housing needs of this largely imported workforce and easily defended the necessity of these towns.[6] In addition, miners guaranteed the coal company control over their lives by signing strict, mandatory housing agreements—a move that coal companies also justified as essential to operation. Such authority over the living space of a miner and his family allowed the company to crush any activities that might threaten the company's bottom line. If an employee "got out of line," the employee could be terminated, and he and his family would be promptly removed from the company housing.[7] Ruling these towns with an iron fist, the company rendered the miner (and his family) virtually powerless.

Some scholars have debated the severity of treatment afforded miners in company towns and stressed that miners possessed the option to move from company town to company town, thereby limiting some of the control the companies had over workers.[8] Nevertheless, miners possessed little self-determination and autonomy as they moved from one company town to another, each built on the same power relationship as the previous one.[9] Therefore, the company maintained the advantage when it came to shelter. These company towns were viewed so negatively that the coal operators themselves often felt pressed to defend the company towns' very existence.[10] Many operators viewed with alarm the turbulence in the region and sought to extinguish it through welfare capitalism in the form of the "model company town."[11] Even if operators improved the amenities in their model company towns and offered more fringe benefits, the power structure remained the same with absolute power resting in the hands of the company.[12] These endeavors helped improve the image of coal company towns to outsiders and, in some ways, advanced the quality of life for the towns' inhabitants, but workers did not enjoy true independence. It was this lack of freedom and power over their own lives that inspired many coal miners to support unionization efforts. Power would not be snatched from the corporations easily, however, and the many, often bloody, battles that followed in order to unionize the southern West Virginia coalfields are well known and well documented.[13]

Company towns, as first created, ceased to exist beyond the 1950s; the few company homes that remained in some of the towns were sold to individuals, leaving numerous unincorporated communities in their place. Even after exiting the company-town business, coal companies continued to exercise power over community members who were still economically dependent on mining. In fact, power became even more concentrated over the course of the twentieth century as ownership and control over the industry became increasingly consolidated into fewer, larger corporations.

With the expansion of the railroads in the late nineteenth and early twentieth centuries came the opening up of the southern West Virginia coalfields. Hundreds of independent coal operators leased land from large absentee land companies with the hopes of cashing in on the coal boom. The glut of coal companies resulted in the overexpansion of the coalfields. Even with a plethora of independent coal operators, large companies continued to dominate. Guided by northern bankers, industrialists, and other capitalists, efforts to consolidate the natural-resource-wealthy land into the hands of a few corporations were accomplished early through the buyout of these smaller operators by large coal syndicates. The coal syndicates then consolidated several of the small operations into one larger entity.[14] Early mine operators frequently lived in the mining community, but the owners of the larger corporations were absentees. No longer would the operators personally exercise authority of their own. Now hired managers became agents of the absentee owners whose corporate offices were far removed from the coal towns themselves.[15] This domination of the coal-fields by large, often multinational, corporations accelerated during the twentieth century and persists to the present day.

In his study of power relationships in the Clear Fork Valley of Tennessee, John Gaventa examined the power relationships of community members with American Association Ltd., which exercised extensive ownership in the valley. He explored three dimensions of power: public participation in challenging power structures, manipulation of public issues by those with power, and the reigning elite's usage of propaganda.[16] Gaventa's study portrayed citizens who were subjected to a company-dominated exis-tence since the erection of the company towns that forged the company-dominated power structure. Rather than accepting defeat, residents often fought back only to find a power structure so complicated that the power source was nearly impossible to locate.

This book also looks at the relationships between the power elite and the residents of coal communities, and how these intricate relationships continued beyond the stifling of public dissent to the actual forced remov-al of residents from their homes and communities. With the expansion of MTR, the coal companies no longer needed a substantial workforce. In-stead they needed the hills and valleys where these people lived. The land was taken, mostly through coercion, for the "greater good" by the coal interests. As exercised by this power elite, the process of MTR that entered the coalfield communities affected all aspects of life.

Obtaining coal by MTR is a methodical enterprise that includes sev-eral steps. First, trees and vegetation are removed from the area to be mined, with the trees typically leased to a timber company to be logged and sold. The operator will either save the removed topsoil or spread it over an existing stripped site. Next, the area is pre-stripped to make a foundation for the dragline, the piece of machinery that is most crucial to MTR. The dragline, a large earth-moving machine, can be as tall as twenty stories. It is this machinery that actually digs and removes the earth and coal. The area is prepared for pre-stripping using shovel load-ers and dump trucks. During this phase, access roads are constructed to reach the preliminary operation. This activity continues throughout the life of the MTR operation as area after area is prepared for stripping. The next step is the actual extraction stage. The exposed sub-soil and rock, known as overburden, is then drilled, blasted, and removed from the area. Hundreds of feet may be removed from the top of the mountain during blasting. The now-exposed coal seam is splintered through blasting, and the coal is hauled away. The overburden is compacted and used to re-grade an already mined area. Any excess overburden remaining after the area is back-filled is placed into a valley fill, a valley area (typically at the head of a hollow) used for MTR waste disposal. Then, reclamation (i.e., attempts to restore the area to a useful standard) occurs. This involves using the graded and compacted topsoil on the now-stripped site, and reseeding it for vegetation.[17] MTR, a quick and efficient way to obtain coal, experienced an upsurge in popularity during the 1990s, though it had been used in earlier decades as well.

MTR came into widespread use to meet the demand created by the 1970s energy crisis, but with the subsequent decline in demand during the 1980s, the method was expanded because it was cheaper for the compa-nies. Demand for southern West Virginia's coal once again exploded with the enactment of the 1990 amendments to the Clean Air Act. The new amendments proved auspicious for the West Virginia coal industry, espe-cially the inclusion of provisions to reduce emission standards of air pol-lutants. A quick and cheap way to reduce emission standards was to use low-sulfur coal, so coal-burning power plants needed a readily available, easily obtainable source of this low-sulfur, high-volatility coal to meet the new requirement. One place they found it was in the hills of southern West Virginia. By 1994, the U.S. Department of Energy anticipated an in-crease of as much as 24 million tons of coal from the central Appalachian coalfields, much of this from southern West Virginia, as opposed to 12 million from the Powder River Basin in Wyoming.[18]

The quickest way to obtain low-sulfur coal was through MTR. Util-ity companies recognized the importance of obtaining the quality coal as cheaply as possible. American Electric Power acknowledged its support of MTR as a way for the company to meet its own need for coal at low prices. In 1999, American Electric Power was the largest purchaser of West Vir-ginia coal, and the majority of that coal was obtained via MTR. It was the low-sulfur emissions requirement of the Clean Air Act that ensured the utility would continue to purchase southern West Virginia coal.[19]

The ultimate goal of the act was to decrease air pollutants, but two unanticipated consequences were the increase in MTR in southern West Virginia and the mining companies' employment of fewer and fewer miners, since MTR required less manpower than more traditional mining meth-

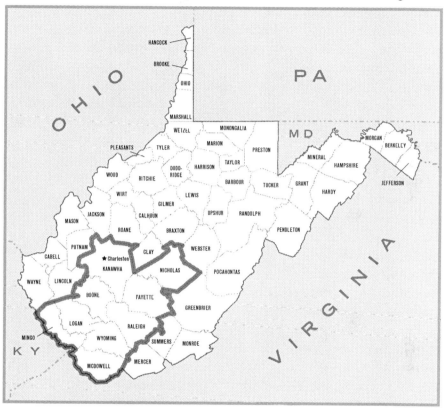

Map 1.1. The southern coalfields of West Virginia

ods. While the area endured decades of environmental problems from previous mining activities, MTR exponentially increased those problems. Once again, the peripheral region of southern West Virginia was sacrificed for the benefit of the core region. Some counties were, of course, more affected than others. Boone, Logan, and Kanawha counties, for instance, produce at least two times as much coal from MTR as other forms of surface mining. Still, other counties such as Wyoming and Raleigh are

7

at the beginning stages of MTR, with the total economic and environmental effects yet to be realized. While still an important part of the economy, coal employment is minimal in these areas as increased mechanization has led to fewer and fewer jobs.

Mountaintop removal mining is pervasive in nine of the southernmost West Virginia counties: Boone, Fayette, Kanawha, Logan, McDowell, Mingo, Nicholas, Raleigh, and Wyoming. (See Map 1.1.)

Production numbers for the counties change from year to year, but according to the 2003 *West Virginia Coal Facts*, these nine counties were responsible for more than 67.2 percent of the total production of coal in West Virginia. Surface mining accounted for 82.9 percent of the coal mined in these counties, with 82.3 percent of the surface-mined coal coming from MTR.[20] The nine counties have a total of fifty-eight coal-slurry impoundments within their boundaries, with the capacity to hold in excess of 85.3 billion gallons of slurry, the toxic by-product of cleaning coal.[21]

The twenty-story draglines used in MTR cost $25 million or more, and are so large they must be brought in piece by piece and can take years to assemble.[22] Because of the capital investment required for MTR, only very large companies with vast economic resources can afford to enter the business. In West Virginia, the two leading MTR producers are Arch Coal Inc. and Massey Energy Company. Faced with the encroachment of this newest mining technique on their communities, many residents of southern West Virginia have found themselves unlikely environmentalists and activists, joining with neighbors directly affected by MTR.

MTR has had a massive impact on communities in southern West Virginia. By the time it entered West Virginia in 1970, the state was firmly entrenched as a rural-industrial state with the southern coalfield region dependent on coal extraction for its economic survival. Since then, counties have witnessed a decrease in employment and an increase in environmental degradation. These communities continue to turn into ghost towns, and it is important to document their existence. Ironically, these communities that once flourished because of coal mining are now being destroyed by the same industry. The cycle has come full circle. In the end, it is certain that the cost of this latest way to mine coal is unaffordable, especially to those opposing it and to the land that stands in the way.

1

MAKING MOLEHILLS OUT OF MOUNTAINS:

Power Relationships and the Rise of Strip Mining

in Southern West Virginia

I will lift up mine eyes unto the hills
from whence cometh my help.
—Psalm 121:1

In a small storefront in Whitesville, West Virginia, a hand-lettered sign spells out "Coal River Mountain Watch." Flyers adorning the window advertise meetings to discuss the halting of mountaintop removal. Inside the sparsely furnished headquarters are a couple of tables, a few computers, and a bevy of energetic, determined volunteers. Since 1998, this grassroots organization, situated in the heart of the southern coalfields of Boone County, has actively opposed the mountaintop removal mining that has dismantled its small communities one hollow at a time. Often subjected to blatant hostilities from those who are employed by these MTR sites, the group continues to take part in lawsuits, make presentations, and participate in other informational activities in an attempt to keep their message in the public eye. Coal River Mountain Watch (CRMW) knows that it takes tenacity and a concerted effort to compete with the bombardment of propaganda generated by the large conglomerates that operate MTR mines. Grassroots organizations like CRMW lack the sophisticated networking systems that could grant them access to the powerful political players who could help them in not only the MTR struggle but the power struggles that chart the sustainability of these communities.

One state over and a world away sits the headquarters of Massey Energy Company, the target of much of CRMW's efforts. The coal company's modern, multistory brick building is a stark contrast to the small office that houses CRMW. From the Richmond-based office, Massey operates a billion-dollar business with coal holdings throughout southern West Virginia as well as southwestern Virginia, Tennessee, and eastern Kentucky. Massey's annual report for 2005 indicated that the company had 2.2 billion tons of reserves and a multi-million-dollar annual revenue.[1]

Both factions—grassroots groups like CRMW and vast coal entities like Massey—are just the most recent players in a drama that has unfolded for more than one hundred years in resource-wealthy southern West Virginia. The question has always been, who would decide the fate of the land and, ultimately, the fate of the people living there? Would it be the outside interests who frequently owned the mineral rights, or the southern West Virginians who lived and died in the region? Time and again, that struggle has led to a tense compromise between the industry and the people; although the people have often been dependent on the industry for employment, they have also remained fierce protectors of the land. This uneasy dance has its roots in the earliest development of the area.

Most of the nine counties this book focuses on were formed between the mid- to late nineteenth century. Kanawha County alone was formed in the late eighteenth century. From the onset, these counties were overwhelmingly agricultural with the exception of Fayette County, where most people supported themselves by hunting. The full-on assault of the coal-mining industry would change these areas economically, environmentally, socially, and culturally. Although it had been no secret that coal was present in the area, the resource was not exploited until the burgeoning national economy increased the demand for coal and necessitated trains to haul it long distances. In the 1880s, railroad construction made the extraction and transportation of the rich resource from a rugged, harsh environment economically viable. Development came with the railroads, and with that development a greater dependence on the fluctuations of a marketplace outside the region's boundaries.

It would, however, be a mistake to think that the new development was shunned by all of the inhabitants. There were many in the rural backcounties who embraced it with entrepreneurial spirit. Most would certainly have had little idea of the repercussions that would accompany these irreversible changes—their society would be transformed from one based on farming and bartering to one based on wage labor.[2] The penetration of the railroads farther into the region assured that these changes would occur quickly. For, once the railroads were established, money flowed not into the pockets of southern West Virginians but into the pockets of absentee landowners. Without that revenue, southern West Virginians could not create an infrastructure that would allow the area to develop beyond a one-resource economy. It is this lack of infrastructure and economic diversification that is at the heart of why the region, with the exception of Kanawha County, remains so far behind the rest of the state. It is not merely the rough terrain of the southern coalfield region that stopped a diverse economy. "Inaccessible topography" also pervades northern West Virginia, but Clarksburg, for example, has flourished in recent years in spite of its rugged landscape. Development in the backcounties of West Virginia occurred at a slower pace than the more populated areas and depended mainly on natural-resource extraction. The repercussions of a single-industry economy continue today, as job choices are still minimal in these areas.

Connection to outside markets came early for the southern coalfields territory, and it was that connection that led to the speculation of the area.[3] The legacy of these acquisitions resounds today when more than two-thirds of the state's non-public land has been gobbled up by absentee landowners.[4] Of the nine counties included in this study, all but one (Kanawha) have more than 50 percent of their acreage controlled by outside interests. One county, Wyoming, has outside landownership that exceeds 100 percent as a duplication of mineral and surface rights surpasses the total acreage in the county itself.[5]

Since outside interests hold such a large amount of land in the nine-county sub-region, economic diversification is nearly non-existent there. Direct coal-related employment continues to decline, causing an exodus of residents from the region. All counties have seen a decrease in coal-mine employment accompanied by an increase in overall coal production. Central to this phenomenon is the "advancement" in mechanization embraced by the larger companies that pervade the area, in particular the process of MTR. MTR, however, could not be embraced until surface mining itself had been accepted. This happened gradually over nearly seven decades.

The rise of MTR in the southern coalfields is the latest development in the overall history of strip mining in West Virginia where the goal is to feed America's ever-insatiable need for cheap energy. Although underground mining dominated the coal industry in West Virginia through most of the twentieth century, strip mining also had its place. Northern West Virginia operators were the first to introduce strip mining to the state in 1916. World War I brought with it a high demand for coal to fuel the war effort both at home and abroad as coal shortages occurred across the country. Miners were encouraged to mine coal as a patriotic duty.

The heightened demand along with the negligible start-up capital required for these operations made surface mining more attractive to investors. These mines employed a fraction of the miners of underground operations, and as new operations, the strip mines were not burdened with previous contractual obligations and placed highest priority on the new markets created by the war. At a time of nearly unlimited demand, coal meant big profits.[6] The heightened need for coal during the war resulted in strip mining becoming more respectable and gaining easy entry into the mainstream coal industry. Still, massive strip mining in the region did not occur until World War II, by which time equipment for stripping had improved and more roads had been surfaced, allowing surface workers to extract the coal more easily.

With better access to the coal seams and a renewed need for the product, strip mines once again thrived in the region. From 1938 through 1942, strip-mine coal companies operating in the state increased from two to forty-one.[7] Strip mining supplied the demand for coal faster, with fewer casualties and higher productivity per man, than underground mining. In fact, during World War II, strip mining was considered a significant contributor to the war effort.[8] This increase in demand created new business opportunities. Strip mining necessitated heavy equipment operators, and while many of the new mining contractors had been engaged in highway construction and were unfamiliar with mining, they had the equipment and the trained manpower to obtain the coal. In his essay "The First

Fifty Years of Strip Mining in West Virginia, 1916–1965," Robert F. Munn noted that "[p]roduction increased ten-fold between 1939 and 1943." He identified 1947 as "the peak year" and reported that 10 percent of all West Virginia coal was obtained through strip mining. While largely contained within the northern part of the state for twenty-five years, strip mining made its way to the southern part of the state, entering Raleigh and Fayette Counties first, and was firmly established by 1943.[9]

Strip mining leveled off during the 1950s and began to expand again during the 1960s. From 1962 forward, the importance of strip mining to the coal industry increased until it became an integral part of West Virginia's natural-resource-dependent economy. It was not until the 1970s, when large-scale stripping took place on a regular basis, that West Virginians began to pay attention to it. Equipment became larger, and massive strip-mining jobs became much easier and cost effective for the companies.[10] As the state witnessed a decrease in coal mining employment, the tonnage steadily increased. In 1970, 45,261 West Virginia jobs were supplied due to coal mining, and 143,132,284 tons of coal were produced. Thirty-two years later, in 2002, 15,377 people were employed by the coal companies, and together they produced 163,896,890 tons of coal.[11]

Mechanization has continually made coal jobs obsolete; however, with MTR, the overall number of jobs has gone down even faster. As Figure 1.1 illustrates, surface mining production held steady in the nine counties during the 1970s but saw significant growth beginning in the 1990s. Since 1990, a definite trend can be seen, with surface mining employment consistently decreasing even as production increases. Underground employment has plummeted while underground production has also decreased. Even with its decreases, underground production still exceeds surface production. As noted above, larger coal companies are responsible for the vast majority of MTR since the necessary machinery is extremely expensive. However, MTR requires far less manpower than traditional underground and even traditional surface mining (see Figure 1.1 on page 14).

Surface mining brought with it new ways for the residents of coal communities to lose self-determination and power. Mechanization had progressively decreased coal mining jobs, and the men who worked surface mines were heavy-equipment operators, and largely non-union. Not until the operations became so large that the resulting scars could be witnessed

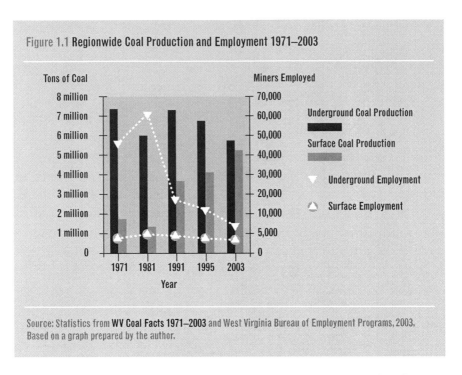

Figure 1.1 Regionwide Coal Production and Employment 1971–2003

Source: Statistics from WV Coal Facts 1971–2003 and West Virginia Bureau of Employment Programs, 2003. Based on a graph prepared by the author.

on the landscape did any major protest against the practice take place. By that time, a whole new type of hopelessness had emerged in the coalfields. On one hand, MTR mines polluted streams and filled in valleys; some of these valley fills are among the largest man-made earthen structures in the world.[12] On the other hand, while residents found themselves despondent about the consequences of MTR, many felt that they had little or no choice but to accept things the way they were, in order to preserve coal-mining jobs. In this way, West Virginians felt torn between the desire to preserve the land and the need to earn a living.

Although strip mining did not flourish in the state until the second half of the twentieth century, West Virginia became the first state to pass a strip-mine control act much earlier than that, in 1939. Significantly, the framers of the measure realized legislation was necessary "because strip mining 'causes soil erosion, increases the hazards of floods, causes the pollution of streams of water . . . and creates dangerous hazards in life and property.'"[13] There was little fanfare and little enforcement of the sparse law, and strip mining continued to grow in the region.[14] The act was amended in 1945 to legislate more extensive post-mining use, but again the lack of enforcement rendered the amendments nearly moot. Further amendments were passed in 1963, but they only weakened an already anemic law. The amount of money required as a bond was reduced, and operators were no longer required to declare what area a permit would cover.[15] These revisions left the people with even less legal redress than before. The strip miners essentially were given carte blanche to mine in any manner without regard for the public welfare; if that meant ruining the land of a private citizen to secure the coal, then so be it. Mineral rights were given far higher priority in the law than surface rights.

In the spirit of President Lyndon Johnson's Great Society community action programs, antipoverty workers helped form a citizens' movement against strip mining in the southern coalfield counties, including Boone, Fayette, Raleigh, and Wyoming, in 1967.[16] The movement idled soon after, but it was revived in 1970 by then–gubernatorial candidate Jay Rockefeller, who used his own money to start Citizens to Abolish Strip Mining. Rockefeller abandoned the strip-mining cause in 1972 after losing a gubernatorial bid to Arch Moore. In 1971, the West Virginia legislature considered a bill banning strip mining completely in the state. Supporters of the bill quickly pointed out that the jobs-versus-land argument did not apply since the majority of strip-mine workers were not local but from out-of-state. Proponents also noted that these workers were *not* miners (they were heavy-equipment operators with transferable skills) and that surface mines actually took away jobs from underground miners.[17] The legislature did not pass that bill, only a two-year moratorium that applied to one-half of the fifty-five counties. There was never enough legislative support for an overall abolition; many of the legislators counted the coal industry among their major contributors.[18]

But the tug-of-war over strip mining was not confined to West Virginia or its politicians. In the 1970s, the concern with environmental degradation in West Virginia—and indeed in all of Appalachia—stretched even into the religious sphere. Formed in 1965, the Commission on Religion in Appalachia (CORA) supported antipoverty and community empowerment commitments at the grassroots level throughout Appalachia. In 1970, CORA compiled a "Dialogue Focuser" on strip mining in Appalachia. Realizing the economic, social, and political importance of strip mining, the document hoped to create a forum for both sides to express their views on the issue. At the time of the report, the debate over whether to allow strip mining at any level was intensifying. The companies' viewpoint focused on the need for coal for an energy-strapped nation and postulated that the surface-mined coal reserves could not be obtained by traditional, underground mining. Opponents of strip mining argued that the energy needs of the nation *could* be met with the abundance of coal available from traditional, underground methods.[19] The document covered topics ranging from environmental effects to legal and political ramifications, and illustrated the seriousness of the strip-mining debate just as MTR was beginning in Fayette County.

Nationally, federal legislators were getting involved in the strip-mining debate because states failed to enforce even the weakest state laws and court judgments favoring strip-mine operators made federal intervention necessary. West Virginia Congressional Representative Ken Hechler introduced a bill to ban surface mining in February 1971 at the same time that anti-stripping forces in West Virginia carried the battle into the state legislature. The federal and state efforts were doomed to failure. Two more attempts would see congressional passage of regulations only to meet with presidential vetoes in 1974 and 1975.[20] It was only with the passage of the 1977 Surface Mining Control and Reclamation Act (SMCRA) that federal regulations were finally approved for strip mining. Though a far weaker bill than its two predecessors, the act did provide for some control and entrusted regulation to the states. The act prohibited the dumping of debris on steep slopes, provided an abandoned-mine reclamation program funded by a coal tax, and established the Office of Surface Mining in the Department of the Interior.[21] SMCRA also allowed concerned citizens to call for inspections of surface mines, gave them the right to participate in those inspections, and let them file lawsuits against those regulators who failed to enforce the law.[22] Among the noted allowances in the act was permitting MTR. Finally the people had their protective legislation but still no power of enforcement or redress. Now residents were dependent on the regulators to enforce even more rules, and they still had not achieved the outright ban of strip mining that many had sought.

Legislators and those who supported the ban on surface mining almost certainly could not have imagined the huge twenty-story machines that were on the horizon. MTR began in West Virginia in 1970 when Cannelton Industries Inc. began mining Bullpush Mountain near the Fayette-Kanawha County line.[23] However, it was not until the 1980s, with the introduction of these massive, efficient draglines on MTR sites, that MTR enjoyed vast growth in the state. Throughout the 1980s, permits covering 9,800 acres were granted. In 2002, within a nine-month period, enough permits were granted to cover 12,540 acres.[24]

As strip mining increased in the 1980s, particularly MTR, and as demand for coal decreased during the decade, coal mining and related employment continued to plummet. Corporations needed to produce coal with the cheapest bottom line possible. With large machinery doing the work of hundreds of men, MTR did just that. As the method became increasingly common throughout the 1990s, a new era of MTR protests took off. Citizen groups sprang up throughout the coalfields in an attempt to mobilize residents against the perceived oncoming environmental and employment disaster. One of the first of these groups was the Ohio Valley Environmental Coalition (OVEC) formed in 1987. Located in Huntington, West Virginia, it was originally formed as a citizen's group opposing the construction of a chemical hazardous waste incinerator near Ironton, Ohio. By the end of the 1990s, halting MTR had become the group's top priority. The West Virginia Highlands Conservancy (WVHC) was yet another state environmental group that embraced the cause of educating the public to the dangers of MTR and halting the mining technique. CRMW is one of the most recent additions to these groups; its members act as an important voice against the practice directly affecting their homes and environment. Since they are located in the county with the highest MTR coal production, their work is particularly notable and crucial.

Conclusion

Since coal mining began in southern West Virginia, underground mining has been the dominant form of extraction, but strip mining has steadily increased its market share. As equipment changed and surface mining became more common, the environmental and aesthetic problems associated with surface mining gained the attention of citizens throughout the coalfields. Huge draglines introduced in the 1980s led to the expansion and proliferation of MTR in the 1990s. The nine southernmost coalfield counties overwhelmingly depend on coal mining to fuel their economies. This lack of diversification has proven devastating as continual mechanization has resulted in fewer mining jobs and in environmental destruction. The increase in MTR led to the mobilization of various citizen groups. Among those were CRMW, OVEC, and WVHC. These groups continue to become more vocal as MTR expands throughout the southern coalfields and as the United Mine Workers of America (UMWA), once a stalwart for coalfield communities, continues to support MTR where some members have employment.

2

SOLIDARITY FOREVER?

The UMWA and Southern West Virginia

I stood for the union and walked in the line.
I fought against the company.
I stood for the U. M. W. of A.
Now, who's gonna stand for me?
—Billy Edd Wheeler, "Coal Tattoo"

The United Mine Workers of America organized in 1890 in Columbus, Ohio, in an effort to unite coal miners for "action and purpose, in demanding and securing by lawful means the just fruits of [their] toil."[1] Throughout its tenure, the union strove to secure better working conditions and decent pay for its members. Its efforts can be seen through many important pieces of legislation—the eight-hour workday, collective bargaining rights, previously unheard of health and retirement benefits, and the enactment of better federal coal-mine health and safety standards. For many members, it served as a surrogate or extended family, and for decades it provided an avenue by which miners could improve their economic advantages in a hostile world. The union also acted as a mediator between the workers and the coal companies, and presented a united voice for thousands of miners.[2]

Coal fueled the nineteenth-century industrial revolution, and the United States coal industry grew to meet the high demand. Southern West Virginia, with its abundant coal reserves, witnessed firsthand the changes brought by the industrial revolution at varying speeds. Because of its rugged landscape, the southern coalfields were a special challenge to coal operators. Only when railroads were constructed in the backcounties could coal and other natural resources be brought to the national marketplace.[3] From the late 1890s until 1933, the union was thwarted at nearly every avenue. Companies fiercely fought efforts to unionize West Virginia's southern coalfields through coercion and paternalism. The companies formed alliances among themselves to resist unionization efforts, hiring outside agencies (such as Pinkerton agents and Baldwin-Felts detectives) to enforce their anti-union mandates. While a few operators resisted resorting to such brute force, the majority of operators stayed firm in its use.[4]

Coal mining remained a difficult vocation complete with physical challenges, health hazards, poor pay, and low social status. Therefore, the union was attractive to miners because it gave them a chance to improve not only their pay but also their dignity. To that end, the miners were willing to make great sacrifices. The union struggled to make headway into the southern West Virginia coalfields. While the union made some inroads in the early twentieth century, it did not secure its position in the area until 1933—after the federal government gave workers the right to unionize. The southern coalfield counties were the most difficult to organize, and the companies would stop at nothing to keep their coalfields union-free. Southern West Virginia witnessed numerous wars between miners trying to unionize and the hired company thugs with the lone goal of stopping their efforts. The Battle of Stanaford, the Paint Creek–Cabin Creek Conflict, the Matewan Massacre, and the Battle of Blair Mountain are all part of the rich history of the UMWA in West Virginia. From the nearly forgotten to the legendary, the battles highlight the complicated relationships between labor, industry, and community.

The Battle of Stanaford is a little-known, but interesting, battle that erupted in 1903, when organizers and supporters of the UMWA engaged in a gun fight with U.S. Marshals. Although no consistent telling of the battle exists, much can be gleaned from the varying accounts that do. In 1902, some 259 miners walked out of Raleigh County's fledgling coal industry in an attempt to bring the union into their county. In late February 1903, a U.S. Marshal met with threats when he tried to deliver a court injunction against the walkout to thirty-three miners who had marched from Fayette County to what is now East Beckley. The marshal then formed a posse of some fifty "special marshals" and was joined by the Raleigh County sheriff and a Baldwin-Felts detective working with the C&O Railroad. A UMWA official had tried to contact the strikers to tell them to give up quietly, but he later reported that his messages were refused delivery since coal operators owned the phone and telegraph lines. The posse approached Stanaford City in the early morning and attacked the striking miners. At the end of the battle, three men were dead and eight more would soon succumb to their wounds for a total of eleven deaths. Some miners were incarcerated for their part, while others fled. Mary Harris Jones, better known as Mother Jones, visited the area afterward. She recounted seeing the remains of miners who had been killed while sleeping.

By the summer of 1903, the UMWA had withdrawn from the New River coalfield. While minimal scholarship has been focused on the Battle of Stanaford, it was a great defeat for the union and effectively drove the UMWA out of the county as, afterwards, mine owners doubled their efforts to keep the mines union-free. This union-free stance helped cement the power relationship in the New River coalfield heavily in favor of the coal companies. Successful organization of the county would not occur until 1933 when President Franklin Roosevelt promised to send armed forces into West Virginia if the workers were stopped from their newly acquired right to unionize.[5]

A decade later, in April 1912, the small inroad the UMWA had made in the Kanawha coalfield was jeopardized when the coal operators in the Paint Creek area refused to renew their contract. Paid 2½ cents less per ton of coal than other area union miners, they had hoped to secure equal wages, and when they didn't, they walked out on strike. They were soon joined by the non-union miners on Cabin Creek.[6] Before too long, Baldwin-Felts guards forcibly removed them from their company homes. In response, the miners erected tent colonies and took up arms. They petitioned Governor William E. Glasscock to intervene on their behalf, but he responded that he could not tell men (in this case, Baldwin-Felts guards) where they could and could not go.

In July, after the death of two men, the sheriff asked Governor Glasscock to intervene by sending in the National Guard. Although Glasscock complied, he chastised the sheriff for failing in his duty to arrest the perpetrators. Within four months, the strike had spread to nearby Cabin Creek. A rally in the state capital of Charleston brought out six thousand miners and supporters, featuring Mother Jones as speaker. As the sheriff still refused to arrest offenders, the governor felt he had no choice but to declare martial law so that the National Guard could make the arrests instead. Miners who had committed criminal acts were tried before a military court.[7] Mine guards were forced from the strike area, and one month later, with order restored, Glasscock lifted martial law. Coal operators quickly organized to bring in strikebreakers, a move that was met with violence from the strikers. While not permitting Baldwin-Felts agents to return, Glasscock allowed "watchmen" approved by the National Guard to come in.

The violence continued, culminating in February 1913. A train known as the Bull Moose Special made its way into the tent colony under the blanket of night, and its occupants fired upon the sleeping residents, killing one. The miners attacked mine guards in Mucklow in retaliation, leaving sixteen more dead on both sides. In total, Glasscock ordered three separate periods of martial law. In the end, he failed to successfully mediate the strike, and his successor, Henry D. Hatfield, was left to pick up the pieces.

Hatfield did not repeat the mistake of lifting martial law. He realized the tactic was necessary to maintain order and to force the coal companies to come to the table to work out an agreement. This move halted the coal companies' intimidation tactics as represented by the bullying Baldwin-Felts agents and the hired watchmen. The agreement that Hatfield was eventually able to hammer out allowed workers "the explicit right to join the UMW without discrimination" as well as the right to hold meetings on "company property."[8] In the end, the miners were only slightly better off than they had been before the strike, which is often described as the first West Virginia mine war.

The next decade brought with it even more turmoil as miners throughout southern West Virginia struggled for some sense of power in their relationships with the coal industry. During the 1920s, Mingo County was known as "bloody Mingo" because of the violence that erupted there as the UMWA tried to unionize. Company-hired Baldwin-Felts detective agents stopped them at every attempt, and the tension culminated on May 19, 1920. An exchange of gunfire between the detectives and Matewan's police chief had numerous repercussions in addition to the ten initial deaths. A subsequent twenty-eight-month-long strike led to two dozen deaths. The gunfight resulted in "West Virginia's longest and most controversial murder trial to date, a United States Senate investigation, the retaliatory assassination of [Matewan Police] Chief [Sid] Hatfield, and the largest armed civilian insurrection since the Civil War," at Blair Mountain, Logan County.[9] This uprising became known as the Battle of Blair Mountain. It took the U.S. Army to stop it, representing the first time since the Civil War that armed military was used against Americans. At the Battle of Blair Mountain, nearly ten thousand coal miners were determined to bring "democracy" to the workers of Mingo and Logan counties. After fighting with the sheriff of Logan County and his "special deputies," the U.S. Army was called out to halt the insurgence. With the rebellion crushed, the union was unable to mount another offensive in the southern coalfields until 1933.[10]

Not all efforts to curb unionism were violent. Some companies sought a softer way to prevent unionization attempts by creating model company towns. These endeavors embraced the idea of welfare capitalism, or paternalism. Born from the nineteenth-century industrial revolution, welfare capitalism hoped to secure worker loyalty by offering benefits such as healthcare, death benefits, housing, annual and sick leave, and recreational facilities. The movement was at the height of its popularity during the 1910s through 1920. Model towns worked in much the same way as traditional company towns, with some notable exceptions. Model towns had numerous amenities that could not be found in traditional company towns, such as sturdy houses with indoor plumbing and appliances. The company often supplied the latest in entertainment, and some towns had restaurants, movie theaters, well-stocked grocery and mercantile stores, well-kempt lawns and gardens, and sidewalks. Companies hired doctors to tend to their employees' needs and erected schoolhouses and sometimes even churches.[11] The model town infused coal camps with paternalism in an effort to keep unionization in check. The companies were selective about the tenants they allowed into the model towns, which often helped the companies' cause by passively pressuring workers into being fiercely loyal.

One of the last model towns of the southern West Virginia coalfields was Kopperston in Wyoming County. Generally speaking, model towns reached their peak in popularity between 1910 and 1920,[12] nearly two decades before Kopperston was formed. But by the end of the 1930s, coal was being mined in Wyoming County in full force. Some of the richest deposits rested in the Toney Fork area just outside of Oceana. By the end of the decade, Koppers Coal Company of Pittsburgh, Pennsylvania, purchased some ten thousand acres of this mineral-rich land, which consisted largely of wilderness and farmland.[13] As construction of homes began, the area was named for the coal company: Kopperston.

By 1943, more than 230 individual houses stood in the new mining community.[14] The company told tenants that only the best could live in this coal camp—their model company town. Everyone who lived in the coal camp, of course, worked for the mine, but not all of the miners who worked for Koppers lived in the coal camp. Some of the men who worked for Koppers had a long lineage in the valley with families who had lived in the region for more than a hundred years. These miners already owned their own land and homes, so they commuted back and forth. Having so many workers with existing roots in the area, Koppers realized the importance of providing not only exemplary housing and amenities for newcomers or those wanting to live in the camp, with its close access to work and modern conveniences, but for commuting workers as well. With this slightest tweak of the typical model town, Koppers was able to obtain loyalty from workers both inside and outside the company town. They offered the town's numerous amenities to all of their employees and their families, regardless of whether or not they lived in the coal camp. Because of all the benefits that accompanied being employed by Koppers, just working for them became a privilege of sorts, much like living in their model town. The community boasted playgrounds and included a farm baseball team that was nearly semiprofessional; its own health service, complete with a doctor, a nurse, and ample medical supplies; a restaurant and soda fountain; a mercantile; places of worship; and schools. Koppers even had a summer camp, Camp Lightfoot, for employees' children. Thomas Lightfoot, the director of the company's welfare and compensation division and for whom the camp was named, summed it up best:

Many of the youngsters living in our mining towns some day will hold jobs with the company. The boys who attend the camp will, we hope, be our foremen, our superintendents and executives of the future, and we feel that their development is a matter of great importance for us.[15]

Lightfoot's reasoning provided a perfect example of welfare capitalism in the model towns. The company, by promoting an employee's goodwill through benefits and amenities, could create an ideal capitalist man who believed that his continued personal success was permanently tied to the company's best interests. In essence, doing the best for himself and his family equaled doing the best for the company. If a company was successful in creating this environment, it would surely be successful in creating a loyal workforce. At the time Kopperston was built, it was recognized as an exemplary model company town. Thirty-five years later, praise was still being heaped on the coal camp. Two 1978 *West Virginia Gazette* articles examined the community, one dubbing it "the classiest coal camp in Appalachia."[16]

The union established itself in the area on November 4, 1938, with the charter of Local Union 7604,[17] and the Koppers Coal mine was organized soon afterward. Still, the paternalism spawned by Koppers' initial effort at welfare capitalism benefited Eastern Associated Coal Company, a subsidiary of Eastern Gas and Fuel, who gained control of Koppers' coal holdings in the late 1940s. By all accounts, the workers and management had a good relationship. Eastern maintained Camp Lightfoot, the summer camp for miners' children, and many of the other amenities for decades. The company store, for instance, did not shut down until the 1980s.[18] Employees typically spoke well of their treatment by Eastern. While the area miners did walk out during the wildcat strike of 1976, they were not walking out on Eastern but against the Bituminous Coal Operators' Association.[19] Even though Eastern had sold the coal-camp houses to the residents in the 1950s, and even though the numerous amenities that made the model company town so special were lost over the decades, the welfare-capitalism experiment succeeded in Kopperston, though perhaps not in the manner the company had initially hoped:[20] loyalty to the company may have remained, but the desire to hold off the union failed.

While the coal companies seemed to supply much for their model communities, miners still looked to the union to have a voice in their own fate. To that end, the union worked to secure an eight-hour workday and was instrumental in creating legislation that provided for the health and safety of miners. In a show of solidarity, union members banded together to ensure health and retirement benefits for their members and for the widows of union miners. Even with its history of protecting worker rights, the UMWA witnessed a stark decline in its membership. During the 1940s and 1950s, when coal employed hundreds of thousands of workers, most were union miners. By 2000, only 20,522 of the 71,000 miners throughout the United States belonged to the union.[21] (See Figure 2.1.)

Membership had decreased so much that by the early 1990s, District 17 merged with Beckley-based District 29. By 2001, District 17 membership

Figure 2.1 **Nationwide UMWA Membership 1941–2000**

1941	1951	1955	1960	1965	1970	1985	1989	1995	2000
300,000	349,406	185,499	139,038	94,229	92,565	85,000	65,000	37,226	20,522

Source: See Endnote 20

(which includes southern West Virginia as well as southwestern Virginia and eastern Kentucky) had declined from thirty thousand members in 1979 to four thousand members.[22] By the beginning of the twenty-first century, union miners produced "less than a fifth of American coal."[23]

Much of this decrease can be attributed to the declining number of miners overall. Figure 2.2 shows the reduction of coal-mining employees in West Virginia over a fifty-four year period. Many miners replaced by machines must have felt betrayed when the UMWA, led by John L. Lewis, officially embraced mechanization to ensure the "long-run stabilization of the whole industry."[24] Dictates of the marketplace forced the union to accommodate mechanization as more and more small coal operators were pressed out of business by larger coal companies that could afford the new machinery. The decreases in mining employment, and hence union membership, left hundreds of thousands of people out of work. As the number of unemployed miners increased, the number of West Virginia residents decreased accordingly, a trend that persisted from the 1950s down to the present-day lows (see figure 2.2 on following page).

The union faced additional, and bitter, opposition from the large multinational coal companies now doing business in the southern coalfields,

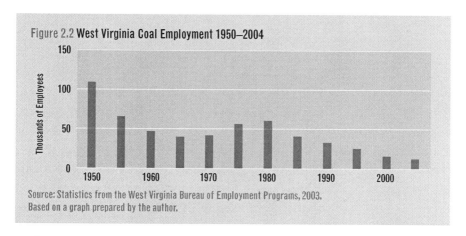

Figure 2.2 West Virginia Coal Employment 1950–2004

Source: Statistics from the West Virginia Bureau of Employment Programs, 2003. Based on a graph prepared by the author.

such as Massey, and by other large coal companies, such as Pittston, who tried to avoid the company's agreements with the union regarding health-care benefits for widows and retirees. In 1989, three years after yet another failed strike against Massey, the UMWA participated in a bitter strike against Pittston that resulted in large fines and strained relations. Ultimately, the fines were dismissed by the U.S. Supreme Court. The strike seemed to mobilize the union, especially after its Massey defeats, and it proved once more that the UMWA was not afraid to stand up for workers and their families.[25] Massey remains largely non-union, reporting that in 2003 only 193 of its 4,428 employees (or 4 percent) were members of the UMWA. Massey cited "an increased risk of work stoppages and higher labor costs" with workers represented by the union.[26]

The fierce anti-union sentiment witnessed throughout southern West Virginia is particularly offensive to a union that fought long, hard, and often bloody battles to gain recognition in the coalfields. The continued growth of non-union mines in southern West Virginia—the traditional stronghold of the UMWA—certainly hurt the union.[27] It also hurt the coal miners. As many companies turned to surface mining, heightened mechanization, and contract labor, miners found themselves part of an increasingly expendable workforce. The loss of influence was especially important to the communities themselves. In the past, the UMWA had improved not only the work environment of its members but also the work environment of all miners. It endorsed political candidates who advocated for labor and coal communities. Having learned from past episodes of massive unemployment, the union currently sponsors UMWA Career Centers Inc. to help unemployed members and their families obtain new job skills after coal-mining layoffs.[28] It remains to be seen if the present upsurge in coal demand will see any real increase in coal miner organization, especially in the southern West Virginia coalfields. In spite of the obstacles, the union has continued to evolve, organizing workers outside of its traditional coal-mining-targeted recruitment, and has gained some success by changing with the times.

The UMWA's stance on MTR has vacillated between the silence of acquiescence and outrage at opponents of the process. It has been a very precarious balancing act between protecting the interests of UMWA members who work on the sites, underground miners, and the communities affected by MTR. As membership continues to decrease, the UMWA has had little choice but to attempt to unionize MTR workers. Often such attempts at unionization have been spurned by surface workers who carry out their duties in a far safer environment and are better paid than underground coal miners.

The union has consistently followed a policy of trying to ensure fair wages for both segments of its membership—a tricky maneuver, since the interests of underground miners were often antithetical to those of surface workers. In the 1970s, UMWA leadership under Arnold Miller supported the strictest reclamation of strip-mining sites, instinctively knowing that many of these jobs would go to unemployed miners,[29] but the union faced stiff resistance in convincing workers on surface mines to cast their lot with the UMWA.

Until the proliferation of MTR in Appalachia during the 1990s, the union focused its attention on efforts to organize western surface workers. The bread-and-butter issues of the union—safer working conditions, better healthcare, and higher wages—were not real issues for these workers who already enjoyed these benefits. In addition, western surface mine workers did not have a long history of bloody unionization efforts to rally around, and most were not from mining traditions.[30] Most of the western surface workers remain unorganized by the UMWA.

Until recently, the UMWA has been conspicuously quiet regarding MTR. When addressing communities struggling in the face of a Massey MTR operation, union leadership expressed its opposition and encouraged people to fight against the operation. A 1998 editorial written by the UMWA's president, Cecil Roberts, indicated that the union strove to achieve a balance between mining jobs and environmental concerns. Unlike coal companies who often repeat that same mantra, Roberts detailed that the union was not in favor of either extreme (the environmentalists or the coal companies), which he claimed favored outlawing all coal mining or allowing the industry to operate without regard for community welfare. He heartily defended the union's right to protect the workers of these MTR sites, but he asserted that the union could both protect those jobs and speak up for the communities. Roberts stated:

> The UMWA strongly believes that coal companies should not be permitted to destroy local communities in the process of mountaintop removal mining, including by blasting. Community residents with homes and farms should be protected from the consequences of such damage. The UMWA believes that there should be additional legal protections to ensure that blasting damage can be easily and completely compensated by coal companies . . . [W]ith regard to any property within 1-mile radius of a blast, there should be a rebuttable presumption that the blast caused any property damage.[31]

Roberts called for better federal enforcement of the surface-mining act, and a halt to the allowance of fish and wildlife habitat and recreation lands as an acceptable post-mining use. He maintained that southern West Virginia mountains with historical significance, such as the historical parts of Blair Mountain and the Stanley family farm on Kayford Mountain, should not be mined at all. He also noted that mining provided jobs in areas where few jobs were available, and that the taxes generated by mining, including surface mining, were important sources of public revenue. Even though he maligned Massey's MTR activities in the past, he did not mention Massey in his 1998 editorial. However, Roberts seemed to defend Arch Coal, another MTR operator, as a good and responsible corporate steward.[32] Not surprisingly, some of Arch Coal's employees are union employees. By shrewdly allowing the unionization of many of its MTR employees, Arch Coal ensured itself an unholy alliance with the UMWA, one that left the UMWA unable to adequately speak out against the process now that it was bound to protect its MTR members.

This protectionist stance was seen during and after the 1998 *Bragg v. Robertson* case, heard by Judge Charles Haden II—a case explored more thoroughly in chapter five. Soon after the judge's preliminary injunction effectively halted the expansion of Arch Coal's Dal-Tex mine, 1,500 union miners and industry supporters marched on the state capitol in protest. At risk were 387 union jobs at Dal-Tex. District 17 president Bob Phalen spoke of Haden's decision as a workers' issue, rather than a union–versus–non-union issue, and declared that the ruling would cause the "economic devastation [of] the state."[33] Those opposing MTR were painted as "extreme" environmentalists. Phalen went on to say that a line must be drawn "when extremists set out to destroy an entire industry and destroy the lives of tens of thousands of workers."[34] A union once proud to speak for the coalfield communities, not just its members, showed how much things had changed when it denounced community members affected by MTR who were now suing for the enforcement of federal regulations. At least one of the plaintiffs in the case was a disabled underground coal miner and union member.

The UMWA's position in *Bragg v. Robertson* illustrated yet another break from community involvement by union leadership. So fervent was the union in its support of MTR in West Virginia that President Cecil Roberts requested a debate with Cindy Rank, one of the leading environmental opponents to MTR, to discuss why "West Virginia needs mountaintop coal mining (and mining in general) done responsibly and by the law."[35] What Roberts failed to acknowledge was that the plaintiffs in the case *did* sue for mining to be "done responsibly and by the law," and that Haden had ruled that neither had taken place. More appropriately, the union might have discussed the very concerns of the plaintiffs and how illegal activity might be reined in. Arch Coal had the opportunity to submit a legal application for expansion of the mine in question at any time before the injunction was handed down, but the company erroneously assumed the court would rule in its favor and that members of West Virginia's federal delegation would intercede on its behalf. In supporting Arch Coal in this matter, the union was in blatant denial. As a *Charleston Gazette* editorial stated, miner layoffs rested squarely at the feet of Arch Coal, not the residents and citizen groups that brought forth the lawsuit.[36] When contacted regarding the union's official stance on MTR, Roberts's response remained consistent: a need to balance good jobs, including MTR jobs, with environmental concerns.[37]

The union's fierce protectionist attitude toward MTR infuriated some out-of-work underground miners. A 1999 *Charleston Gazette* letter to the editor voiced some of those frustrations. The author indicated that he was one of thousands of laid-off underground union miners. He questioned the lack of UMWA publicity for the loss of those underground jobs, while the union lavished attention on the potential loss of a few hundred jobs at Dal-Tex. The author clearly believed that the UMWA had created its own problems by championing MTR at the expense of underground coal miners. He also believed that if the union had been as supportive when the underground jobs were in jeopardy, many underground miners might have been able to keep their jobs. It should be noted that Randy Sprouse, the author of the letter, was apparently so disgruntled with the inattentiveness of politicos and his union to the degradation occurring at the hands of MTR mining that he formed the community action group Coal River Mountain Watch in 1998.[38]

Indeed, balancing the interests of the two factions became more and more difficult for a union determined to maintain its dignity and traditions while in desperate need of members. Although the union sided with residents against Massey, its archenemy, it staunchly defended MTR, thereby limiting the amount of collaboration it could engage in with the community groups. For these reasons, the UMWA's influence in coal communities continued to diminish. Many coal-community residents were no longer able to depend on the union and found themselves forced to organize grassroots organizations to oppose the injustices of the coal companies, injustices that the UMWA failed to adequately recognize and address.

Conclusion

After decades of struggle in the southern coalfields, the UMWA is now facing opposition by the numerous anti-union coal mines operating in southern West Virginia. For much of its existence, the union played an important role in the lives of miners, their families, and their communities. However, the UMWA has recently found itself on opposing sides of many coalfield residents.

As union membership in the southern coalfields declined, so did the union's influence within coalfield communities. Influence continued to decrease as the newest wave of mechanization embodied in MTR forced more workers out of their jobs. Although residents used to experience the influence of the union on a daily basis, the union's new alliance with MTR often pitted it against them. Today the union continues to struggle to balance the needs of both factions of its membership. Many residents who are disappointed in their treatment by MTR companies, whether unionized or not, know they must take action if their communities are to survive. They have formed their own organizations to combat adversarial relationships with coal companies that the union, at one time, would have battled with them.

3

TO DANCE WITH THE DEVIL
The Social Impact of MTR

There are two roads in life, a right one and a wrong one.
There is no in-between path to take.
—Pauline Canterberry, resident of Sylvester, West Virginia

As the nineteenth century gave way to the twentieth, West Virginia's rural backcounties experienced a fundamental transformation. Natural-resource speculators pervaded the area. Chief among them were the coal and timber industries, along with their handmaiden, the railroad industry. Throughout West Virginia, beautiful hardwood forests came crashing down until, by the 1920s, nearly all of them were gone.[1] Railroads penetrated the rugged countryside to whisk the natural treasures of timber and coal away from the state and into the large cities beyond. Older agricultural communities were soon joined by the new industrial towns that dotted the landscape for the express purpose of providing homes for workers and their families. The repercussions of this rapid-fire change resonated throughout the southern region. Subsistence farmers accustomed to bartering soon found themselves usurped by wage-earning laborers who toiled in the mines rather than in the fields.

As the industrial age shifted to the information age, coal miners struggled for their economic lives. Technology had rendered them nearly obsolete. Underground miners saw their ranks slashed as the continuous miner and longwall machinery replaced tens of thousands of men. Surface workers witnessed the introduction of twenty-story draglines that performed work previously requiring hundreds of workers. Coalfield residents were affected by these changes, too. Few alternative economic opportunities were available in these areas where coal had been in power for more than one hundred years and where shortsighted politicians had done little to advance economic diversification. While many individuals migrated from southern West Virginia, others stayed because of personal ties to their families and communities. Those who refused to migrate were placed in the most precarious position of all, caught between dwindling coal jobs, particularly as communities transitioned to MTR, and the desire to protect their own homes and families from what they deemed a very unpromising future. These social complexities still pervade the southern West Virginia areas currently being mined by MTR.

Pauline Canterberry and Mary Miller live in Sylvester, Boone County. Sylvester is a small, incorporated town of some 195 people on the outskirts of Whitesville.[2] Sylvester was founded in 1952 in the hopes that it would be a haven for those who did not want to live inside a coal camp while making a living mining coal.[3] The town has seen a number of coal companies on its fringes during its more than five decades of existence. Both Miller and Canterberry note that previous underground coal companies had bosses and supervisors who lived in the town, which ensured that the companies had a vested interest in the health and safety of the community.[4] Then came Massey's huge MTR operations. Initially, nothing was out of the ordinary as coal trucks carried out vast amounts of coal just as the other companies had done. All of that changed in 1997 when Massey opened its Elk Run Coal Company preparation plant just outside the Sylvester city limits. This preparation plant cleaned coal derived from some of Massey's underground mines at Elk Run as well as its surface-mined coal from its Progress mine.[5] With Massey's new preparation plant fully operational, the town and its residents began to experience significant problems.

Many residents have their first encounter with MTR when a coal company contacts them about plans for blasting. The letter residents receive offers homeowners the chance to have their property surveyed in case there is damage incurred. The purpose of the survey is to make it easier to distinguish preexisting damage from damage that resulted from the explosion. Anyone owning property within half a mile of blasting receives the letter.[6] Before blasting can occur, the mine operator has to formulate a plan to protect the public from the negative impact of the operation. A review of these highly technical plans should reveal the time of the blasting and how close it will be to other structures.[7]

Once blasting commences, the effects can be felt for miles around. Often these blasts disturb properties, separating walls and floors from each other and from the foundation. Blasting can also hurl boulder debris from the MTR site into residential lawns, cause damage to private property, and ruin water wells. Russell Elkins from Rawl, Mingo County, saw his windows fall out of his house immediately after a Massey coal company blasted nearby. Elkins estimates that nine out of ten homes in the hollow were affected by the blasting in some way, but he claims that their owners were afraid to come forward because they or their loved ones were employed by Massey. Dickie Judy from Foster Hollow, Boone County, experienced damage to his home as well, both inside and out, during a blast on a nearby MTR site. His foundation split, and his walls shook so hard that pictures fell. Larry Brown, also from Rawl, observed many kinds of blast-related damage in his church and in other structures in the town—cracked foundations, split windows, ruined wells. Summarizing the problems, he noted, "It's destroying property and the state. The beauty of our state is being cut out . . . torn away from us."[8]

Those far away from the blasting, in some instances miles away, are able to hear the distant rumbling as the dynamite is set off. Those closer to the blasting may experience tremors in their houses and on their property. Flyrock—pieces of rock made airborne by the force of the blast—may also result. An MTR site close to Carlos Gore's home in Blair produced flyrock the size of softballs that pelted his house and landed in his front yard. Emphasizing the danger of such flyrock, Gore commented to regulators from the West Virginia Department of Environmental Protection (DEP), "If a rock this big hits you or your car or your house, you're going to have more than a headache. It's going to ruin your whole week, because there's going to be a funeral."[9] Gore's family is one of fewer than thirty still remaining in the small, historic community of Blair. As the MTR permits have increased, the small community has been dismantled house by house, hollow by hollow.[10] Similar experiences occur throughout the southern West Virginia coalfields.

Federal studies have balked at acknowledging residents' assertions that problems have resulted from blasting and MTR. One such document, the Final Programmatic Environmental Impact Statement (FPEIS) on MTR, declared that:

> [t]he existing regulatory controls provide adequate protections from coal mining-related blasting impacts on public safety and structures including wells [and that] the existing regulatory programs are intended to ensure public safety and prevent damage rather than eliminate nuisances from coal mine blasting activities. Some blasting within legal limits may still constitute a nuisance to people in the general area. As with all nuisances, the affected persons may have legal recourse regarding blasting nuisances through civil action. Consequently, blasting is not considered a "significant issue" and no actions are considered in this [Environmental Impact Statement].[11]

Coalfield residents tell a different story. Noise, dust, and property damage associated with blasting have been frequent complaints.[12] Unlike traditional contour strip-mining where blasting would last from weeks to months, MTR blasts can last (and affect close neighbors) for years.[13] While legal recourse in civil courts is an option, the residents must prove that damage was caused directly by blasting and not through faulty construction. To do this, they must have an independent assessment of their homes with all detailed findings and current damages. Residents within one-half mile of the permit area can request a blasting survey,[14] but those farther out are on their own. These surveys can be costly, especially in a depressed region where people have problems even meeting basic survival needs; thus, many outside the one-half-mile radius do not have surveys completed.

Greta Stone (a pseudonym) lives in the vicinity of Oceana-Kopperston. A forty-year resident of the community, she worked in the Wyoming County school system for more than three decades. She lives within one mile of an MTR site. Huge coal trucks barrel by her house seven days a week, 365 days a year. A layer of coal dust covers most of the area. It is the dust and noise that cause the most problems for Stone and her husband. She says, "Coal trucks run all day and the noise is so bad. They pass each other constantly."[15] The coal company does attempt to sweep the streets periodically, but this often only stirs up the dust and creates more work for Stone and her husband. Like many people in the area who are aware of the mining site in their backyard, Stone feels torn. "You're so concerned [about jobs], and you don't want to bite the hand that feeds you. The coal companies and timbering companies provide jobs. No one wants to see anybody put out of a job, because we have to work . . . We have to work."[16] According to Stone, during the 1970s, when surface mining was hotly contested throughout the state, some students would become upset when anyone mentioned the environmental drawbacks of strip mining because their fathers worked on strip-mining sites. Teachers, in return, had to be extremely careful about how they approached the subject, if they approached it at all.[17]

Contrast yesterday's reality to today's reality where in Boone, Logan, McDowell, and Mingo counties, teachers can get grants and materials to teach their students about coal through a collaborative effort with the coal industry and local businesses. Coal Education Development and Resource of Southern West Virginia Inc. (CEDAR) is a non-profit, volunteer corporation that is helping the industry's cause. Their goal "is to facilitate the increase of knowledge and understanding of the many benefits the coal industry provides in daily lives by providing financial resources and coal education materials to implement its study in the school curriculum."[18] The organization's three programs include a regional coal fair that allows students (K–12) to enter "coal projects" in science, math, literature, art, music, technology/multimedia, and social studies. Cash prizes are awarded.[19] Similar programs do not exist for curricula focused on the environment or a diversified economy.

The noise and dust created from the constant coal-truck haulage also pose certain problems in these communities. In 2003, the legal weight for hauling coal in fifteen southern West Virginia coal counties increased to 120,000 pounds from the previous 65,000–80,000-pound limit. The roads in many of these areas are very narrow, and even at the previous low rate of sixty-five thousand pounds, these behemoth machines got into accidents with coal-community residents on numerous occasions. Sometimes the accidents were fatal.

Many citizens of the fifteen counties opposed raising the weight limits, fearing for their safety. They knew the roads and bridges in their neighborhoods were not meant to bear so much weight, and they had seen the results of illegal overweight trucks running through their neighborhoods—demolished roads that were rarely, if ever, repaired, and unnecessary deaths.[20] Those against the tonnage increase used such arguments, but their protests went unheard, and West Virginia's 2003 legislature increased the amount. This should have surprised no one familiar with the history of overweight coal trucks in the southern coalfields. The trucking industry indicated that they were only competitive for contracts if they hauled over the legal limits. Otherwise they risked being underbid for contracts. Of course, if the truckers were caught hauling illegal loads, the truck company was responsible for the fine, not the coal company. Allowed to run illegally for decades, many truck companies were vulnerable when, prior to passing the new weight limits, the state began to crack down on overweight coal trucks.

It is common knowledge in the industry and coal communities that these trucks have run illegally for at least twenty years while authorities turned a blind eye.[21] This inaction resulted in the purchasing of even larger trucks while the state continued to ignore their illegal activity. Even when the state tried to address the situation in late 2001, through increased fines on the overweight trucks, it met with resistance from truckers in the southern coalfields who were effectively shut down for several days because of enforcement.[22] Bickering between the two factions continued well into 2002. In March 2002, about a dozen coal-truck drivers rallied around the state capitol, blowing their horns in support of new, higher weight limits. At the same time, a group of close to one hundred legislators, community activists, and union members gathered at the capitol in a rally focused on keeping and enforcing the current eighty-thousand-pound weight limit.[23] Proponents of the increase saw their livelihoods at stake. Opponents saw public safety at stake. Caving in to pressure, the state continued its enforcement efforts, watered down, and in the end, the legislature made legal activity that had been occurring illegally for decades.

Perhaps the best example of the consequences of illegally hauling coal is the town of Sylvester. The town experienced firsthand the noise, dust, and other problems caused by huge coal trucks. So troublesome was the dust in Sylvester that in 2001, 154 of the town's residents filed a lawsuit against Elk Run, a subsidiary of Massey. (Their lawsuit is discussed at length in chapter 5.) Mary Miller stated, "[Y]ou're a prisoner in your own home, breathing this coal dust twenty-four hours a day."[24] In what was for many an amazing turn of events, Boone Circuit Judge E. Lee Schlaegel Jr. ruled against Massey and declared that the coal company must contain the dust that was polluting the town or cease operations. Massey complied by erecting a huge nylon dome over their preparation plant. Massey had originally asserted that the pine trees they had planted in front of the plant were enough to keep the dust to a minimum. But the trees were small and in no way could have cleansed the area. The dome worked better, but it has ripped twice since its construction and had to be replaced.[25] The extent of the dust problem is evident by a quick drive through the town: coal dust blankets almost everything, including patio furniture that is protected by a cover. Even spraying homes with power hoses becomes futile, considering that a few weeks later, they will once again be coated with coal dust. Residents remain concerned about the possible health hazards the coal dust presents.[26]

The process of cleaning coal is a dirty one. Coal is washed to remove the ash.[27] What is left over is a thick, gooey substance known as slurry. Slurry is contained by an impoundment that holds vast amounts of the impurities and wastewater left over from the washing.[28] The holding capacity for a coal-slurry impoundment can range from millions to even billions of gallons of slurry. In addition, slurry impoundments are frequently hundreds of feet deep and encompass several acres. One such impoundment is the Brushy Fork impoundment that was built about five miles from the Sylvester-Whitesville neighborhood. This impoundment, owned by Massey, is nine hundred feet high and will hold 8.166 billion gallons of slurry once it is completed. This will be the largest impoundment in the nation.[29] One of the main fears voiced by Sylvester residents is the escape plan on file at the DEP in case of a break, which suggests an exit route that has the community leaving *toward* the flow of the impoundment break.[30] Mary Miller noted, "[T]hey are . . . trapping us down here in these valleys with no hope of escape."[31]

Hydrogeologist Rick Eades performed a survey of the Brushy Fork impoundment. He, too, was alarmed that the evacuation plan prepared by

Marfork, the Massey subsidiary that owns the impoundment, instructed the citizens of Sylvester to travel four miles into the path of any sludge release. He called for a new emergency evacuation plan to be constructed, one that would not have inhabitants driving into the danger.[32]

In October 2000, a Massey slurry impoundment in Martin County, Kentucky, broke through the underground mine it rested above. From there, the 300 million gallons of slurry poured through local creeks, eventually reaching the Tug Fork of the Big Sandy River, on the border between West Virginia and Kentucky, as well as the Ohio River.[33] While no one died, one hundred miles of streams were polluted and any life forms there were obliterated.[34] Eades has noted that consultants who work for the coal companies are under a huge amount of pressure to provide data that is favorable to the consultant's client. He stated, "[C]onsultants must find the 'least-case scenario' of environmental risk, somewhere within their credible methods, to enable coal companies to do whatever they want to do."[35] He did not make such assertions lightly, noting that he had been employed as a government and commercial consultant for sixteen years.[36] He worried that the mine's pillars did not have enough coal left in them to support the additional load from the Brushy Fork slurry impoundment, despite Eagle Fork Mine's claims that all was well. Constructing impoundments over underground mines could leave the impoundment vulnerable to breakthroughs, putting the communities near the impoundment in direct harm. Eades's concern stemmed from the fact that coal companies would never leave that much coal in a mine, and to suppose that the company had any prior knowledge that a slurry dam would be built above it is illogical.[37]

The fear of impoundments and dust problems grip the entire town of Sylvester. Even employees at the now-closed Sylvester grade school were affected during the course of their workday. In the school cafeteria, coal dust blanketed the cooks' equipment so much that the cooks were forced to wash it off before they could use it. Finally, the cooks decided to store their pots and pans in plastic bags to keep from having to wash them twice.[38] Just a year before the local elementary school shut down, the school had conducted practice emergency evacuations of the students in case of a slurry-impoundment break. Officials at the school timed the children as they moved from the school to the tallest knoll in the area, which most of the town would be clamoring to reach should an actual slurry-impoundment break occur.[39] "There's children in these valleys, too," Pauline Canterberry said. "I might be old and ready to go, but a lot of these people are not. They still got life ahead of them."[40]

Many Sylvester residents, as well as other southern West Virginia coalfield residents, are angry that politicians and coal companies do not seem to treat their communities (and particularly the young children living there) as if they were worth being saved. Some children are so frightened of flooding and slurry breaks that when it rains, they sleep fully clothed. The same problem occurs with the elderly, who fear flooding and the incessant noise associated with blasting and coal trucks.[41] The problems associated with the stoker plant above Sylvester and the dust it created were severe enough to cause the Boone County Board of Education to close the Sylvester school, rather than maintain its newer facilities, and consolidate it with Whitesville Elementary.[42] Whitesville Elementary has been repeatedly flooded and is older than the Sylvester school.[43]

Unfortunately, Sylvester and Whitesville are not isolated cases in southern West Virginia. Huge coal-slurry impoundments have been built above schools elsewhere, and in some instances, schools have even been built in valleys below a dam. In Wyoming County, for example, the new Wyoming County East High School was built less than two miles from the high-hazard Itmann Preparation Plant impoundment (formerly the Joe Branch impoundment). Like the Martin County, Kentucky, impoundment that dumped more than 300 million gallons of coal slurry into tributaries that flow into the Tug Fork,[44] the Itmann Preparation Plant impoundment was built partially over underground mines. In addition, the impoundment had been constructed at least twelve years prior to the building of the new high school. The March 14, 2003, emergency evacuation plan that Consolidation Coal Company submitted to the DEP indicated that if a "fair weather break" were to occur, the slurry would crest at 21 feet at New Richmond (home of the school), 11 feet at Pineville, 11.4 feet at Mullensville, and 11.4 feet at Marianna. These communities are 2.4, 7.7, 13.7, and 17.9 miles, respectively, from the impoundment.[45] The high school consists of nearly six hundred students and employees, is downriver from any potential breakthroughs, and, as illustrated by the company's own evacuation plan, would be devastated should a breakthrough ever occur. (The company is quick to note in its evacuation plan the unlikelihood of this ever occurring, in spite of the dam's categorization as a high-hazard impoundment.)[46] It is unclear if the Board of Education did not realize the danger existed or simply chose to ignore the fact when it decided to construct the school in its present location. Also downstream from the impoundment is a retirement home in New Richmond and several small communities. It is likely that Pineville, the seat of Wyoming County, would be hurt drastically by any breakthroughs, since it is a mere seven miles from the site.[47]

The danger associated with these impoundments being so close to communities is real, and deaths of schoolchildren due to such impoundments is not just speculation. On October 21, 1966, a similar impoundment in Wales spilled over its boundaries and landed in the coal town of Aberfan below. The disaster resulted in a loss of 144 people, 116 of them schoolchildren who had met their death after the rushing sludge completely covered three classrooms of their school.[48] Disasters such as Aberfan should be cautionary tales for those constructing coal dams above communities. The British government did create warning documents and distribute them to interested parties both inside and outside Britain. One of those interested parties was the coal company operating above Buffalo Creek, Logan County, West Virginia. The company had even consulted with British experts. Yet in 1972, Buffalo Creek was virtually destroyed and 125 people died when a coal dam above the community collapsed. Only after this loss of life would coal-dam failures receive attention in the U.S.[49]

In another instance in Raleigh County, West Virginia, Marsh Fork Elementary School rests 225 feet from a coal silo and four hundred yards from a slurry impoundment. In 2005, the Massey subsidiary responsible for the two structures proposed a coal-loading silo 220 feet from the school. The permit was initially approved by the DEP who viewed it as an extension of an existing permit, one that had been approved in 1975 before the passage of SMCRA that outlawed such construction within three hundred feet of a school.[50] Two months prior to the June 30, 2005, approval by Environmental Protection Secretary Stephanie Timmermeyer, Massey began construction for the new silo's foundation, assuming the financial risk that came with finishing this initial stage of construction prior to the permit's final approval.[51] The *Charleston Gazette* revealed that the boundaries of the original permit had been altered over the previous eight years on maps turned into the DEP by the company. No expansion was ever requested, or approved. After their own review of the boundaries, the DEP rescinded their initial approval and ordered the company to tear out the foundation and reclaim the area. The DEP concluded that the maps used to allow the permitting had been inaccurate and that the proposed silo was actually outside of the previously permitted area, thus making it a new permit and not an extension of a permit.[52] Massey appealed the decision with the state Surface Mining Board.[53] In March 2006, that group upheld the DEP's decision to revoke the permit.[54] In August 2006, the DEP once again denied the coal-silo permit request.[55]

A number of residents from the affected community made their dissatisfaction with the permitting process and their concern for their children known. In the midst of this activity was Ed Wiley. Wiley had a granddaughter attending Marsh Fork Elementary and was concerned for the health of those attending the school. During the silo dispute, Wiley conducted a sit-in on the capitol steps for five hours and even met with Governor Joe Manchin about the school. Manchin ordered an investigation into the school's conditions.[56] By September 2005, the results of that investigation concluded that the school was safe.

Coalfield residents were not convinced, and many, including Wiley, felt that their neighborhood still needed an alternative to the Marsh Fork school.[57] The state's top epidemiologist cautioned that the health risks to students remained unknown, even as the school was cleared by the West Virginia Department of Education for another school year.[58] In spite of the epidemiologist's caution, Manchin's general counsel informed Coal River Mountain Watch that state agencies did not believe that any further testing was warranted.[59] CRMW then launched their "Pennies of Promise" campaign to raise money for a new school for the Marsh Fork students.

Wiley took action, too. Frustrated by what he saw as a lack of response from local and state leaders, he began a walk from Charleston, West Virginia, to Washington, DC, in August 2006. He concluded his 366-mile walk on September 13, 2006, with a meeting with Senator Robert Byrd.[60] At the time of this writing, no plans have been made to build a new school or to close Marsh Fork Elementary.

Seven years earlier, in 1999, Larry Gibson took a similar walk across West Virginia to bring attention to MTR. Gibson logged 493 miles in a walk that took him across the state, finally ending in Charleston. In spite of tenuous health (Gibson had undergone angioplasty surgery just two weeks earlier and had previously undergone bypass surgery), he surpassed his original goal of 490 miles, representing the number of stream miles lost to valley fills on MTR mines. Along the way, he conducted presentations and provided information to people.[61] Gibson maintains the Stanley Heirs Park at Kayford Mountain, and he also founded the Keeper of the Mountains Foundation. He has repeatedly refused to sell out to Arch Coal, who mines the area all around his property. His little piece of land is one of the few spots where it is possible to see an active MTR site.[62]

All of the problems associated with MTR notwithstanding, there is an unquestionable need for jobs in an area where the unemployment rate runs as high as 11 percent, representing some of the highest numbers in the state. The recent loss of thousands of residents in search of work has resulted in a population made up mostly of the elderly and disabled. The few remaining working-age individuals lucky enough to have jobs work for the coal companies, the school system, or the supporting welfare system. Well-paying jobs are sparse in the coalfields, and while many southern West Virginians oppose MTR, others staunchly support it. Some of the most vocal protectors of the practice are the workers whose livelihood depends on the continuation of MTR.

In 1998, when Arch Coal's Dal-Tex mine was trying to secure a controversial expansion permit, workers at the operation showed up in droves at a public DEP hearing. They complained about the high unemployment rate in their area and spoke of the desperate need for good jobs. Dal-Tex encouraged their outspokenness: before the hearing, the company enclosed notices with their employees' paychecks, which read, "There will be people there who don't want this permit issued. They don't care about your job. Please attend this hearing and show that you support the future of our jobs here at Dal-Tex. Encourage your family and friends to join you. Arrive early to get your 'I'm proud to work at Dal-Tex' T-shirts while supplies last."[63] At the hearing, one miner, a resident of Boone County who was employed at the Logan County mine, asked, "What are we going to give the next generation to live on? How are they going to make it? What are we going to do for jobs for our families?"[64]

Carlos Gore, a resident of Blair, asked the supporters how many of them lived in the area where the MTR was taking place. No one in the audience resided in Blair. Gore responded that there was something wrong with that scenario. Gore then asked all of the audience members who did not live in the area to raise their hand. His request was met with a flurry of hands in the air. Gore then emphasized, "We're not trying to shut you people down. We've got rules and regulations that these [DEP] people are supposed to enforce. That's all we want."[65] Even the president of the local UMWA appeared at the meeting in support of the community. He tried to calm the audience down and explain that the residents wanted the mining to be done according to law and that the company had an obligation to either mine around the residents or buy them out at a reasonable price.[66]

Still, those depending on the mine to support their families were not easily consoled. Noting that the mines provided one of the few avenues to secure a livable wage, a miner at Hobet described how his household consisted of ten people, including a son and daughter-in-law who traveled to Charleston every day for $7-an-hour jobs. He asked a very good question: "What are we going to do for jobs?"[67] It was a question that neither state nor federal politicians have adequately addressed. Community leaders in the affected towns were just as adamant as the MTR employees. An administrator for the Logan County Commission declared that there was no other way for the county to support itself except through the coal industry, stating, "If the mining process is stopped or impeded, Logan County would suffer devastating consequences. The county commission is not saying coal mining is perfect. But we cannot lessen the degree of dependence on coal that currently exists."[68]

Other industries dependent on MTR were also quite vocal in their support and suspicious of the environmental impact of the process. Stephen Walker, the president of Walker Machinery, said, "Do not blame the modern coal industry for water-quality problems in Southern West Virginia today. Modern coal mining does not pollute."[69] Coal-industry representatives were indignant. At another hearing about mountaintop mine permits in October 1998, Bill Raney, lead lobbyist for the West Virginia Coal Association, told EPA representatives at the Logan County hearing, "Today's hearing isn't about streams. It's about jobs, and families and kids, and a way of life."[70] At this hearing, opponents of MTR may have far outnumbered proponents, but proponents at the meeting were still especially vocal.

Rather than addressing legitimate concerns posed by opponents of MTR, one union member working for Arch Coal lashed out at opponents and questioned their legitimacy as functioning community members when he said, "Most of the people who are doing all the talking couldn't tell a dozer from a loader. Most of them are on a check or too old to have a family to raise."[71] A company manager added, "All we have are Chicken Little environmentalists claiming the sky is falling, and they have a sympathetic press to help their cause."[72] Opponents implored the EPA to ignore the pleas about jobs and to do their job of enforcing the law and protecting the environment.

As in the previous meeting, Carlos Gore was vehement about his right to protect his home, even though he understood the workers' desire to keep their jobs: "You put a pond and valley fill in my hollow. I had two streams running, and I had well water. Now I don't have anything. I've got a right to live there. I lived there before the mountaintop removal came in, and I'll be there long after it's gone."[73] Supporters of MTR expressed anger with what they perceived as flawed priorities. UMWA member Terry Vance, a vocal proponent and employee at an MTR mine, stated, "You need to take a good look around at what you're impacting. We're people, not crawdads or spotted salamanders . . . We're not going to go into the ranks of the unemployed quietly."[74] In January 2007, the U.S. Army Corps of Engineers issued a Clean Water Act permit for Arch Coal's Spruce No. 1 Mine. While scaled back from 3,113 acres to 2,278 acres, this is the same permit at the core of the 1998 Dal-Tex controversy, the center of a series of protests by UMWA members. Since that time, Arch Coal transferred the operation to its Mingo Logan Coal Co. subsidiary and will operate the mine with non-union workers.[75]

Workers and others who depended on MTR to make a living sometimes used violent rhetoric when speaking of judicial attempts to monitor it. One operator of a local trucking company commented on Judge Haden's decision to halt the expansion of the Dal-Tex site, "It could get ugly. I'm surprised that some of these guys that have lost their jobs haven't taken it into their own hands with this judge."[76] Tensions became so severe that in September 1999, when trying to commemorate the Battle of Blair Mountain, a group including long-time West Virginia political mainstay Ken Hechler was attacked by proponents of MTR who erroneously blamed the re-enactors for lost jobs. Hechler served as a United States congressman from West Virginia from 1959 to 1977 and as West Virginia's secretary of state from 1985 to 2001. Throughout his tenure as a congressman, Hechler was a true friend of the coal miner and, typically, enjoyed an excellent relationship with the UMWA. He was such a staunch ally for the miners that he had been known to go against not only the coal interests but also UMWA leadership itself when its actions were not in the best interest of the miners it represented. Such was the case during the corrupt UMWA presidency of Tony Boyle when Hechler stood up for stronger safety measures and accountability from coal companies. Hechler's public service saw him repeatedly speaking up for the blue-collar worker when others elected from the state remained silent.[77]

History was lost to those lashing out at the re-enactors. Acting more like the company thugs who historically strong-armed the union than actual union members, laid-off UMWA workers and others kicked members of the re-enactment group, ripped the signs from their hands, and pelted them with eggs. Some re-enactors even had their eyeglasses broken. Hechler himself was slightly injured.[78] The protestors would have been better served to lay their anger with the company who failed to obey the law and used quick extraction methods that would hasten the end of coal.[79]

Coal-industry propaganda was able to convince some underground miners that any ruling against MTR (or enforcement of laws regarding MTR and, in turn, enforcement of laws that made certain valley fills illegal) would lead to an eventual end to underground mining. In truth, however, experts have concluded that Haden's ruling would not have affected that many underground mines. Still, the fix was in and had some underground miners on the defensive. One underground miner commented, "Until we quit letting the environmentalists come in and tell us what we can and can't do, we aren't going to have any mining."[80] Terry Vance commented that he and his family lived near an MTR site and that it was not hazardous. If it had been, he would have moved his family. His opinion was in stark contrast to his Logan County neighbors that filed a lawsuit against the damage the process was having on their property. One electrical engineer for Arch Coal, and a native of Logan County, commented that streams at the foot of one of his company's valley fills were clearer than the ones he had grown up around. He went on to suggest that communities focus on cleaning the sewage out of the streams instead of coal refuse.[81] Still, others living in the shadow of MTR contend with rivers, like Coal River, that are so polluted they have earned a place on the most endangered rivers list.

Clearly, those who stand to lose their jobs if MTR is halted or curbed have a vested interest and will do whatever is in their power to ensure its continuation. These individuals do not seem to realize that while MTR does provide a few high-paying jobs, the jobs typically are not long-lasting. The coal on MTR sites is obtained so quickly that it is depleted far faster than with traditional mining methods. Coal communities have always struggled to strike a balance between their need to maintain jobs and their need to preserve the environment, but with MTR, the balancing act has become even more delicate.

The problem is so pressing that even the Church has weighed in on the subject. By 1999, in a rare political move, Methodists, Catholics, Episcopalians, Lutherans, and Presbyterians had all passed declarations opposing MTR.[82] Their pronouncements were certainly important, but they were not assertive enough to enact any real social change—even though they represented a unified front, and even though religion is a cornerstone of the rural communities in southern West Virginia. Members of these communities, whether they belonged to religious organizations or not, banded together to create their own safe harbors, known as "free spaces," in their neighborhoods. The Church may not have generated direct results for them. The political process may have offered them no respite. The UMWA may have allied with the very mode of industry that was destroying their communities. But in free spaces, concerned citizens could gather together to air their grievances, voice their opinions, and urge each other on in the fight.

Free spaces are "environments in which people are able to learn a new self-respect, a deeper and more assertive group identity, public skills, and values of cooperation and civic virtue."[83] To expand the idea further, historical free space, as defined by political scientist Richard Cuoto, includes a "sense of connection with past or other current effort to achieve dramatic change, allowing the understanding of democratic efforts as being related and not isolated."[84] Free spaces provide people with an intimidation-free environment where they can express their beliefs and brainstorm new ideas without fear of retaliation from those who hold power. Free spaces are few and far between in the southern West Virginia coalfields. Still, some residents have been adept at creating free spaces in spite of a history of oppression at the hands of the coal industry and the politicians who favor it.

The free spaces created in the coalfields of southern West Virginia lend a collective voice to those trying to protect their homes and environment from encroaching MTR. Two of the most vocal of these groups are the Ohio Valley Environmental Coalition and the Coal River Mountain Watch. Formed in 1987, OVEC hoped to protect the environment of West Virginia and parts of Ohio and Kentucky through education, grassroots organizing, and media efforts. Presently, the organization's main focus is MTR. CRMW was formed in 1998 by a group of concerned citizens in the neighborhood of Whitesville, West Virginia. Originally headed by laid-off underground coal miner Randy Sprouse, the organization hoped to organize the residents of Whitesville and the surrounding countryside directly affected by MTR into a vocal coalition. Both organizations have their own newsletters to address the organizations' current campaigns. OVEC's *Winds of Change* (formerly *e-notes*) and CRMW's *Messenger* are free to the public. In the March 2006 edition of the *Messenger*, articles can be found about coal sludge found in well water and a Massey sludge spill in the Coal River.

CRMW is a particularly impressive entity as it is stationed in the middle of some of the most active MTR sites in the state and is home to some of the most contentious struggles over MTR. The individuals that organized CRMW have remained committed to the protection of their communities. Knowing that there is strength in numbers, it gives individuals a collective voice that is harder to ignore. Through their organizational efforts, protests, and educational activities, CRMW acts as a free space for its community members.

CRMW's past director Julia "Judy" Bonds has become nationally and internationally recognizable among American environmental activists. In 2003, Bonds won the Goldman Prize, an award that has been called the Nobel Prize for the environment. Her passionate fight against MTR climaxed in 2001 when her family history came full circle. Six generations ago, her grandfather had been the first person to move into Marfork Hollow; she was the last person to leave Marfork, and the last generation of her family to live in the hollow, after being driven out by MTR. Holding out was sometimes a dangerous venture for her. She remembers being "run off" the narrow hollow roads into ditches by supporters of the mine.[85] Bonds spent the first forty-eight years of her life in what she found to be an ideal place to raise children, to live, and to die. According to her, there had been continuous mining on Marfork Hollow for decades, but it had not been so intensive, and its effects not so devastating environmentally. In 1993, Massey began actively moving people out of the hollow and started its rigorous MTR operations. Bonds could only watch as her small town died:

> When they first moved in there, we had a thriving community. It wasn't as thriving and prosperous as it was when I was a child because of the employment factor in this area, but it was still a thriving community with children and, of course, people that were retired lived there and it was still a thriving community. We had our little store that was always there—the Pantry Store— but I noticed people started moving out . . . the houses at the head of the hollow first from Marfork and Birch . . . Old Man Pop Aliff was the last house in Marfork, and he did not want to move. They moved him out because he was living on company land. He had a lifetime lease. He lived six months after he moved. Six months after he moved. He was heartbroken. Certain people there that didn't own their own land that was just leasing land, they were the first people to be moved out.[86]

Bonds also watched as family cemeteries were disinterred and moved to other places. As far as Bonds was concerned, those were the lucky ones; other cemeteries were just pushed into valley fills.[87] Both Pauline Canterberry and Mary Miller have seen cemeteries being unearthed similarly.[88] Regardless of how the graves are removed, the upheaval of what were thought to be "final resting places" can result in traumatic stress for those left behind.

Bonds witnessed the annihilation of her small community as one by one the families sold out to the coal company as the MTR operation came closer and closer to their homes. The majority of people in the hollow owned their own land, but they trickled out of town as the incessant blasting, noise, and coal dust worsened, driving them to quieter, more stable locations. Bonds was amazed by the ease with which the company tore down once lively homes:

> There was a beautiful home there that Harry and Cheryl Dickens owned. A beautiful brick home and of course they sold, too. Everybody started moving out. The closer you were to their mining prep plant, the more people moved out. I remember after they bought that house, they brought a backhoe over there and just took the backhoe, I remember the handle of the backhoe, the shovel part of it just . . . stuck it in the middle of that house and just pulled it back and that house just crumbled. That was so strange. I don't understand how they can do anything like that, you know. It was a beautiful home and it crumbled, crumbled and it was gone in the matter of an hour. It was gone . . . It was all just completely gone.[89]

Marfork Hollow no longer exists except in the memories of its former residents. Excluding one family cemetery, the rest of the hollow has been consumed by MTR. The company quietly accumulated acreage, expanding its presence before residents realized what was happening. While some changes seem subtle, they are actually drastic. The mountains provided protection from the sun, wind, and floods.[90] As the mountains have disappeared, so has that protection. Late 1997 through early 1998 was the period when Bonds first became aware that the mining had begun its slow encroachment on her home. Bonds related how the company put up cameras along the mine to monitor the activities near the company's property:

> The camera they had pointed at the house sitting in front of me and one right up above my house. Legitimately they could say that they had the camera on the one in front of [me] and on [their] property. They bought up around me . . . So it was an intimidation factor.[91]

Less than four years later, she had moved from her ancestors' home-place. Bonds had not wanted to leave, but, as she noted, "the last blackwater spill . . . came right up to the bank of our creek that was right in front of our house."[92] The blackwater spill—combined with the noise, the safety issues, the dust problems, and her family members frantically encouraging her to leave—was enough to make Bonds pack up and move out of the hollow in 2001.[93]

When Massey first moved in, company officials held a town meeting with community residents and assured them that Massey would be a good corporate neighbor. Many of the residents were not convinced since they had already heard otherwise from neighboring communities. While Armco Inc., an underground coal company that used to do business in the area, didn't form a perfect relationship with nearby residents, it was regarded as more sensitive to its workers and the community than Massey was. Armco managers lived in the area, which helped to create a sense of community between the company and the town and made the company more mindful of the effects the mining had on the area. Contrast that with Massey, which had no high-level officials living in either Whitesville or Sylvester. Prior to the onslaught of MTR, the underground coal companies like Armco had an unwritten policy of doing more neighborly things such as sending cards and food to employees and their spouses when a loved one died. With large companies such as Massey, civic gestures no longer occurred.[94] Now the companies were large, multinational corporations directed from distant headquarters and too removed from the community to entertain such ideas.

Residents lament the fact that coal corporations devoured common land where hunting, fishing, berry picking, and medicinal-herb gathering used to take place. They have even noticed an increase in flooding since MTR came into the area.[95] Streams that were not covered up by a valley fill had often been rendered unusable by pollutants from mining or slurry ponds. Noise from MTR sites was also a problem, including the massive number of loud trucks that traveled on roads too narrow for heavy traffic. And the dust, of course, was pervasive.

These are not isolated incidents. Throughout the southern coalfields where MTR is taking place, residents have had similar experiences. In a written response to the Draft Environmental Impact Statement (DEIS)—the precursor to the FPEIS—the Ohio Valley Environmental Coalition presented collected responses from coalfield residents to show the government. Like residents of Whitesville and Sylvester, respondents spoke of the destruction of the commons once used by multiple members of a community, as well as increased flooding problems. One man commented, "We live in fear. The whole hollow is in a state of anxiety now every time it floods." The same OVEC document noted how people in these affected communities had lost insurance on their homes and, in some cases, how the homes had been condemned. Residents' homes have endured cracked foundations, walls, and ceilings; destroyed water wells; and overall devaluations.[96]

The value of Mary Miller's home fell from $144,000 to $12,000.[97] Hers is a beautiful, large brick house with hardwood floors throughout. In a moderate to large city, it would certainly be appraised at a far higher value than $144,000.[98] Miller accounted the lower appraisal to the extensive mining occurring near her home, particularly the huge preparation plant, complete with nylon dome, that sits just behind her home and that can be seen from her well-maintained lawn.[99] Additionally, her town has experienced a decrease in population and has recently suffered the closing of their elementary school.

West Virginia's history of out-migration has fluctuated from boom to bust. Earlier out-migrants traveled to the manufacturing centers of the Midwest, particularly Ohio and Illinois. Today, a lack of good-paying jobs for highly educated people has created a drain as many highly educated West Virginians leave for places like Virginia, Pennsylvania, Ohio, North Carolina, and South Carolina in search of employment.[100] The lack of economic diversification has hastened the exodus of educated citizens just as mechanization drained the blue-collar workforce once employed in the coal mines.

In 1951, West Virginia coal mines produced 163,448,001 tons of coal and employed more than one hundred thousand people. In 2002, the state's mines produced 163,896,890 tons of coal, slightly more than the 1951 amount, but the southern coalfield region lost 15,094 employees from 1970 to 2003 (from 32,139 employees in the nine counties in 1970 to 17,045 employees in 2003).[101] Continuing mechanization is largely responsible for these figures. The amount of surface-mined acreage has continually increased since 1982, and surface-mining production has been on the rise since 1991.[102] This is largely attributable to the newest surface-mining machinery, such as that used in MTR.[103] Since the introduction of the twenty-story dragline in the 1980s, coal-mining employment has plummeted from 59,700 in 1980 to 15,200 in 2004.[104] Coal production has increased minimally as well, but the bottom line for companies has vastly improved since the highest cost of operating, labor, has been virtually eliminated.

In spite of it all, many of the people continue to live near the coalfields, even if it means putting their property, and themselves, at risk. They do so largely because of ties to the land, their communities, and their families. On the surface, it would seem far easier for the companies to simply buy out these homeowners, securing complete control of the entire area. In many places where significant MTR has occurred, this tactic has been used. The town of Blair, for instance, has seen a sharp decline in its population. By 1998, fewer than thirty families still remained in the area, down from 180 families just years earlier.[105] In Blair, Arch Coal bought out both residents and businesses. The businesses were purchased first, resulting in the loss of the taxes they would have generated and the convenience they offered. Residents would soon find themselves traveling miles for milk and bread. Then, massive buyouts of the residents in the area took place, and population decline forced the closure of school systems, often the death knell for a small community.[106]

From the standpoint of the company, it made perfect sense. David Todd, vice president and spokesman for Arch, provided the company's philosophy in a court deposition: "Our philosophy is not to impact people and if there are no people to impact, that is consistent with our philosophy."[107] In its quest to limit the adverse effect MTR has on communities, the best solution equaled removal of the communities. In truth, the communities hinder the expansion of mining corporations; only by eliminating them can corporations take over their land. Whether this elimination comes from paying someone to leave or creating nuisances so severe that they force people to sell out is not an issue. The end result is the same: depopulation of the coalfields and easy access to the coal. Arch Coal and its Logan County operations usually did not offer to buy out residents. Rather, they relied on the increased activity at the mines to force residents to ask them for a buyout, thus ensuring that Arch could pay less money for the residents' property. Residents then signed an agreement stating that they would not come back to the communities, would not speak out against the mining activity, and would withdraw any previous complaints they had made about the mining. Such wording is illegal, but the people who signed the agreement didn't know that. These buyout plans affected eleven hollows near Blair Mountain.

If not through buyout or coercion, communities may be destroyed by environmental accidents that occur because of MTR. One small Logan County community, Yolyn, was dismantled after summer flooding resulted in the partial collapse of a valley fill into the middle of the road. Residents complained to state agencies, and the mining corporation then began evicting residents from the company-owned property in retaliation.[108]

Arch Coal is not the only entity to embrace depopulation as a solution. Some industry lawyers openly applaud and encourage the removal of people. In 2000, a Charleston, West Virginia, lawyer made multiple presentations to various groups of citizens about that very subject. The attorney is employed by a well-respected, well-established Charleston law firm that handles labor, government, environment, and energy litigation, including coal-related cases.[109] The lawyer is part of the firm's department that represents corporations in permitting and penalty negotiations as well as appeal hearings and rulemaking proceedings. The firm has noted its wide-ranging experience identifying and minimizing environmental liabilities for its clients.

One of the attorney's presentations detailed the presumed problems with MTR in southern West Virginia. Ridding the area of its inhabitants for the sake of the company's growth was presented as worthwhile—an example of the ends justifying the means. The effects on wildlife were dismissed. It was asserted that saving wildlife, particularly any endangered species that might be affected, was not worth the social or economic cost: "People will always be more important than insignificant species whose only value is spiritual."[110] The attorney did not address the environmental problems that would still remain regardless of population numbers. The hundreds of miles of streams that would be affected, for instance, run into other streams and would negatively affect those water outlets as well.

In the course of arguing in favor of MTR, the attorney lauded reclamation, noting the "hardwood saplings up to three feet tall" that are the result of successful reforestation practices on reclaimed land.[111] Left unmentioned was the scientific proof that such endeavors have rarely been successful.[112]

Additionally, the attorney dismissed residents' claims of home and well damage due to blasting, stating that most complaints have no merit, that the homes already had damage before blasting took place, and that both home- and well-damage claims would decline with pre-blast surveys.

The attorney further argued that MTR removes more coal than traditional mining techniques do (the presentation quotes removal rates of 98 percent and 70 percent, respectively) and provides employment. The starkest argument in the presentation, however, was the claim that MTR-assisted depopulation was a good thing—the only way to solve the long-term poverty found in the coalfield counties. Rather than encouraging economic development in the area, the presentation noted the huge financial drain on the miners who, it asserted, pay the majority of the taxes, with two-thirds of the taxpayers dependent on the one-third that worked as coal miners. The "core problem," as the presenter sees it, "is too many people. Way too many people."[113]

The attorney set out various proposals to handle this problem. One proposal encouraged the state to eradicate dilapidated coalfield homes. Another proposal suggested that the state provide grant money to help people settle outside of West Virginia and to revoke the grant if they moved back to the state. Yet another idea entailed offering free college education for coalfield kids whose families relocated, as well as to single adults and childless couples. The main goal would remain getting people to move. A final suggestion: if "stubborn people" refused to move, their land could be condemned, taken over by the state, and sold to companies who wanted it for MTR. The companies would then reimburse the state for any expenses incurred in securing the land.[114]

In the presentation, the attorney admitted that a West Virginia government would likely never embrace such suggestions, declaring that the government lacked the political fortitude to depopulate the southern coalfields. The attorney still believed the coalfields would be depopulated, but in a more agonizing way than necessary, and without the assistance that the attorney outlined in the presentation. It is certain that such depopulation would allow the companies total control of the coal-rich southern counties. It is also certain that the tactics employed so far by many coal operators seem to embrace the idea of depopulation, which increases the power of a coal corporation.

As MTR is currently practiced, three distinct stages of power relations can be discerned among communities affected by MTR. Stage 1 is the infancy/beginning stage. In this stage, community members often trust that the company has their best interests at heart. They welcome the company for the employment and tax revenues it will generate. Initially, the community sees the company as the savior who will deliver it from its economic plight.

Stage 2 is the intermediate or middle stage. Community members become shocked, dismayed, and angered as MTR begins to directly affect them in a negative way. Those with jobs at the site may still praise the company for providing them with work and see the company as protecting their homes. Many others leave in search of work or to escape the effects of MTR; steady migration from the area begins. As the company begins to offer to buy out households, residents band together in an effort to save their communities. The role of savior begins to crumble, and the company instead finds itself in the dual role of protector of jobs and robber baron of the land.

In Stage 3, the final stage, massive buyouts of homeowners and businesses take place, intense depopulation occurs, and migration escalates and soars. The coal company essentially gobbles up the community as MTR expands, consumes the surrounding land, and displaces residents. Once established, Stage 3 cements the company in the role of destroyer. The stage is complete when all members of the community have moved and the community itself is dissolved, with all associated local businesses and schools closed.

As the stages progress, the number of residents plummet, MTR acreage increases, and employment begins to slightly increase, followed by a tapering off of employment as MTR expands. The need for manpower is replaced by the need for huge draglines. It is expected that more and more southern West Virginia communities will experience these stages as MTR becomes more widespread there. Throughout all three stages, the power relationship remains the same; coal corporations enjoy the upper hand.

The old argument pitting jobs against the environment remains. By 1920, West Virginia's bountiful hardwood forests were nearly eradicated. It took eighty years for the forest to replenish itself. Coal, of course, is a finite resource and will not replenish itself. Four generations have passed since the decimation of the state's hardwood forests and the birth of the railroads that would take West Virginia's bountiful natural-resource treasures of coal and timber to places outside the region. The repercussions of constantly extracting coal with no thought of the future consumed those within the region. There were jobs, but at what cost? At the turn of the nineteenth century, West Virginia's inhabitants learned a difficult lesson about what such a "dance with the devil" could do. In this present struggle, once again balancing economics with community needs for a safe and functioning environment, this generation has now done the same.

Conclusion

For generations, southern coalfield communities have been at the mercy of the coal industry that provides the only viable economic opportunity while simultaneously destroying the communities themselves. As the mechanization of MTR increased in the region, both employment and population decreased. As larger companies, many of them non-union, began to dominate the southern coalfields, the make-up of coal communities changed. No longer did supervisors and mine foremen live in the communities where they worked. As MTR became more pervasive in these areas, fewer of these employees lived in the communities where they worked. Thus, the connection with the community itself decreased while the effects the mining had on the community increased. Small communities felt the brunt of this transformation.

The reality of living in a single industry economy has burdened these communities and often set neighbors against one another. While MTR has well-known repercussions on the environment and those living near the sites, this knowledge has not stopped the embracement of the few high-paying jobs these operations produce in areas notorious for high unemployment. Those economically benefiting from the jobs are directly pitted against those who believe the cultural and environmental cost of extracting coal by MTR is a much too expensive price to pay. In the past, the region's residents have borne the consequences of a non-diverse economy fixated on natural-resource extraction. The present generation is grappling with the same dilemma. Whether it decides to face the problem head-on, demanding that politicians and those in control provide economic diversification and alternative employment options, or once again relies on a one-resource economy has yet to be seen. In the beginning of the twenty-first century, the coal industry, aided by sympathetic politicians, keeps its chokehold on southern West Virginia communities and looks to remain in the same position for the foreseeable future.

4

YOU SCRATCH MY BACK, AND
I'LL SCRATCH YOURS:
The Political Economy of Coal

[W]hether we like it or not, West Virginia's hills will be stripped, the bowels of the earth will be mined and the refuse strewn across our valleys and our mountains in the form of burning slate dumps. This refuse will continue to be dumped into our once clear mountain streams. We are paying a fearful price to allow the coal to be extracted from the hills of West Virginia . . .
—Gov. William C. Marland (1953–1957)

From its inception, West Virginia supplied numerous opportunities for the business entrepreneur, and its earliest political leaders acted as its biggest salesmen. An abundance of largely untapped natural resources offered a variety of ways to make a fortune, attracting businessmen looking for new capitalist ventures. The backcounties of southern West Virginia failed to develop at the same rate as other regions of the state. Politicians saw the coming of the coal industry as an opportunity for unlimited expansion of industry to the areas that heretofore had been too remote to see any real industrial development. When describing his and Governor Aretus B. Fleming's participation in this development, Governor William A. MacCorkle went so far as to state that the two of them served as "advertising agents on a large scale."[1] Since its first exploitation, coal has remained the sole economic driving force for most of southern West Virginia and has continually wielded more political power in the area than it did in other coal regions of Appalachia.[2]

In West Virginia, development of the coal industry equalled progress. The lines between the two primary political parties became undetectable as support for the coal industry superseded all other allegiances. In fact, alliances formed around the coal interests with the singular purpose of defeating any threats to the established economic system, especially any legislation that endangered the powerful coal industry. Ex-Governor Fleming had firsthand knowledge of such ties, going so far as to tell a potential gubernatorial candidate that he was not in politics for any particular side but to defeat anyone fighting against the coal interests.[3]

The coal interests realize the importance of having a politician on their side during key legislative battles and in important government jobs, and they are diligent in forming their alliances with politicians. There are key positions at the state level that could aid the coal interests—governor, legislative leaders, tax commissioner, and the Department of Natural Resources director. Tax commissioners have the power to set favorable rates on taxes for coal companies. Many have done just that. A 1972 study by the Appalachian Regional Defense Fund found that once they had left their posts, many former tax commissioners found corporate jobs within the coal industry or at a coal-dependent enterprise.[4] The same can be said of West Virginia's ex-governors. Since the time of the 1972 study, every governor has been closely aligned with the coal industry, often obtaining employment with a coal company after leaving office or continuing to support the coal companies in his political career. These politicians realized that political success hinged upon their backing the coal industry. The economic policies embraced by West Virginia's politicians are inextricably linked to coal and have become a solid part of the region's history. Citizens, in turn, are caught in a vise between politics on one side and the coal industry on the other. The large amount of absentee landownership ensured that outside interests would take precedence over the well-being of actual residents of the region.

West Virginia Democrats and Republicans are quite similar in their alliance with coal companies. The majority of West Virginia's governors, for instance, have been affiliated with the coal industry either as owner, manager, or lawyer, a fact that has greatly benefited the industry. In essence, political and business leaders are so closely aligned that differentiating between the two roles is nearly indiscernible. One example of this occurred during Governor Cecil Underwood's second term (1997–2001). Underwood, a former Island Creek Coal Company executive, relieved several coal companies of more than $400 million in unpaid workers' compensation premiums and interest by dismissing lawsuits initiated by Underwood's predecessor, Gaston Caperton.[5] The larger companies contended that they did not owe money to the workers' compensation fund.[6] However, a 1993 workers' compensation law had made the larger companies responsible for any unpaid premiums incurred by their subcontractors, and the lawsuits alleged that the larger companies had subcontracted with smaller contractors specifically in order to avoid paying the premiums.[7]

Underwood received more than $500,000 from coal-industry donations for both his campaign and the subsequent inaugural ball. It was some of these coal donors that benefited from the dismissal of the workers' compensation lawsuits. During Governor Bob Wise's tenure, however, the lawsuits were re-filed, and fifteen coal companies agreed to pay $56.6 million to settle the case, far below the $400 million originally owed.[8]

Taxes are the main avenue by which the state recoups monies from natural-resource extraction. While politicians, executives, and some inhabitants alike laud the amount of taxes put into the system by the industry, it is arguable that the amount of severance taxes and taxes on the industry itself is still not enough to sustain these communities and correct the damage that occurs at the hands of the very industry that provides for the area's economic life. The industry-biased tax code was forged by West Virginia's earliest leaders who intentionally shaped the tax policy to encourage industry and to shift the tax burden to non-corporate citizens. The state's tax base never kept up with the demands of its growing populace, and the citizenry of West Virginia has borne the brunt of taxation.[9] Out of the 15 million acres that constitute West Virginia, 3 million acres are publicly owned. Two-thirds of the remaining 12 million acres are owned by outside interests.[10] Unimproved land (such as coal-rich land which has yet to be mined) is taxed at a much lower rate than improved land. These factors greatly diminish the tax base of the area.[11]

It was not until 1971 that West Virginia allowed an appraisal of the coal itself. Still, each county appraiser has the authority to assess the property between 50 and 100 percent of the assessed value.[12] This practice results in the coal reserves being taxed at different levels from county to county and all at a very low rate. When that fact is added to the amount of tax revenues lost to the 3 million acres of publicly owned land, it simply results in a debilitated tax base. A 1980 study showed that the average tax on mineral land owned by corporations was between $1.08 to $1.51 per acre.[13] Corporations are also able to drive down the amount of taxes owed by leasing land they own to individuals. This drops their tax rate and effectively cuts their property taxes for that piece of land in half.[14]

Realizing the loss in tax revenues from the current tax system, the state has made attempts to address the problem. As recently as June 1997, Governor Underwood formed a Commission on Tax Fairness (also known as the Fair Tax Commission) with the stated goal of re-creating West Virginia's tax system. The bipartisan commission recommended repealing personal property taxes and replacing the numerous business taxes with a flat 2 percent business tax. A family of four earning $25,000 would have saved more than $300 per year while a coal company's taxes would have risen by a little more than $300,000.[15] The recommendations were met with dissent. The Affiliated Construction Trades Foundation (ACTF) sponsored a study that showed the newly proposed tax structure benefited wealthier West Virginians and increased the tax burden on the middle class. The Commission continued to stand by its original suggestions.[16] In 1999 and 2000, state legislators failed to act on the recommendations, opting instead to keep the tax system as it was.[17]

In July 2004, the state, through the secretary of tax and revenue, sought to clarify the tax code as it pertained to the extraction of natural resources. For partially mineable and partially mined-out property, the tax would remain at five dollars per acre. For mined-out land, the property would be taxed at one dollar per acre. Barren coal acreage would also remain taxed at one dollar per acre.[18] Conversely, average private property owners would continue to be assessed based on any improvements they might have made. Again, the amounts would vary greatly from county to county, but most assuredly they would be more than one dollar an acre. The state continued to suffer from a tax system that left the heaviest burden on individual taxpayers rather than the corporations. A September 2004 report by the Massachusetts Taxpayers Foundation showed that West Virginia, the poorest state in the nation, had the eighth highest tax burden in the United States in 2002 per personal earnings.[19] A 2000–2001 study revealed that the majority of West Virginia's taxes came from its citizenry with a full 73 percent of taxes attributed to either personal income taxes (38 percent) or consumer sale and use taxes (35 percent). Business taxes accounted for 25 percent of the tax base with the remaining 2 percent being described as "other." Still, West Virginia's future will most likely not include any increase in business taxes since West Virginia is forced to compete with other states to attract business. While West Virginia business taxes make up far less of the tax base than what citizens pay, it is still relatively high compared to that of most surrounding states.[20]

One of the most contentious business taxes has been the severance tax. The struggle to enact a severance tax on natural-resource extraction remains a good example of the political influence of the coal companies. This much-debated and much-maligned tax on natural-resource extraction suffered three distinctive defeats before finally becoming law in the late 1980s. The early 1900s saw the defeat of severance tax initiatives by Governors Albert B. White and Henry D. Hatfield (1901–1905 and 1913–1917, respectively). Historian John Alexander Williams noted that West Virginia tax reform surrounding natural-resource extraction has been debated in "agrarian circles since the 1880s."[21] The failed Tax Commission of 1903 was the most ambitious endeavor up to that point. Corporations fought tirelessly against reforms such as the complete overhaul of fiscal administration, larger corporation license taxes, and, in particular, the notion of a severance tax. In the end, the corporations proved victorious and the ambitious program was thwarted.[22]

Some fifty years after this attempt, Governor William C. Marland (1953–1957) made another failed effort to pass a severance tax on natural resources. Marland was from a coal-mining—*not* coal-baron—family, grew up and lived in a mining town in Wyoming County, and had worked in and around coal mines. From the onset, he made it known that he would not kowtow to the land barons and industrial giants that ruled the state. He was motivated by the desire to see that the companies gave back to the communities that were sacrificing so much for the coal to be extracted from their mountains. As usual, the cry of "ruination of the industry" arose from the coal industry. Marland's attempts at tax reform were quickly halted, and he was soundly defeated by a state legislature firmly wedded to the coal interests.[23]

Marland's political and professional careers were ruined. He opened a law practice and industrial-consulting business after leaving office, but he could not secure the lucrative coal-industry business because of his prior support of a severance tax.[24] After two failed attempts to become a West Virginia senator, Marland moved to Chicago where he worked as a sales director for West Kentucky Coal Corporation for less than a year before his long-standing drinking problem began to get the better of him. In the summer of 1961, he was fired from his job with the coal company, received treatment for alcoholism, and by 1962 was employed as a taxicab driver in Chicago. His plans to return to his native West Virginia to work for a political friend were tragically halted when he was diagnosed with pancreatic cancer and died at the age of forty-seven.[25] None of his successors attempted to stand up to the coal companies in such a way as Marland did, and arguably none have met a fate as harsh as his. While dogged by personal tragedies of his own, Marland at least tried to gain some degree of state compensation for extracted natural resources. For this, he was effectively destroyed as a politician and as a person. His coal severance tax would not be realized until 1987.[26]

Before the severance tax could become law, the state had to experience a surge in reform movements spanning the 1960s and the 1970s. The 1960s saw the formation of the Human Rights Commission, the West Virginia Industrial Development Authority, and the Department of Commerce, among others.[27] The Black Lung Association and the Association of Disabled Miners and Widows fought for the rights of disabled miners and widows in obtaining compensation for black lung. Under Arch Moore's first administration (1968–1972), pressure from these groups, along with a 1969 wildcat strike of UMWA miners in support of making black lung compensable, assisted in the passage of both state and federal regulations recognizing black lung as an occupational disease.[28]

Moore's first two administrations (1969–1977) also witnessed other far-reaching reforms, such as programs for the aging, dam-control regulations after the Buffalo Creek disaster, and the "Sunshine Law" to allow open public meetings.[29] As he entered his third and final term as governor

(1985–1989), Moore inherited the worst economic conditions since the Great Depression. While the severance tax was enacted on his watch, it was also during his administration that "super tax breaks" provided massive tax credits for existing industry—largely benefiting the coal industry, which enjoyed 90 percent of the total super tax breaks.[30] These tax credits were part of Moore's efforts to rejuvenate the quickly plummeting coal industry. Efforts were made to cut coal production costs, and a 30 percent reduction in workers' compensation fund contributions was also provided to the coal industry. In spite of these efforts, coal employment continued to plunge, and a 1990 super tax break study showed that the coal industry had lost 1,300 jobs even though the industry witnessed a 13.3 percent increase in overall coal production. The tax credits had been used by some coal companies to avoid paying the newly enacted severance tax, costing the state millions of dollars in state revenue.[31] In 1985, super tax breaks cost the state $600,000. By 1989, that amount had surged to $48.2 million. Abuse was so prevalent and apparent that by 1990 legislation was enacted to stop further exploitation. The 1990 efforts produced a minimum severance tax to be paid, and this overhaul, along with 1993 reforms, resulted in a decrease in the amount of lost severance tax revenue to the super tax breaks from $48.2 million in 1989 to $30 million in 2000. The super tax break cost on other taxes was an additional $12 million.[32]

The economic benefits of coal, particularly coal obtained via MTR, remains a contentious issue, the roots of which stem from West Virginia's historical marriage of industry and politics. People in business need politicians, and politicians need businessmen to fund their political careers. While working under the guise of what is best for the state and its residents, it is not uncommon for politicians to protect the interests of their wealthy business benefactors even as the economic impact of the industry diminishes. A 2001 study conducted by the University of Kentucky's Center for Business and Economic Research, and sponsored by the Appalachian Regional Commission, found that the impact of the coal industry on Appalachian communities was expected to drop within the decade, "particularly with respect to employment and earnings," which is expected to decline by 25 to 30 percent.[33] Even the impact of collected taxes, such as severance, payroll, income, and retail taxes, is expected to drop by 20.4 percent in the Central Appalachian region that includes the southern West Virginia counties.[34] From 1980 to 1999, the national coal industry saw a decrease of 108,000 employees (from 192,000 to 84,000 employees) even while production increased to more than 1 billion tons per year.[35] The largest surface mines in Appalachia are located in West Virginia, and in both 2001 and 2002, nine out of the top ten largest-producing surface mines in Appalachia were found in the southern West Virginia coalfields.[36] While the overall employment has declined, employment by independent contractors has actually "more than tripled" from 1980 to 1999.[37]

The high level of employment by independent contractors works favorably for the larger companies because it carries less responsibility for adhering to federal environmental and safety laws as well as excluding the larger companies from paying workers' compensation deductibles for these employees. The company does, however, still reap the financial benefits of the production of these employees. Production per employee has also increased, with the average surface-mine employee producing 18,436 tons per year in 1999 compared with the 8,488 tons per year per underground coal miner in 1999.[38]

These statistics clearly show why surface mining is such a desirable alternative for many coal companies: each employee can produce more than twice the amount of coal as his or her underground counterpart. This, combined with the recent upswing in demand for the low-sulfur, high-volatility coal that the southern West Virginia coalfields are noted for, has meant an increase in sales revenues. In May 2004, a *Charleston Gazette* article noted Massey's upbeat outlook and reported that the company estimated that sales on the global market could reach $80 to $90 per ton.[39] With the high demand and increased prices for low-sulfur coal, the mining industry in 2003 extracted 1.7 billion tons of coal. In 2004, the industry slightly exceeded its 2004 goal of 1.1 billion tons, mining 1.122 billion tons. In 2005, 1.133 billion tons were extracted.[40]

While the coal industry's bottom line has been improving, West Virginia's economy has been on the decline for decades, and the loss of mining jobs has hit the southern West Virginia region particularly hard. Since 1970, the nine counties have witnessed a loss of 21,968 jobs (or 66 percent of total mining jobs), from 33,263 mining jobs in 1970 to 11,295 coal-mining jobs in 2003. At the same time, total production has increased from more than 27.1 million surface-mined tons from all surface-mining techniques throughout West Virginia in 1970, to more than 38.7 million tons mined in the nine counties by the MTR method alone in 2002. This is a marked increase in surface production and shows that MTR is leading the way in that increase.

As the coal industry mechanized and as surface mining became more common, fewer and fewer people were able to make their living in the coal industry. As MTR expanded in the 1990s and a few large corporations monopolized the industry, the number of small companies rapidly declined. This growing domination allowed the larger companies to become more competitive with the western coal industry, particularly Wyoming's Powder River Basin. Massive companies, such as Arch Coal and Massey, with large MTR sites have pushed other companies to the side in overall production measures.[41] And, of course, along with the increased production and increased surface mining (including MTR) has come a decrease in overall mining jobs.

The subsequent decrease in employment has resulted in an increase in welfare and food stamp recipients.[42] Statistics from the Department of Health and Human Resources show that the number of families receiving food stamps steadily increased from 89,446 in August 2001 to 101,561 in August 2003 at a time when the population for the state had consistently declined and when eligibility requirements had been tightened.[43] A 2003 article in the *Charleston Daily Mail* quoted Secretary for the Department of Health and Human Resources Paul Nusbaum as saying that he believes there is "a direct relationship between poor economic conditions and increasing benefits" paid out to recipients; he also noted that while the number of eligible recipients swells, the state does not have the tax revenues to pay for it.[44] The nine southern West Virginia counties shared in this burden. In 1998, transfer payments—such as Social Security Disability, Supplemental Security Income (SSI), Temporary Assistance for Needy Families (TANF), retirement benefits, and unemployment—accounted for more than 20 percent of each county's total personal income (except Kanawha County where it accounted for 19.8 percent).[45] Of the other eight counties, McDowell had the highest percentage, at 46.2, followed by Wyoming at 34.9 percent, Logan at 34.5 percent, Fayette at 34.1 percent, Mingo at 32.1 percent, Nicholas at 29.7 percent, Raleigh at 26.6 percent, and Boone at 25.5 percent.[46] Larger and larger numbers of people in each county are receiving public assistance of some sort, and fewer and fewer employed individuals contributing to the tax base of each county. McDowell County, for instance, showed nearly 50 percent of its population dependent upon some means other than employment for their survival, and the other 50 percent provided more of the county's tax base. The end result is a lack of services for the county overall. The per capita payments for three income maintenance programs—TANF, SSI, and food stamps—is twice as high in Central Appalachia as in Northern and Southern Appalachia.[47]

By the end of the decade, in 2010, an increase is forecasted in all of the maintenance programs for Central Appalachia. An increase of 5.77 percent in per capita TANF payments, 4.8 percent in SSI payments, and 11.35 percent in food stamp payments is expected along with a noted decrease in population. In terms of real dollars, that correlates to a $6.2 million annual increase in TANF payments, a $17.7 million increase in SSI payments, and a $24.3 million increase in food stamp payments.[48] For an already economically depressed area, such increases indicate fewer individuals paying into the tax system, which could prove devastating to an already depleted tax base. The weakened tax base and the minimal number of jobs in these areas ensure that the power structure will remain the same and that the residents will stay beholden to the coal industry.

Whether receiving transfer payments or not, citizens of the southern coalfields depend on federal and state regulators to oversee and protect them and their environment. Politicians often have more sympathy for, and alliances with, corporations than inhabitants, and go so far as to encourage the delay of studies aimed at considering the concerns of residents. In 1999, the U.S. Department of Environmental Protection, the U.S. Office of Surface Mining, the Fish and Wildlife Service, and the Army Corps of Engineers agreed to partly settle a lawsuit brought against them regarding the legality of valley fills.[49] The agreement stated that an environmental impact study would be conducted to examine the environmental, social, and economic effects of MTR, especially addressing the environmental impact of valley fills on the communities. The study was supposed to be finished by 2000. The 2000 deadline came and went, and no draft appeared. Politicians and bureaucrats were once again dragging their feet. Before President Clinton left office, his administration attempted to release an earlier draft of the study but met with complaints from

West Virginia officials, namely Governor Bob Wise, Senate President Earl Ray Tomblin (from Logan County), and House Speaker Bob Kiss (from Raleigh County).[50] The *Charleston Gazette* was able to receive an early January 2001 draft of the environmental impact study in May 2002 through a Freedom of Information Act request. At that time, the report was two and a half years overdue. It would not be for another year and a half, in January 2004, that a more complete DEIS would be officially released. The official study, the Final Programmatic Environmental Impact Statement, would not be completed until October 2005.

The DEIS was met with fervent responses from both sides. In comments written to the DEP regarding the DEIS's treatment of surface-mining valley-fill impacts, the coal interests, including the West Virginia Coal Association, responded collectively in a single 138 page statement. They pointed out how valley fills are used by both underground and surface mines and stressed that they wanted extra emphasis added to that fact. They stated that the DEIS failed to "acknowledge [the] interrelationship of surface mining to underground mining," and that many of these "underground mines exist solely to provide blending stock for coal produced through surface mining methods as part of a large mining complex."[51] To drive their point home, they declared that surface-mined coal is "generally of a better quality" than that obtained via underground methods and that this underground coal would "not produce a marketable product unless blended with a surface mined product."[52]

Taken at face value, this statement is hard to believe, especially considering that southern West Virginia coal is of the highly marketable, low-sulfur, high-volatility variety—whether mined by surface or underground methods. The marketplace does not support their assertion either; statistics from 1996 through 2000 show that surface-mined coal, on average, brings less per ton than its underground equivalent.[53] (See Figure 4.1.) The price difference is larger between the 2002 and 2003 figures for southern West Virginia coal prices by method. In 2002, the cost per ton of underground coal was $30.20, and it increased slightly to $30.72 by 2003. In contrast, surface-mined coal brought $28.77 per ton in 2002 and $29.25 per ton in 2003.[54] While the difference in price is not large, they obviously do not support the coal interests' previous assertion at all. What MTR lacks in pricing, however, it makes up for in sheer volume as the companies are able to mine far more coal using MTR than underground methods. This, in turn, drives down the cost of production per unit, which results in larger profit margins than more expensive underground mining.

Within the DEIS and the final product, the framers remarked that there are other methods to obtain low-sulfur, high-volatility coal besides MTR. The coal interests' united front begged to differ. They asserted that most seams currently being strip-mined and using valley fills "cannot be recovered using underground mining. The seams are either physically too thin, the overburden too unconsolidated to allow for safe mining or the reserve so isolated or small that underground extraction is either impossible or hopelessly uneconomic."[55]

One concern raised by the industry in their response is the lack of emphasis on the use of valley fills by underground mines as well as surface mines that could not exist without these massive constructions. Industry is correct to note that underground mining also uses valley fills. What is left unmentioned is the small number of valley fills that underground mining actually uses in comparison to what is used by MTR. The DEIS noted that of the 6,697 valley fills observed for the study, only 11 percent (or 719) were associated with underground mines. Surface mines accounted for 85 percent (or 5,688) of the valley fills. The remaining 4 percent (290) existed on other sites such as preparation plants, tipples, and load-outs.[56] For the coal industry to encourage the FPEIS to include underground mining in its definition of mountaintop mining by noting the comparatively few valley fills[57] associated with underground mining is blatantly deceptive and an obvious attempt to manipulate the final report. In their response to the DEIS, the coal representatives stated, "As this statistic reflects, underground mines in this steep sloped area also require the construction of

Figure 4.1 **Price per ton of West Virginia coal by method of extraction**					
	1996	1997	1998	1999	2000
Underground	27.31	27.64	28.25	26.21	25.79
Surface	25.04	24.60	24.50	22.39	24.67

Source: See Endnote 50

valley fills."[58] This statistic actually shows that surface mines, and in particular the excessive overburden created by MTR, are largely responsible for the proliferation of valley fills.

Furthermore, a Kentucky mining engineer reviewing the decision of Judge Charles Haden II in *Kentuckians for the Commonwealth v. Rivenburgh* (May 8, 2002) stated that the decision would *not* affect underground mines. In that case, Haden effectively blocked the Army Corps of Engineers from issuing most valley-fill permits unless the companies included a post-mining land-development plan. He asserted that underground-mining fill permits would not, either in the short or long term, be negatively affected, and that underground and surface mines had "little potential" for immediate closings and decreased production.[59] While eventually appealed and overturned, the decision would not have been the catastrophe the coal companies made it out to be. However, MTR is the one arm of the coal industry that is dependent upon valley fills. If the process were not so extensive, and more time were taken, valley fills as they are currently executed would not be made necessary by any criterion except expediency. Companies could reclaim as they go rather than tearing up all the land to get a huge dragline in and hurriedly dumping excess overburden into the valleys and streams below. Mining the top of a mountain in this manner certainly results in larger valley fills, and it diminishes the possibility of safer and more effective methods of saving the rock and soil overburden in a separate area to use in later reclamation.

Vast amounts of extracted coal resulted in the need to export the product. This caused an increase in coal-truck traffic and the rise of another controversial topic: coal-haul tonnage. Truckers wanted increased weight limits to more quickly meet demands; residents wanted safe roads. In response to coal haulers' requests to increase the limit and coalfield residents' demands to enforce the law, competing legislation attempted to end the debate. After much back-and-forth, the 2003 West Virginia legislature passed a highly controversial bill that almost doubled the previous coal-truck weight limit (from 65,000 to 120,000 tons). The law only applied to fifteen southern West Virginia coal-producing counties. All other areas of the state would still have to operate within the previous limits.[60] Testifying before the West Virginia Joint Commission on Economic Development concerning raising the truck-hauling rates, Don Blankenship, CEO of Massey, stunned spectators by dismissing the death of West Virginians in coal-truck accidents as "no more than might be expected given the many miles that coal trucks travel each year."[61] The death of coal miners has typically been viewed as an acceptable means to an end. It is no secret that legislative reforms have been written with the blood of miners, victims of an often reckless industry, with little safety enforcement. Statements such as those made by Blankenship give the impression that deaths of coal-county citizens are also acceptable casualties and "part of the cost of doing business."[62]

Coal-county roads were not built to meet the higher weight demands, and the prospect of upgrading the roads to make them more accessible to the heavy coal trucks seems unlikely because of its hefty price tag. Only about 600 miles of nearly 7,500 miles of southern West Virginia roads were intended to hold more than sixty-five thousand pounds. Most of the bridges that these oversized coal trucks will travel are not equipped to handle more than eighty thousand pounds; only 150 miles of roads within the fifteen counties meet these standards.

West Virginia Transportation Secretary Fred VanKirk noted that repeatedly exceeding this load could cause "fatigue" and "wear the bridge out."[63] The Department of Highways, using a 1980 study, estimated that it would cost $2.8 billion to update the 3,600 miles of coal-haulage roads that needed upgrades. That amount is more like $6.5 billion in today's marketplace.[64] It should also be noted that while the legislature passed the law to allow more tonnage in fifteen southern West Virginia counties, it failed to provide any new funding for "upgrading highways and bridges in the Coal Resource Transportation System," as the targeted area has been dubbed.[65] The law does, however, increase the amount charged for permits to haul the larger loads and is expected to generate "between $200,000 and $1 million in fees" each year, falling well below the billions needed for updating the roads and bridges.[66] These fees will certainly do little to undo the damage that the heavier trucks cannot help but make, nor are they remotely adequate to begin upgrading the roads to handle the heavier loads at all. In essence, if these upgrades are to be made, it is the tax-paying citizen, not the coal companies, who will foot the bill. The economic impact of this bill has yet to be seen, but it surely will be a negative one for the citizens of the coalfields.

While coal unarguably brings in millions of dollars to these counties, surface mining also contributes to millions of dollars worth of destruction due to ever more frequent flooding, exacerbated by the lack of groundcover that accompanies massive timbering and MTR. A June 2002 Flood Advisory study concluded that MTR contributes to flooding in the southern West Virginia coalfields by increasing runoff in the study watersheds.[67]

After the 2001 floods, Governor Bob Wise commissioned studies from two consulting groups, Parsons Brinckerhoff and Tischler & Associates, to ascertain some viable solutions for these flood-ravaged areas. The results were not well publicized. Parsons Brinckerhoff, a Kentucky firm, concluded that in McDowell and Wyoming counties (the focus of the study), only two communities, Mullens in Wyoming County and Welch in McDowell County, were sustainable. The other communities were not sustainable without significant investment. The main task of the consulting firm was "to work with citizens and community leaders in McDowell and Wyoming counties to develop long-term redevelopment plans."[68] The consulting groups as a whole believed that the strip-mined area was ripe for development as well as for housing new communities for those devastated by flooding.[69]

Remarkably, they suggested using the flat land developed by MTR, the very source of the flooding problems. An employee with the Wyoming County Economic Development Authority admitted that convincing people to move from their longstanding communities would be a difficult task. It was suggested by the consultants that residents be given "the opportunity to move out of old, flood-prone communities but keep them within the area by building new housing and industrial developments at higher elevations along two proposed highways, the King Coal Highway and the Coalfields Expressway."[70] Pineville and Oceana in Wyoming County were also regarded as sustainable with some restructuring. The other nine municipalities in the two counties were deemed unsustainable. Developing new communities on the newly stripped land near the new highways was declared most viable. The consultants also suggested that the town governments and utility services of small, incorporated towns in the two counties may have to be combined to ensure sustainability. The group recommended new development along the shared boundaries of the two counties.

Tischler & Associates noted the area's positive characteristics as well, such as low cost of living, recreational opportunities, low utility costs, and rail transportation. These were offset, however, by such negative factors as low levels of education, stagnant income, limited access by roads, and little land that could be developed.[71] In essence, their solution was depopulation and consolidation. In the case of McDowell County, all other communities besides Welch were considered "physically worn out."[72] Sweeping aside concerns about the impact of strip mining—particularly MTR—on flooding, State Senator Billy Wayne Bailey (D-Dist. 9) told the Mullens City Council and the Wyoming County Economic Development Authority to look at the recent flooding as though "God has wiped the state clean"[73] and given them the opportunity to build better communities elsewhere. The Wise administration wanted to make sure that residents in these areas realized that moving was an option but that no one would be forced to move. The consultants' idea was to "guide and lead" rather than to "push and shove."[74]

Floods such as those that occurred in 2001, which devastated most of Wyoming County and part of McDowell County, repeatedly cost millions of dollars in financial destruction to economically strapped communities. A March 2004 editorial in the *Raleigh Register-Herald* of Beckley, West Virginia, underscored that "[t]axpayers have borne the cost—to the tune of hundreds of millions of dollars—of putting communities back in order after flood waters pour through them."[75] It is not the coal companies that pay the bills for these disasters. It is the West Virginia taxpayer—and, through federal assistance programs such as the Federal Emergency Management Agency (FEMA), the national taxpayer—who pays in the long run. While MTR companies hail the number of good-paying jobs they bring to the region, the actual number of jobs associated with MTR is limited. The cost associated with rebuilding homes and property after flooding must also be considered. The presumed benefits of MTR will never be realized if residents are constantly doling out money because of the damage this type of mining inflicts. Southern West Virginia has always suffered flooding, but not at the present rate of frequency and strength. In November 2003, for example, Wyoming County suffered more than $2 million in flood damage. FEMA assisted many of the residents,[76] but others have been told that this was the last assistance FEMA would provide if they continued to reside where they did.[77] Therefore, many of these homeowners have sold their homes and moved away. Since the federal government now owns the land, less revenue is generated for local governments.

According to a 1999 *Charleston Gazette* article, banning MTR altogether would cut the state's total coal production by 10 percent.[78] The *Gazette* drew this figure from an industry-sponsored study which also claimed that the coal industry stood to lose about $490 million in revenues each year, based on an estimated sale price of $28 per ton of coal, and declared that both state and local governments stood to lose $37 million in yearly tax revenues.[79] While these figures, admittedly, show an impact on the coal industry, they are hardly as dramatic as many industry executives claim.

Some coal company executives would have inhabitants believe that they continue to mine coal in southern West Virginia for largely altruistic reasons, citing statistics that the companies are not making much money from the coal business. In an April 1999 column, the general manager of Arch Coal made such an implication. He pointed out that $18 million of Arch's $30 million profits for 1998 came from "land and property sales." He detailed how the other $12 million, while made from extracting coal, only equaled fifteen cents on each of the 80 million tons of coal that it mined.[80] He went on to describe the massive amount Arch paid out in wages (nearly $100 million), to other support industries (more than $130 million), and in state taxes (more than $31 million).[81] If this executive's arguments are to be believed, then it would seem that the destruction of thousands of acres of some of the most diverse forest system in the world, the covering of thousands of miles of Appalachian streams, and the rendering of entire areas uninhabitable is an awfully steep price for the people of West Virginia to pay when the coal companies are "barely" turning a profit.

It has been so ingrained in the people that the removal of mountaintops attracts businesses that one individual in Marmet, Kanawha County, wanted to use mountaintop removal to clear his thousand acres in hopes of luring a Wal-Mart distribution center to his property. The local economy was deteriorating, and the man hoped that the huge retailer would bring in jobs. Wal-Mart said that the company had no plans to build a distribution center near Charleston, West Virginia.[82] Similarly, a Williamson, Mingo County, mayor planned to apply for a federal grant to allow the mountaintop removal of one of Williamson's mountains. The mayor hoped that the newly flattened land would be used for an industrial park, a recreational area, shops, and restaurants.[83] The mayor must not have been aware that of the thousands of acres left flattened by MTR, most are not used in the ways he proposed. After three decades, the first MTR site in Fayette County is still waiting to benefit from its MTR experience. No industry, or any type of construction, exists there.

While businesses have not been attracted by flattened mountaintops, tourists continue to flock to West Virginia to enjoy its natural beauty. The DEIS acknowledged the importance of tourism to West Virginia's economy. In fact, a study by the West Virginia University Bureau of Business Research showed an economic impact of $2.54 billion in 1991. The DEIS listed hunting; fishing; whitewater rafting; hiking; camping; skiing; golfing; and visiting national parks, state parks, fairs, and festivals as some of the activities that visitors to West Virginia participated in. It also emphasized the importance of keeping areas environmentally healthy if they are to continue to attract tourists.[84] The study noted that tourism in the southern coalfield region is below the West Virginia average and goes on to say that this "suggest[s] that the study area is not a major tourism destination."[85] The drafters of this study missed the point. Numbers cannot show what might have been; they can only show what is. There is no study that estimates the loss in tourism dollars because of land destruction in the counties experiencing massive MTR and surface mining.

The New River Gorge National River occupies seventy thousand acres in Fayette County, West Virginia. One can easily imagine the magnitude of financial loss that would occur in Fayette County should MTR sites ever move close to this major tourist destination. The natural beauty of the area can sustain many generations of employment and tourist dollars for the county. Other southern West Virginia areas also have beautiful natural surroundings but enjoy far less success. A combination of inaccessibility, lack of advertising, and the ugliness that comes with industrial waste all contribute to marring the visual beauty of the unprotected landscapes. Also diminishing the beauty are the rusting remains of coal tipples and the scars from the contour and auger mining that transpired throughout the region for decades. Since the 1990s, the scars have become larger as MTR has expanded, creating vast moonscapes and valley fills.

The economic effects of MTR for these southernmost counties are—superficially—positive, but coal is a finite resource that will be exhausted within the next few decades. A Massachusetts Institute of Technology professor, hired by the state development office to identify specific industries that the state should target for its development efforts, concluded that manufacturing and coal should continue to be the focus.[86] Still, the region must diversify its economy. A June 1998 *Register-Herald* editorial addressed how Wyoming and McDowell counties were among the poorest in the state because of their dependency on "King Coal." It mentioned the development of industrial parks in both counties as well as plans for the first four-lane highway for either county. The editorial also spoke of the development of the Hatfield-McCoy Trail System, an ATV trail system that, once completed, would span eight southern West Virginia counties, and bring tourism dollars to the area.[87] As of March 2007, the four-lane highway, the Coalfields Expressway, has yet to become a reality. Its completion is looking ever more unlikely, considering that while it is still on the state's six-year highway-improvement plan, there is no state funding for it.[88] In fact, no roads in southern West Virginia are on the top 10 list in the state's six-year highway-improvement plan.[89] Transportation Secretary Paul Mattox stated that the money to finance southern West Virginia roads was just not there. A consultant's report to lawmakers noted that other regions were growing at a quicker rate and new roads were "needed to accommodate that development" and that southern West Virginia had failed to pass "an economic development and growth standards test."[90] Thus, the state has focused its funding on completing projects in every part of the state but southern West Virginia. Delegate Richard Browning noted that the funding disparities were ". . . an insult to Congressman Rahall" who, Browning noted, provided "the bulk of money here" and whose "district is getting the least amount." The state, he said, was "not doing anything to help us climb out of the hole."[91] Browning went on to note that at any point, Governor Manchin could change the plan and provide much-needed funding to southern West Virginia roads. It is simply a matter of wanting to do so. This lack of funding continues a trend. In the past decade, District 3, which houses southern West Virginia, received $1.5 billion in highway spending as opposed to $1.8 billion in District 1 and a whopping $2.5 billion in District 2. The current six-year plan provides

$1 billion dollars each for Districts 1 and 2 and half that amount for District 3.[92] Further construction on roads which would benefit the southern West Virginia counties—such as the King Coal Highway, the Coalfields Expressway, and WV 10 in Logan County (one of the most dangerous roads in southern West Virginia)—have been relegated to the status of "specially funded projects" and will continue only as funds are made available from Congress.[93] The Department of Highways' criteria for highway construction consists of population, traffic demand, and the potential for economic development. Wyoming and McDowell counties, for example, would benefit from the Coalfields Expressway, but they do not meet these criteria. Yet without this road, the two counties seem destined to continue their current plight of low employment and mass exodus.

This fact is not lost on county politicians. Wyoming County Clerk David "Bugs" Stover walked 134 miles to make Governor Joe Manchin pay attention to the need for this highway construction.[94] The road still has not made it back to the list of highway projects. The absence of funding for such needed infrastructure is certain to anger southern West Virginians whose roads are being obliterated through heavier weight limits on coal trucks and whose very economic existence has been stymied through its state-supported dependence on coal. The needed economic diversification cannot occur without a change in infrastructure, and a good road system is one of the most important parts of an adequate infrastructure.

Using land donated by many land companies, including coal-affiliated land companies, the Hatfield-McCoy trail has opened, and one need only drive through a county with growing traffic (such as Wyoming County where the trail opened in Spring 2004) to see the efforts the residents have made to attract tourists. The trail has the potential to be an economic boom for the financially strapped area, and handmade signs have sprouted up all over the place, welcoming riders of the Hatfield-McCoy trail. With 21 percent of riders coming from Ohio, 19 percent from within West Virginia, and the remaining 60 percent from the rest of the United States and Canada, southern West Virginia has the potential to receive a much-needed economic boost from tourism.[95] The trail is only a very small portion of the tourism industry that southern West Virginia could attract if the natural surroundings were protected. Matt Ballard, then–executive director of the Hatfield-McCoy Trail Authority, noted, "There's no doubt that this has created an economic impact. You can see the new construction in these towns. What you can't see is that it hasn't just created new businesses and jobs; it's saved existing ones."[96] Ballard highlighted that the entrepreneurship residents experienced was new for the area and "is a way for southern West Virginia to take control of its own destiny."[97]

While certainly not a cure-all, the trail and other such tourism ventures provide an alternative to total coal dependency and illustrate the region's eagerness for new economic opportunities. Potential negative environmental impacts from the trail remain to be seen and certainly should be explored. Still, massive strip mining, such as that associated with MTR, and a healthy tourism industry cannot coexist. Former state senator Si Galperin perhaps stated it best in his 1971 appearance before the Mines and Mining Sub-Committee of the U.S. House Interior Committee, which was debating the regulation of the surface-mining industry:

> Both stripping and the recreation and tourist industry which employs four times as many people are today growing rapidly. But they cannot both continue to grow. One must force out the other. Either we will have a state of beauty which West Virginians and Americans can continue to enjoy at great profit to ourselves, or we will have a stripped state enjoyed by none at great profit to a few giant, absentee corporations.[98]

In March 1999, the State Senate passed and Governor Cecil Underwood signed legislation reforming MTR in the state. Coming on the heels of Judge Haden's controversial *Bragg v. Robertson* decision, Senate Bill 681 created the Office of Blasting and Explosives as well as the Office of Coalfield Community Development, which it placed in the West Virginia Development Office. The controversial bill was purportedly voted on and passed unanimously before some senators even had a chance to read it. This bill also rolled back Senate Bill 145, another controversial bill signed by Underwood in 1998 that "nearly doubled the amount of a watershed that can be filled with excess rock from large-scale strip mines."[99] The purpose of the Office of Coalfield Community Development was to assist coalfield communities affected by strip mining in creating plans for economic development. The office would also help property owners determine a fair market value for their homes in areas where market prices had plummeted because of strip mining. The West Virginia Council for Community and Economic Development, a fifteen-member panel, set the policy for the office and immediately proposed that economic development professionals be involved in the mining permit process from the beginning to ensure the most cost-efficient, achievable post-mine development.[100] Still, the fact remains that most areas impacted by MTR are undeveloped.

The need for economic diversification cannot be overstated. Coal is a finite resource. In the southern coalfield counties that have failed to diversify their economy, coal is an economic albatross. While a few people benefit from direct employment and the higher wages offered by coal mining, these counties consistently have the highest unemployment and poverty rates. In short, coal counties represent the poorest counties in one of the poorest states in the nation. The short-term economic boosts to the coal counties' economies due to MTR are indisputable, but the boosts are just that—short-term. Nevertheless, the number of acres permitted for MTR continues to increase. In November 2003, a nine-month review of permits showed an increase of 3,727 acres since 2002, from 8,813 to 12,540 acres.[101]

With the ever-present dependency on a one-source economy, the state government tends to turn a blind eye toward growing amounts of environmental degradation, since it is often seen as necessary for sustaining local economies. In 2002, Jim Pierce, a West Virginia DEP engineer, admitted that the regulations were not working. The purpose of the law was to diminish disaster risks to a "tolerable" level. He went on to make the following analogy: "When you get on an airliner, it might crash. It's deemed a tolerable risk because they don't crash every day but when they do, it's bad. We put up with the small risk because we reap much bigger benefits. Mining's the same way."[102] These comments seem startling coming from an agent of the DEP. Such an analogy is fallacious on its surface, since those who choose to board a plane realize the risk involved and take it willingly, unlike coalfield residents. Actually, only those working on the mining operation would be in a position to realize and assume risk. One would assume that the DEP would be more concerned with protecting the state's citizens than calculating risks for the companies.

The power of coal is felt in all aspects of politics in the Mountain State. An obvious example is the public political persuasions of Massey's CEO

Don Blankenship. The vast profit made by Massey has greatly benefited Blankenship who uses his personal wealth to influence the political process and the power relationships in West Virginia. Beginning with the 2004 West Virginia Supreme Court race, Blankenship has become a vocal political player.

Under the guise of a non-profit organization, "And for the Sake of the Kids," Blankenship altered the face of the court system in West Virginia to create a friendlier court atmosphere for the coal industry. Warren McGraw, a West Virginia Supreme Court Justice, had ruled against the coal industry—and Massey—in a number of cases. Backed by Big Coal dollars, "And for the Sake of the Kids" had no difficulty distorting facts of an event totally unconnected to coal to the ultimate benefit of the coal industry. Since McGraw was seen as a nemesis, his reelection offered a unique opportunity for the coal interests. They knew if they could latch onto an issue that would alienate him from his constituents, he would be vulnerable to defeat from the little-known, industry-friendly candidate, Brent Benjamin. Tony Arbaugh Jr.'s tragic lifetime of abuse offered the perfect Achilles' heel for Warren McGraw and provided an easy opportunity for exploitation by the coal interests' new non-profit organization, "And for the Sake of the Kids." In what became a well-known case in the Mountain State, "And for the Sake of the Kids" targeted Arbaugh, who at the age of fourteen was tried as an adult for sexually assaulting his younger brother. Other sexual assault charges against him were dropped in a plea bargain, but he was still sentenced to fifteen to thirty-four years.[103] Arbaugh was himself a victim of years of molestation. His mother was sentenced to forty-five years for selling him and his younger sibling for drugs and money and for using them in a drug trafficking scheme. In addition to the family abuse, Arbaugh was targeted by a sexual predator who was also his school teacher. That school teacher, Ferlin Heavener, is now serving eighty years for a series of child molestation convictions where he targeted the most easily victimized children entrusted to his care. Arbaugh himself had successfully settled a lawsuit with the Pendleton County Board of Education for its failure to act upon obtaining knowledge of the teacher's behavior.[104]

These facts were apparently lost on "And for the Sake of the Kids," who instead turned the court's decision to give an already beaten-down young man a second chance into something lewd and lascivious. "And for the Sake of the Kids" launched a successful campaign, and the populace bought it hook, line, and sinker. In the end, Brent Benjamin replaced Warren McGraw, a member of one of West Virginia's most well-known political families. Prior to losing to Benjamin, McGraw had commented that he would rather exit public life than destroy the life of a young man who was himself a victim of sexual abuse. McGraw seemed to fully understand that the power behind the Arbaugh controversy had very little to do with protecting kids and everything to do with protecting the coal interests.[105] With complete disregard to the impact that a campaign based on distorted facts would have on Arbaugh, the nasty 2004 West Virginia Supreme Court Justice campaign illustrates the length that the coal interests are willing to go to in order to advance their agenda.

Heavily funded by the coal industry, and headed by Carl Hubbard, a Beckley coal-mining-equipment vice president, "And for the Sake of the Kids" would be more appropriately titled "And for the Sake of the Coal Industry." Interestingly, Hubbard himself had some experience with the legal system, having several run-ins with the law in Mercer County. Between 1977 and 1981, Hubbard pleaded guilty to two counts of destruction of property, three counts of public intoxication, and two counts of battery. Hubbard seemed to dismiss his past problems as youthful indiscretions and seemed offended that they were even brought up during the court race.[106] But many people go an entire life without accumulating the number of "mistakes" that mark Hubbard's past. While he certainly could have changed, he should have expected these problems to resurface when he decided to head a group called "And for the Sake of the Kids" and to target a political mainstay such as Warren McGraw.

With the McGraw defeat as impetus, Blankenship has announced his plans to use his immense fortune to alter West Virginia's political landscape further. As a coal-industry advocate, he has asserted his intent to oust a number of incumbent legislators and another Supreme Court Justice—this time, Justice Larry Starcher. Starcher, too, has ruled against coal companies, and his ousting would cement a firm, conservative, industry-friendly majority on the court.[107] While Blankenship publicly states that he is acting as a private citizen and not as an industry advocate, his targets are overwhelmingly Democrats and more likely to be labor-friendly candidates.[108] His intentions are so blatant and his threats so feared that in late July 2006, the Raleigh County Democratic Executive Committee met at a "we appreciate you" rally that the *Raleigh Register-Herald* characterized as an anti–Don Blankenship gathering. One of the points of their discussion was finding ways to fight off the onslaught of the millionaire's attacks on Democrats in the November 2006 election.[109] In fact, the Democratic Party made Blankenship, who ran for no office, a target in the election. State Party Chairman Nick Casey made a number of statements denouncing Blankenship in press conferences. In public statements, the party chair was quick to note Blankenship's high salary—$92,000 per day—and compare it with Massey's starting salary for new miners—$10.25 per hour.[110] In the end, Blankenship's efforts were unsuccessful: candidates that he backed consistently lost to their Democratic rivals.[111] In reflecting on his party's numerous losses, Republican Party Chair Doug McKinney stated that Blankenship's efforts actually hurt his party in the election since Democrats successfully linked Blankenship to the Republican Party.[112] Blankenship provides a face and an easy target for anti-MTR advocates. He is not the only player in this power struggle; he is merely the most visible. Without a visible, flamboyant leader, Arch Coal, for example, rarely experiences as much negative attention from media and opponents as Massey does, but their MTR activities are just as devastating.

Those elected to the state legislature are frequently affiliated with the coal interests. The coal industry has always exerted considerable political power in the state, and those who have challenged that authority have found themselves at the losing end of many political races. It is widely regarded that state policy, those forging it, and the agencies responsible for enforcing the laws have bent over backwards to appease the coal industry. It is also widely regarded that the state serves the benefit of out-of-state coal companies at the expense of its citizens. A guest column in the *Charleston Gazette* expressed this belief when it declared that MTR could be justified only if the state forced the coal companies to serve the public interest rather than forcing the people to serve coal.[113]

The alliance of state politicians with the coal industry is a West Virginia tradition. The practice is easily traceable through campaign contributions. Senate President Earl Ray Tomblin received $21,300 from the coal interests for his 2004 reelection bid. This donation was second only to those made by health-professional special-interests groups. During the 2004 elections, coal donated $299,312 to various State Senate and House races, far surpassing the $1,855 donated by environmental groups. In other words, environmental groups contributed less than 1 percent of what the coal interests gave to State Senate and House races.[114] Before Bob Wise decided not to run for reelection, coal had donated $187,400 to his campaign—or 17 percent of the total amount.[115] Donations by the coal interests often included candidates from both major political parties, thus ensuring allegiance from whoever won the race.

Current federal politicians also show their bias in favor of the coal industry. West Virginia's congressional delegation frequently protects the industry by fighting against the passage of hostile legislation, or attaching riders onto bills to guarantee favorable treatment for the coal industry. Although congress members' favoritism is frequently cloaked under the guise of helping their constituency, time and again this has been proven false, especially in the case of MTR where the majority of West Virginians are soundly against the practice. Only one representative, Nick J. Rahall II, represents southern coalfield residents. Still, even he could not logically say he is voting the conscience of his constituency, considering that a poll of West Virginia voters showed that a full 54 percent of southern West Virginians, encompassing the district that Rahall represents, oppose MTR while only 27 percent favor it. The other 19 percent remain undecided.[116] West Virginia's other two representatives are elected in parts of the state where MTR is not so readily utilized, or in the case of senators, represent the entire state. U.S. senators who embrace these bills supporting MTR actually go against the majority of their constituents. They may truly believe that they are helping the state, but in the end they are doing more harm than good.

Rahall was first elected to the United States Congress in 1976 and began his freshman term in 1977. Since that time, the people of southern West Virginia have continually elected him as their representative. Throughout his career, he has championed himself as a defender of the coal miner and coal-mining-safety issues. To that end, he has been a vocal advocate for coal miner's health benefits, black-lung issues, and coal-mining-safety legislation. He has also been active on issues related to veterans and the Appalachian Regional Commission, both of which are concerns for the southern West Virginia population. But he has been squarely behind MTR as well. Rahall attributes the problems of MTR to inadequate legal enforcement, not to the practice itself. In this assertion, he has been consistent. In 1998, he joined with then-Congressman Bob Wise and called for the Office of Surface Mining to scrutinize the post-mining land use for coal companies granted an MTR variance in southern West Virginia. The duo was responding to a *Charleston Gazette* exposé which revealed that a full 75 percent of mines permitted for MTR were not granted an approximate original contour (AOC) variance. Approximate original contour, as defined within SMCRA, requires surface reconfiguration through backfilling and degrading of the mined area so that the surface resembles the land prior to mining and complements the drainage pattern of the terrain.[117] The drafters of SMCRA compromised by putting in wording that required the land to be returned to its AOC. They also mandated that companies would have to state post-mining uses for the land before being granted a permit. In order to receive an AOC variance, the company must show that the now-mined land is going to be used for a greater and higher purpose. This would have required the coal companies to present post-mining plans showing the area would be used in a way that was equal to or better than the way it was used before mining. Because MTR mines cannot achieve AOC, these surface mines necessitate an AOC variance and should request this variance in the permitting process.[118] For his part, Rahall called for the Office of Surface Mining to more closely regulate MTR in southern West Virginia. Specifically, Rahall called for a crackdown on the post-mining use of land as outlined in SMCRA and the need for this property to be transformed for industrial, commercial, residential, or public uses. Rahall emphasized that the people of southern West Virginia should have economic opportunities in exchange for the variance allowed to mine via MTR.[119]

True to form, Rahall stated, "This is not a case of whether you are for or against mountaintop removal operations. This is a matter of whether or not there has been compliance with federal law as it relates to how permits for these types of operations are reviewed and granted."[120] He has also pointed out that obtaining an AOC variance comes with the price of viable post-mining land use such as "industrial, commercial, agricultural, resident or public facilities."[121] Rahall noted that this rule was designed so that local inhabitants would be left with something economically viable "once the coal is gone."[122] In a December 21, 2002, *Register-Herald* interview, Rahall vehemently supported MTR. He postulated that regulators had not made the coal companies adequately prepare, which led to present court cases. As a freshman congressman, Rahall helped draft SMCRA. He stated that the act was a "give-and-take" piece of legislation and was "an effort to head off those who wanted to abolish strip mining completely."[123] He pointed out that there was never any intent to abolish strip mining, because it provided jobs, and that he believed reclamation could be done effectively. Rahall proclaimed, "I support the law [SMCRA] and it does allow mountain-top mining."[124] In a 2002 interview, Rahall said, "[T]he fill material from a mountaintop operation is properly regulated under section 404 of the Clean Water Act."[125] He also affirmed that he did not agree with the buffer-zone ruling of the *Bragg v. Robertson* case, and was pleased that the ruling was overturned on appeal. Yet, he believed that regulatory improvements were being made in West Virginia as a result of the *Bragg v. Robertson* settlement, and he had "always found that all the coal industry wants to know is what the rules of the games are. They will, for the most part, abide by those rules of the game."[126] The article also contains a picture of Rahall in his DC office with the caption "Rahall, friend of the coal industry."[127]

Nevertheless, Rahall is concerned about the environment of West Virginia. The Wilderness Society even awarded him one of their highest honors in Summer 2004, the Ansel Adams Award, for his "lasting contributions to the stewardship of America's natural treasures."[128] In June 2004, he and fellow West Virginia congressman Alan Mollohan called for an investigation of the impact of windmills on West Virginia's environment. Both Mollohan and Rahall were concerned with the effect these large structures would have on the tourism industry in the heavily visited Potomac Highlands section of West Virginia. Mollohan declared that "there is nothing more beautiful than my West Virginia hills . . . and I don't need windmills to re-landscape God's glory and my West Virginia hills."[129] Rahall shared the sentiment, stating:

> We now have a situation where speculators are staking claim to some of our most scenic areas and erecting these monstrosities that produce little energy and are only made possible by a tax credit. . . . [N]obody has examined the

impact these facilities will have on our people and wildlife ... Folks go to visit places like Pocahontas County to hunt, fish, camp, canoe, hike and bike, not to stare at giant wind scrapers straddling the ridgetops ... When they stand at the top of Snowshoe Mountain, I think people would prefer to see the beautiful, unending vista that is there today, not a view horribly marred by a phalanx of steel-girder pinwheels.[130]

Granted, an environmental impact study is appropriate for any activity that might affect the environment, but digging in on wind turbines seems disingenuous coming from Rahall and Mollohan. MTR sites also represent what once were "beautiful West Virginia hills." Still, West Virginia's elected delegation has yet to make an outcry about this issue. Similarly, Mollohan feared that the harnessing of wind power would result in the continuation of West Virginia being a peripheral region.[131] That is a very real concern given that the majority of West Virginia's natural-resource money does, indeed, leave the area; the major players in the coal industry have headquarters in places like St. Louis, Missouri (Arch), and Richmond, Virginia (Massey). But, unlike coal, wind energy is a new, infinite, and renewable resource. It is a precarious tightrope these congressmen walk, speaking out against the *potential* environmental degradation of windmills while embracing the *proven* detrimental practices of MTR.

When contacted about his position on MTR, Rahall was consistent in his support of the process while praising the environmental regulations that many coal operators fear. Rahall noted that it was Clean Air Act regulations that have led to the increased demand for southern West Virginia coal. He also noted that the upsurge in demand has led to an increase in MTR. While admitting that not all MTR coal companies follow federal regulations, Rahall claimed that "there is a proper place for mountaintop mining" and that "when all is said and done, when all of the court challenges are disposed of, it will continue although perhaps on a smaller scale."[132]

Of all the current West Virginia congressional delegates, Jay Rockefeller is the only delegate who has made a 180-degree turnaround. Rockefeller first entered West Virginia in 1964 as a Vista Volunteer. He soon became part of a movement to halt strip mining. In 1970, while serving as West Virginia's secretary of state, Rockefeller ran for governor. In the same year,

Coal train near U.S. 119 at Danville, West Virginia. For more than 100 years, riches from the state's coalfields have wound their way to economic centers outside of the region. Photo by B. Mark Schmerling.

Mary Miller (left) and Pauline Canterberry laughing at the coal dust monitor placed at the closed Sylvester Elementary School as a result of a lawsuit over the effects of coal dust on the town's air quality. The device consists of a pipe, a cone-shaped apparatus, and a plastic Rubbermaid jar. The duo do not have much faith in its accuracy. Photo by R. Mark Schmerling.

MARSH FORK ELEMENTARY

Above: Marsh Fork Elementary School with coal silo behind it. The school has been at the center of controversy because of its proximity to this silo and to a coal slurry impoundment. Photo by B. Mark Schmerling.

Larry Gibson with his dog (named Dog) overlooking the destruction at Kayford Mountain. Kayford is one of many mountains being decimated by Mountaintop Removal. Photo by B. Mark Schmerling.

Judy Bonds standing outside of Coal River Mountain Watch, Whitesville, WV. Bonds, a local resident, has become a vocal opponent of mountaintop removal after being forced off of her ancestral home by MTR. Photo by R. Mark Schmerling.

Ed Wiley holding a picture of his granddaughter Kayla, a student at Marsh Fork Elementary. Wiley has been a vocal proponent in building a new school for Marsh Fork Elementary students. Photo by B. Mark Schmerling.

A coal sludge dam, the Chess Processing Refuse Disposal Area No. 1, owned by Elk Run Coal Company, a Massey Energy subsidiary. This dam is permitted to hold a maximum capacity of 760 million gallons of sludge. On the left side of the picture, the dome cover-

ing a stockpile at the Elk Run Coal Preparation Plant is visible. In the background is part of the mining operation on Kayford Mountain. Photo by Vivian Stockman, www.ohvec.org,

A massive dragline, dwarfed by the huge scale of the operation, at work on a mountaintop removal operation near Kayford Mountain, West Virginia. Photo by Vivian Stockman, www.ohvec.org, October 19, 2003.

The Elk Run coal processing plant, a Massey Energy subsidiary, Located just outside the
town limits of Sylvester. The dome covers stockpiles of coal and is supposed to protect

the town from the coal dust that emanates from the plant. Photo by Vivian Stockman,

Reclamation of Cazy Mountain in Boone County showing non-native grasses and a few shrubs. Photo by B. Mark Schmerling.

he provided personal funding to support Citizens Against Strip Mining.[133] Soon after, he voiced his opposition publicly, noting that he would have then-State Senator Si Galperin introduce a strip-mining prohibition bill at the beginning of the legislature.[134] He gave a heart-felt speech at Morris Harvey College (now the University of Charleston) in 1972, in which he declared, "It's not enough just to be against strip-mining. In the emotion of seeing a newly-clobbered hill, it's easy to forget the larger justification for abolition. The strongest arguments, other than environmental ones, can be made for abolition on economic terms. And we have to manifest concern for new industries and jobs in West Virginia."[135] (An excerpt from that fiery speech can be found in appendix 1.)

Rockefeller ran his gubernatorial campaign on an anti-strip-mining platform, and for the first time, West Virginians witnessed an important state political contest focused on the environmental and economic destruction of coal mining. While admitting that the prohibition might have a negative impact on the economy, Rockefeller noted that a miniscule number of people were required to work a strip mine—in fact, less than one-half of 1 percent of West Virginia workers were employed in strip mining. To offset the loss of tax revenue that would result from such a ban, he proposed a severance tax on deep-mined coal. His detractors claimed that he underestimated the number of people who would be left unemployed, and also charged that he was leading an assault against property rights. Rockefeller even spoke in favor of anti-strip-mining legislation during the 1971 legislative session.[136] While Rockefeller was successful in winning the Democratic nomination—and doing so against opponents heavily funded by coal-industry dollars—he lost the general election to Republican Arch Moore. Rockefeller erroneously believed that his defeat was because of his stance against strip mining, but in most other state races during the same election, the opponents soundly defeated strip-mining supporters.[137] Still, this loss convinced Rockefeller that he must join the ranks of strip-mine proponents or be an "also-ran." After his conversion, he became an advocate of strip mining in the state, on the grounds of employment and economic needs. It is a position he holds today, supporting MTR as well as traditional strip-mining methods.

Rockefeller was the most vehement among West Virginia senators and Congressman Rahall in extolling the virtues of MTR. He proclaimed that he felt the issue was important, encouraged both sides to talk, and said that he took "every job in West Virginia seriously, and will continue to do [his] best to find a way to prevent the economic harm that this controversy has caused and threatens."[138] Rockefeller's mention of the environment was minimal. He referred to it only in passing while commenting on his hope that all parties can agree on how best to continue the economically important process while "preserv[ing] the land and surroundings as much as possible" and that he hoped for a "solution that would provide peace of mind about both the jobs at stake and the environment."[139]

A discussion of West Virginia politicians and their positions on MTR would not be complete without addressing Robert Byrd. Byrd is a West Virginia institution, with roads, schools, and higher-education facilities named in his honor. His influence throughout the state is deep and his legacy secured. He became a United States congressman in 1953 and began his long tenure as one of West Virginia's senators in 1959. He is the longest-serving senator in United States history. He frequently works on miners' issues, particularly health and safety, and he has recently secured funding for a Coal Mine Impoundment Location and Warning System to monitor impoundments and to educate people living near them about their danger. On the topic of MTR, Byrd is united with other members of West Virginia's congressional delegation in staunchly supporting mountaintop removal.

After the 1999 *Bragg v. Robertson* ruling that halted valley fills because they were illegal under the Clean Water Act, West Virginia's congressional delegation quickly formed a band to reject the decision. Judge Charles Haden's ruling noted that he was merely interpreting the laws as written and, should a change be needed, it would be up to the legislative branch to make it. In a joint letter to the *Charleston Gazette*, West Virginia's congressional delegates committed themselves to do just that. In their own words, they "urged the U.S. Army Corps of Engineers, the Department of the Interior, and the Environmental Protection Agency to join in an appeal of the court's ruling."[140] They also stated that they were "aggressively examining possibilities for a balanced legislative remedy." This was an obvious reference to the rider that Senator Byrd would soon try to push through the senate.

In October 1999, after Haden ruled in favor of the plaintiffs in the highly publicized *Bragg v. Robertson* case, Byrd led the attack against the decision. As the top Democrat on the Senate Appropriations Committee, Byrd used his influence to persuade the Clinton White House to side with the pro-MTR rider Byrd planned to place on a very important spending bill. Not only would this rider have effectively negated Haden's ruling, but it would also have allowed the "dumping of thousands of tons of mining waste onto federal and Indian land."[141] Leading the western contingency was Senator Larry Craig, a Republican from Idaho. Outsiders may find such an alliance strange, but as Craig put it, "Politics makes strange bedfellows. I would not be uncomfortable in Bob Byrd's bed."[142] Soon, the two senators would work together to try to attach a rider that would fit both their needs. Along with the other West Virginia lawmakers, Byrd postulated that West Virginia's elected officials were attempting to ensure the state's viability through protecting its most prolific industry, thus saving thousands of jobs. Byrd's rider was merely following through with a promise the lawmakers had made to the West Virginia people upon hearing Haden's decision.

The Clinton administration waffled when it came to Byrd's ambitious rider. While Byrd was pushing his agenda, other politicians outside the coalfield region were imploring Clinton to uphold the letter and intent of the Clean Water Act and to veto any rider that violated it. Apparently, the Clinton administration feared retaliation from Byrd (a powerful fellow Democrat) more than they feared a backlash from constituents concerned with the environment. The Clinton White House made plans to side with Byrd, going against its usual stance that favored conservation. The same White House that had vetoed other bills because of their anti-environmental impact was set to sign off on a bill that would give coal companies carte blanche in the dumping of mining waste into West Virginia's streams.[143] Once Haden stayed his decision, the White House pulled back its support, stating there was now no need for the amendment.

Standing on the floor of the Senate in November 1999, Byrd angrily decried the judge's decision and the Clinton administration's initial reluctance to support his rider. He declared, "Fie on the White House! Fie for attempting to mislead the people."[144] He proclaimed that he was speaking up for the coal miners, railway workers, truckers, and suppliers that would be affected by Haden's decision. He called those who opposed MTR "head-in-the-clouds individuals [who] peddle dreams of an idyllic life among old growth trees."[145] A *Charleston Gazette* editorial observed that Byrd's speech "contained misinformation and divisive rhetoric that cast opponents of current mountaintop-removal practices as heartless, mindless individuals . . . ignoring the real need for jobs."[146] In fact, Byrd's speech drew a clear line between hard-working miners and "head-in-the-clouds" environmentalists whom Byrd claimed cared nothing about the plight of the families and economy of the southern coalfield communities. "What do they care [about the loss of income]?" the senator stormed. "They will have already thrown down their placards and their banners and gone off somewhere else . . . These dreamers would have us believe that if only our mountains—if only our mountains—remain pristine, new jobs will come."[147]

This rhetoric was as contentious as it was wrong. Many of the most vocal protestors to MTR are people who live and work in the communities affected. Some were once underground coal miners themselves. Byrd was also misleading when he asserted:

> No laws would be weakened by the Byrd-McConnell amendment. No regulations would be discarded. The legislative remedy that is proposed by this amendment is not an either/or proposition. This amendment would permit carefully controlled mountaintop mining while allowing work to continue on a broad environmental study that could spur better oversight and more environmentally friendly mining practices nationally in the years ahead. In my book, that is a win/win situation.[148]

In fact, the amendment, as proposed, would have greatly weakened the Clean Water Act. The amendment, No. 2780, was proposed on November 18, 1999. Byrd's rider would have legalized the unofficial "dredge and fill" permits that coal companies had been using when obtaining permits for valley fills. Haden had concluded that this permitting was illegal under Section 404 of the Clean Water Act because it provided a "more lenient, less protective standard"[149] than had been intended by the Clean Water Act or by the buffer-zone rule of SMCRA. The proposed rider would have "exempt[ed] valley fills from state and federal water quality standards."[150] Byrd's speech indicated that he was concerned with the workingman. He specifically mentioned the dangerous roads many would have to travel to obtain employment if Haden's ruling remained unchanged: "You do not have to drive the dangerous, winding, narrow roads over which these workers would have to commute each morning and evening."[151] Byrd did not address, however, the dangerous roads residents must face every day due to overloaded coal trucks. The senator then launched into a long diatribe about the perils of coal mining that he had witnessed. Interestingly, everything he mentioned pertained to underground, not surface, mining.

In spite of the rhetoric and coercive tactics, Byrd's rider ultimately failed. While still a fervent supporter of MTR, Byrd and the other members of West Virginia's federal delegation have been more restrained in their comments since 1999, and they have not employed the incendiary language that lit up the newspaper columns in the latter half of that year. This restraint may be because of a series of court decisions that have been overturned on appeal to the notoriously conservative Fourth Circuit Court of Appeals in Richmond, Virginia. It is to this court that all West Virginia federal judicial decisions must go when they are appealed. The judicial branch's ultimate decisions have made such outbursts unnecessary. Regarding his position on MTR, Byrd verified his recent silence; he stated that these decisions were "under judicial review in recent years" and that "as a U.S. Senator" he had "no voice in such decisions."[152]

Although the defeat of the rider spared Clinton from having to make such a decision, his administration did entertain the idea of appealing Haden's decision against valley-fill waste dumping and even considered changes to the Clean Water Act that would have given the Army Corps of Engineers the authority to issue permits for MTR sites.[153] Up to that point, under the agency's own rules, the Army Corps of Engineers had been doing so illegally—their own regulations asserted that the agency was not supposed to allow fill material that was used to dispose, primarily, waste. In 1989, a judge ruled that the overburden from mining sites, including all MTR sites, was waste material.

In 1999, Haden further clarified the situation by declaring that since the overburden was waste, the Corps could not legally permit the overburden to be dumped, under Section 404 of the Clean Water Act.[154] Again, Clinton received pressure not to proceed, this time from twenty-three members of the House who wrote, "Any change that has the effect of allowing valley fills to destroy waters of the United States is unacceptable

[and] would be wholly inconsistent with Congress's purpose and intent when it enacted the Clean Water Act."[155]

While West Virginia's congressional delegation shifted between silence on the issue of MTR and an outright protectionist stance, other members of Congress were not so silent. Most vocal of these were Representatives Christopher Shays (R-CT) and Frank Pallone (D-NJ). Their legislation, re-introduced in February 2003, would codify Haden's original decision in *Kentuckians for the Commonwealth v. Rivenburgh* into law. Upon introducing the legislation, Pallone remarked:

> Our bipartisan legislation is needed to ensure our streams and waterways aren't buried under millions of tons of mining and other industrial wastes. While the legal debate continues, it is critical that we support the true intentions of the Clean Water Act and oppose the continued efforts of the Bush administration to use our nation's waterways as dumping grounds for industrial wastes.[156]

Shays concurred:

> It is my hope this legislation signals to the EPA that Congress will not sit silently by as our environment is destroyed. We cannot afford to waste another day, another hour, another minute if we want our children and our children's children to enjoy clean water. We simply won't have a world to live in if we continue our neglectful ways.[157]

The bill had fourteen other sponsors, none of whom were members of West Virginia's delegation.[158] Since its initial introduction, forty-eight other members have signed on to bring the total co-sponsorship to sixty-four. Still, none of West Virginia's delegates have signed on.[159] The proposed legislation, the Clean Water Protection Act of 2003, sought to solidify the definition of "fill" within the Clean Water Act to so that it would mining wastes and other pollutants in the definition. Through this effort, they hoped to halt any further attempts by the Bush administration to rewrite the Clean Water Act. In proposing the legislation, they noted that the Fourth U.S. Circuit Court of Appeals' overturning of Haden's decision made a legislative remedy imperative.[160] As of October 2006, the proposed legislation had been referred to the House Subcommittee on Water Resources and Environment.[161]

Senator Byrd and the other West Virginia legislators who favored MTR would find an ally in George W. Bush when he became president in 2000. The Texas Republican had courted West Virginia voters and vowed to protect the coal interests. Once in office, he kept his promise. Although Haden's initial valley-fill decision had been overturned, the Bush administration took an idea originally born with the Clinton administration and forcefully pursued it. The new administration was taking no chances with a higher court, because by this time, other lawsuits had been filed as well.[162]

So, by 2002, the Bush administration had gone to work rewriting valley-fill rules to legalize the very same valley fills that coal companies had been allowed to construct illegally for years.[163] Not only would the new rules approve those valley fills, but they would also be so broad that they included nearly anything dumped into a stream, including items typically considered garbage, such as old porcelain bathroom fixtures (including sinks and tubs), junk cars, refrigerators, and the like. The proposed rules went so far as to declare that these types of fixtures could be "environmentally beneficial artificial reefs."[164] They were backed by both the U.S. Army Corps of Engineers and the EPA. But so many letters (more than seventeen thousand) were written in opposition to the rules that the proposal did not see the light of day.

Then, in May 2002, Haden once again ruled on a valley-fill issue. This time, he stopped the Army Corps of Engineers from permitting most valley fills. The only legitimate way the Corps could permit such fills, Haden said, would be if they were part of a legitimate post-mining land use. Haden's ruling noted that allowing such dumping, in effect, "rewrites the Clean Water Act."[165] He claimed the Corps and the EPA had overstepped their authority and had no power to rewrite an act of Congress. Furthermore, the Corps had been issuing valley-fill permits illegally, he declared, and to continue to issue permits solely because it had been allowed in the past would be a continued disregard of the law.[166] While Haden was aware of the economic pressures associated with the continued practice of MTR valley fills, he also understood that there were other issues at hand. In his ruling for *Kentuckians for the Commonwealth v. U.S. Army Corps of Engineers*, Haden stated:

> The Court does not rule in a vacuum. It is aware of the immense political and economic pressures on the agencies to continue to approve mountaintop removal coal mining valley fills for waste disposal, and to give assurances that future legal challenges to the practice will fail. Some may believe that reasonably priced energy from coal requires cheap disposal of the vast amounts of waste material created when mountaintops are removed to get at the natural resource. For them, valley fill disposal is the most efficient and economical solution. Congress did not, however, authorize cheap waste disposal when it passed the Clean Water Act.[167]

The Bush administration implored Judge Haden to suspend his ruling until an appeal could be filed, citing the economic consequences of his decision. Federal authorities also believed that the ruling was overly broad and that it should have applied only to the mine site in question.[168] Had Haden only ruled on that particular mine permit, contesting such illegal practices would have placed a heavier burden on the residents bringing lawsuits. It is easy to understand why the coal industry and the Bush administration so fervently support such practices; a more cumbersome process would "occupy" citizens unnecessarily while the courts rendered carbon-copy decisions based on precedence or the literal interpretation of the law.

This time, however, Haden firmly refused to suspend his ruling. His decision against granting the suspension was even longer than his initial decision in favor of the plaintiffs. In denying the suspension request, Haden noted that the defendant's argument that "these fills are required and all mines are dependent on them, is demonstrably false. To stay the Court's injunction would be an invitation to coal operators . . . to save money by continuing their current waste disposal practices, filling miles of Appalachian streams in disregard of the statutory scheme."[169] He clarified that the ruling applied only to the Huntington Corps district as well as to any type of mining pursuing permits by the Corps.[170]

The defendants took up their cause to a higher court—the conservative Fourth Circuit Court. Once again, the conservative court did not disappoint the coal industry. Haden's valley-fill decision was again overturned. Amazingly, the justices concluded that the Clean Water Act actually permits dumping coal-mining waste into U.S. waterways.[171] Their ruling seemed to ignore the fact that the Corps was the agency issuing these permits even though the Corps' own policy stated that they could *not* legally issue them.

Even doing your job can be hazardous in the pro-MTR climate of the Bush administration. Jack Spadaro found that out first-hand when he lost his job as the superintendent of the National Mine Safety and Health Academy, a division of the Mine Safety and Health Administration (MSHA). After the October 2000 Massey slurry-impoundment spill in Inez, Kentucky, which affected areas of Kentucky and West Virginia, Spadaro led an investigation into the causes. The investigation discovered that the same impoundment had experienced a spill in 1994 and that the problems with the impoundment had not been fixed. The investigation into the spill was cut short.

The head of MSHA, Bush appointee Dave Lauriski, tried to secure Spadaro's signature on a watered-down version of the final report, which would have exonerated MSHA's own lack of enforcement. When Spadaro refused, he was demoted. After a four-year battle with MSHA, Spadaro agreed to retire, and MSHA agreed to reinstate his previous pay grade for purposes of retirement pay.[172] In spite of all of this, Spadaro remains an outspoken opponent of MTR.

In January 2004, the Bush administration proceeded with its attack on environmental regulations. This time the administration, through the Office of Surface Mining's director Jeff Jarrett, sought to weaken the buffer-zone rule of SMCRA. The purpose of the buffer-zone rule was to limit mining activity within one hundred feet of intermittent and perennial streams. Under Bush's proposal, the company merely had to do the best they could to minimize stream impact using the most current technology available, not guarantee that there would be no water-quality violations.[173] No decision has been made on that proposal although the Office of Surface Mining is preparing an environmental impact statement on the proposed new rules.[174] With the protection provided to the industry by a presidential administration firmly in its corner and a conservative federal district court poised to overturn most every decision on appeal, MTR proponents have a solid hold on the reins of power, and it appears that they will not have to release them any time soon.

Conclusion

West Virginia continues to serve as a peripheral economic region for the rest of the country, and its economy remains dependent on natural-resource extraction. Exploitation of the state's resources was aided by a political economy organized to favor industry property rights over individuals' property rights. West Virginia's politicians on both state and federal levels historically have been heavily involved with extractive industry, a trend that persists today. The intricate relationship between industry and politics has resulted in economic despair for the coalfield region where economic diversification is minimal.

Increased mechanization associated with MTR has been accompanied by decreased employment. Historically, such increases in demand have boosted employment at least for a short time, but this is not the case in the coalfields now. Demand for coal is up, and coal production continues to climb even as employment dwindles, leaving the paradoxical situation of a jobless coal boom in southern West Virginia.[175] Still, industry and politicians continue to praise the few jobs attributable to MTR and to fight doggedly in the court system to ensure that coal's domination of the state's economy and people remains intact.

5

SHOWDOWN IN CHARLESTON
The Judicial System and MTR

What is not mined today may be mined tomorrow, unless it is determined it cannot be mined under the Clean Water Act, in which case it should not be mined today or in the future.

—Judge Charles Haden

In the southern coalfields of West Virginia, both federal and state laws regulate MTR. Any state law must be as strict as, or stricter than, the federal law. If a state law is weaker, the stronger federal law always trumps it. Most lawsuits brought forth regarding MTR have been based on federal law, or specifically, the state agencies' failure to properly execute its duties under state-run and federally approved programs. The two federal laws that are especially important in regulating MTR are SMCRA and the Clean Water Act, particularly Section 404.

Enacted in 1972, the Clean Water Act regulates the amount of pollutants, both toxic and non-toxic, discharged into U.S. waters. It also regulates the distribution of permits for pollutants released into the nation's waterways. It is in this capacity that the act has proved so important to regulating MTR. Section 404 of the Clean Water Act regulates dredge and fill permits and is the section of the law used to control coal-mining valley fills. The act provides states with the power to regulate permits, and the Army Corps of Engineers the power to issue them. The Clean Water Act also allows for Nationwide Permit 21 in particular, which is often used in surface-mining operations. Nationwide Permit 21 requires little to no delay or paperwork and is, therefore, very attractive to companies looking for expediency. The permit is designed for activities that pose little environmental impact.[1] To obtain it, an applicant must satisfy a number of stipulations: the activity must not harm endangered species or "substantially disrupt the movement of those species of aquatic life indigenous to the waterbody, including those species which normally migrate through the area."[2]

After years of failed attempts on the federal level to pass legislation to regulate surface mining and to provide guidelines on mandatory reclamation procedures, a compromise was reached in 1977 resulting in the passage of SMCRA. A much weaker bill than the one proposed (twice) during the Gerald Ford administration, it was finally passed and signed into law by President Jimmy Carter.[3] The government declared in its "findings" section of the law:

> Many surface mining operations result in disturbances of surface areas that burden and adversely affect commerce and the public welfare by destroying or diminishing the utility of land for commercial, industrial, residential, recreational, agricultural, and forestry purposes, by causing erosion and landslides, by contributing to floods, by polluting the water, by destroying fish and wildlife habitats, by impairing natural beauty, by damaging the property of citizens, by creating hazards dangerous to life and property, by degrading the quality of life in local communities, and by counteracting governmental programs and efforts to conserve soil, water, and other natural resources.[4]

Clearly, the framers of the act recognized that much destruction could occur on the local or regional level as a result of strip mining; however, they sought to balance the energy needs of the nation—then suffering from an oil embargo by Arab nations—with the environmental and commercial realities of strip mining. The framers did not downplay the positive effects mining had on the national economy, also stating:

> Surface and underground coal mining operations affect interstate commerce, contribute to the economic well-being, security, and general welfare of the Nation and should be conducted in an environmentally sound manner.[5]

From these separate findings, it is apparent that Congress, for the good of the nation, was willing to tolerate the negative effects that surface mining had on local and regional economies. The act did allow MTR as long as the land was returned to a state in at least as good a condition as it had been in the past. The act also allowed states to oversee themselves in the enforcement of the act's regulations. However, if the "state fails to implement, enforce, or maintain its approved state program, the Secretary has the duty to prepare and implement a federal program for that state."[6] The act's Abandoned Mine Reclamation Fund helped to ensure that previously abandoned mine lands had a funding source for reclamation.

Since 1998, a number of important cases relating to MTR in West Virginia have occurred. Some of these important cases are reviewed here. The first of these cases was the high-profile *Bragg v. Robertson* case that began in 1998, heard by Judge Charles Haden II. Faced with the impending annihilation of their homes and the destruction of their property due to flyrock, dust, noise, cracked foundations, and destroyed wells, a group of coalfield residents brought forth a lawsuit in July 1998. Plaintiffs in the case claimed that the director of the West Virginia DEP violated SMCRA by approving illegal valley-fill permits for MTR. The plaintiffs cited SMCRA's public citizen suit provision as authority for their suit. The provision allows any citizen to sue state regulatory authorities that fail in their non-discretionary duties under the act.

Bragg v. Robertson claimed that the DEP as well as the U.S. Army Corps of Engineers failed to enforce the federal Clean Water Act and allowed the illegal issuing of valley-fill permits under Section 404. Furthermore, the suit claimed that the Corps of Engineers "lacked jurisdiction" when issuing valley-fill permits under Section 404 because the waste that composes the valley fills is excluded under the Corps' own definition of fill material. They noted that in 1989, U.S. District Judge John Copenhaver defined strip-mine spoil as "waste," and that the Corps' definition of fill does not include such waste. The suit alleged that the Corps had been illegally issuing these permits under Section 404 for years. The Clean Water Act allowed pollutants to be released into the water only if the coal company had received a permit from the U.S. EPA or a state regulatory agency. The Corps of Engineers also possessed the authority to issue permits for dredge-and-fill activities.[7] The suit was filed against Michael Miano, then-director of the DEP, for failing in his duties under SMCRA as well as West Virginia state regulations. The suit also named the Corps of Engineers and three of its employees for illegally permitting valley fills under Section 404, and for illegally issuing Nationwide Permit 21 "without the required analysis."[8]

At the time of the suit, the Corps admitted that under Section 404, they did not have the authority to authorize the dumping of mining waste into waters. The chief of the Huntington, West Virginia, regulatory branch of the Corps, Richard Buckley, stated that they believed the 1989 court decision did not allow for the permitting of valley fills under Section 404, and that the Corps did not disagree with that assertion. Buckley noted that the Corps "stopped issuing 404 permits for valley fills . . . after the agency was made aware of [the] 10-year-old court decision."[9] He further stated, "We're not supposed to authorize valley fills."[10] The suit "ask[ed] for a court order that state and federal regulators have improperly permitted hundreds of valley fills."[11]

In December 1998, plaintiffs agreed to drop the suit against the Corps in exchange for an agreement that the Corps would more closely scrutinize permits and study the effects of MTR. The agreement would streamline the permit process as well as produce tougher environmental standards for the coal companies. It stipulated that federal agencies involved with MTR would "[r]equire complete environmental assessments for all mine permits larger than 250 acres."[12] Still, this agreement did not completely settle the lawsuit.

In November 1998, Miano approved the expansion of Arch Coal's Dal-Tex MTR site near Blair in Logan County. The permit covered 3,100 acres and "was the largest issued in West Virginia history."[13] This particular permit had been targeted in *Bragg v. Robertson*. The federal defendants had asked that this particular permit be exempt from the lawsuit. The plaintiffs, in turn, asked for a preliminary injunction of the permit until the suit was settled.[14] In February 1999, Judge Haden agreed to tour and, encouraged by plaintiffs in the case, do a flyover of southern West Virginia MTR sites. On the flight, he witnessed firsthand "the extent and permanence of environmental degradation this type of mining produces."[15] He subsequently issued a preliminary injunction halting the permitted expansion.[16] By June 1999, the Corps concluded that their chances of succeeding in any lawsuit that might occur because of the permit were "minimal" and withdrew their initial approval of the Dal-Tex mine.[17] The Corps refused to issue a Nationwide Permit 21 to the site, and Arch Coal did not "[submit] a permit that regulators and the courts [would] approve."[18] With the permit revoked, in July 1999, more than two hundred UMWA workers at the site were laid off or had their jobs eliminated entirely. As many as four hundred jobs were predicted to be lost in the end.[19] The citizens and the environmental group involved in the suit signed an agreement with the DEP, the West Virginia Coal Association, and the Western Pocahontas Land Company. The DEP agreed to more stringent regulations that would cause the agency to "enforce federal rules that require companies to rebuild more of the mountains they tear down to reach coal seams" as well as make the industries submit "post-mining development plans," one of which could include free land for low-income people.[20] The judge warned that this was not the final resolution to the problems.

The opposing sides could not reach a decision on the crucial issue of the SMCRA buffer-zone rule—specifically, they could not agree on whether it forbade valley fills in intermittent and perennial streams. This issue would not be decided until the October 20, 1999, courtroom decision. The *Charleston Gazette* headline the next day told the story: "Valley fill mining outlawed: Landmark ruling prohibits mountaintop coal operators from burying state streams."[21] Judge Haden's ruling stated that valley fills were only legal in ephemeral streams, those that flow only when rain falls or snows melt. Intermittent and perennial streams must not have valley-fill waste and material placed into them. Haden's forty-nine-page opinion detailed his reasoning. The defendants had argued that the buffer-zone rule did not apply to streams in their entirety so long as portions of the stream remained viable. Haden was not convinced. He concluded that "the buffer zone rule protects entire intermittent and perennial streams, not just portions thereof."[22] He pointed out that provisions in SMCRA say "nothing therein 'shall be construed as superseding, amending, modifying, or repealing . . . the Clean Water Act.'"[23] The defendants tried to use a Memorandum of Understanding as the basis for their argument that Section 404 allowed valley fills; again, they did not sway Haden, who declared that the Memorandum of Understanding was contrary to the Clean Water Act and, therefore, contrary to law. The Clean Water Act clearly stated that no pollutants should be allowed into U.S. waterways simply for disposal of waste with no higher land use for the fill. He acknowledged that Section 404 might allow valley fills used primarily for land development, along with AOC waivers. Haden then asserted that coal-mine spoil is waste and that the Corps did not have the authority to permit waste disposal under Section 404. He noted that the EPA was the entity that had the authority, under Section 402 of the Clean Water Act, to permit for waste disposal. His ruling stated:

> When valley fills are permitted in intermittent and perennial streams, they destroy those stream segments . . . If there are fish, they can not migrate. If there is any life that can not acclimate to life deep in a rubble pile, it is eliminated. No effect on related environmental values is more adverse than obliteration. Under a valley fill, the water quantity of the stream becomes zero. Because there is no stream, there is no water quality.[24]

He went on to proclaim the reality of valley fills as "waste disposal projects so enormous that, rather than the stream assimilating the waste, the waste assimilates the stream."[25]

Haden's decision rang throughout the region, the state, and the country. With a cacophony of doomsayers at his back, Haden suspended his decision on October 29, 1999, until an appeal could be made to the Fourth Circuit Court.[26] At the same time, West Virginia's congressional delegation worked to circumvent judicial recourse through a rider that Senator Byrd planned to attach to a very important spending bill.[27] A chaotic discourse over the perceived effects of Haden's decision chorused through the state and in the halls of Congress. The coal industry and supporters of MTR rested their hopes for relief on the court. The notoriously conservative Fourth Circuit Court did not disappoint. In April 2001, the court failed to address any of the real issues of the case and instead overturned Judge Haden's decision on a jurisdictional technicality.[28]

Subsequently, in 2002, the United States Supreme Court refused to hear the case, thus upholding the appellate court's decision. MTR would continue. The legal case had broad ramifications for all parties engaged in the coal industry. Important questions were left unanswered, however, and other lawsuits would soon follow.

In October 2003, the Ohio Valley Environmental Coalition, Coal River Mountain Watch, and the National Resources Defense Council filed a lawsuit against the Army Corps of Engineers. Once again, the main concern was the permitting process used for valley fills. This time the lawsuit challenged the use of Nationwide Permit 21. Lawyers for the plaintiffs argued that Nationwide Permit 21 should only be issued, as mandated by law, when it is likely to cause only minimal environmental damage. The plaintiffs maintained that, on the contrary, the Corps had haphazardly issued Nationwide Permit 21, resulting in extreme environmental damage including the burial of hundreds of miles of West Virginia rivers. The plaintiffs argued that the coal companies should adhere to the stricter requirements involved in obtaining individual permits and stressed that the covering of hundreds of miles of streams and the destruction of hundreds of acres of forests do not amount to the minimal environmental impacts stipulated. The suit listed dozens of valley-fill authorizations that were either already approved or expected to gain approval. The list the plaintiffs provided showed "nearly 64,000 acres of mining permits in a dozen West Virginia watersheds."[29]

U.S. District Judge Joseph Goodwin was assigned to the case. He denied requests by coal-industry groups and the Corps to throw out the case, which specifically noted a Nicholas County valley-fill permit issued to Green Valley Coal Co., a Massey subsidiary. Even though the Corps had agreed to have Green Valley seek an individual permit to fill in part of Blue Branch (which flows into Hominy Creek), on March 25, 2004, the Corps approved a Nationwide Permit 21 for the filling of 431 feet of Blue Branch. On April 6, 2004, acting at the behest of the plaintiffs who had requested an emergency ruling on that particular valley fill, Judge Haden temporarily blocked a Massey permit for a preparation-plant waste fill. Granted a ten-day reprieve, the Nicholas County stream that Green Valley had prepared to fill would, for the moment, be "spared." Although Green Valley would be filling in a relatively small amount of the stream, Goodwin observed that once the stream was covered, it could not be repaired. At risk was Hominy Creek, the eventual destination for the disposal and home to a high-quality trout stream.[30]

The fill would have been the beginning of a larger fill for the subsidiary. The smaller fill was proposed to be a temporary, eight-month fix. It was necessary because, as the company claimed, it would allow them to keep 150 of their workers employed. The initial proposal to the Corps would have expanded the company's original permit by seventy-five acres and allowed waste to be dumped into the Blue Branch. The permit would have eventually allowed the placement of "1.5 million tons of coarse refuse and 510,000 tons of fine refuse into the stream"[31] per year, for at least a decade. Green Valley had detailed plans to reroute the stream. They claimed that the water running under the valley fill might even be healthier for the trout because of how cold it was.[32] However, the defendant failed to disclose that if the headwater streams were filled in, the subsequent loss of macroinvertebrates, the trout's food source, would be detrimental.[33]

Within a week of his earlier order, Goodwin heard further arguments and added another ten days to "his initial temporary restraining order," allowing more time for his decision.[34] During the court case, it was revealed that Green Valley had begun filling in the stream in question even before the Corps had approved the company's proposed mitigation plan. The judge seemed astonished at the revelation. At one point, while holding a stack of papers in his hand, he told the Corps lawyer, "Is this a mistake? What good does it do to say, 'Go ahead and fill this, and then later provide us all of the information to show whether it will or will not have a significant impact?'"[35]

On April 26, 2004, Goodwin placed a more permanent halt to Green Valley's valley fill. Acting on a motion for a preliminary injunction or a temporary restraining order in the smaller-fill issue, the judge agreed with the plaintiff's lawyer that the Corps illegally "broke up" the initial permit request into two smaller requests to "avoid a more detailed environmental review."[36] In his decision, the judge ruled that the approval of the smaller fill (called "Revision 5") was "an abuse of [Nationwide Permit] 21"[37] as all documentation in the case made it apparent that the company had not rewritten any mitigation plans. The judge's decision was clear: "[T]he destruction of 431 feet of a stream's small tributary by diverting 8,000 feet of the stream itself is ridiculous. The plan to mitigate so little damage with so much disruption to the watershed is as absurd as the statement by the officer in Vietnam who said he had to 'destroy the village to save it.'"[38] The judge went on to state, "[T]he public interest weighs in favor of OVEC. The public has an interest in the integrity of the waters of the United States, and in seeing that administrative agencies act within their own regulations."[39]

Still, the case was not completely settled. The larger issue of the Corps using Nationwide Permit 21 for valley fills still remained unresolved. On July 8, 2004, Judge Goodwin delivered his decision. "The Army Corps of Engineers could no longer approve mining valley fills through a stream-lined permit process meant only for activities that cause minor environmental damage."[40] Goodwin ruled that the Corps had been issuing Nationwide Permit 21 in violation of the Clean Water Act, and he also stipulated that in addition to halting such permitting in the future, the Corps had to revoke eleven permits it had previously allowed where construction had not yet commenced.[41] On July 22, 2004, OVEC requested an expansion of the judge's original order to include six more permits that the plaintiffs had not known about because, according to the plaintiffs, the Corps had been very secretive about them. On August 13, 2004, he granted the request.[42] A subsequent request by the plaintiffs to clarify the ruling was denied. In refusing the request, Goodwin declared that his orders were unambiguous and that he believed the Corps could enforce them as written.[43]

While *Bragg v. Robertson* faced more vocal critics, *OVEC v. Bulen* was still met with some cries of ruination and economic upheaval from the coal industry. By September 2, 2004, the Bush administration announced its plans to file an appeal with the Fourth Circuit Court. Bush's senior environmental policy advisor, Jim Connaughton, made the announcement at the state Chamber of Commerce's annual luncheon at the Greenbrier Resort in West Virginia. At that time, there had been no layoffs or work stoppages correlated with the decision, yet naysayers asserted that it was only a matter of time.[44] In November 2005, the Fourth Circuit Court stayed true to form, overturning the case on appeal. The three-judge panel disagreed with Goodwin on every point. Specifically, they ruled that the Corps had, indeed, complied with the Clean Water Act. They concluded:

> The Corps identified a category of activities, it determined that those activities would have a minimal environmental impact both separately and cumulatively, and it provided notice and opportunity for public hearing before issuing the permit. The Corps' issuance of [Nationwide Permit] 21 thus fell within its authority under section 404(e).[45]

In February 2006, the Fourth Circuit Federal Court of Appeals refused to reconsider the three-judge panel decision. This time, however, three judges dissented. Two of those judges (Robert B. King and M. Blane Michael) were from West Virginia. Not only did King and Michael, joined by Judge Diana Gribbon Motz, agree to rehear the case, but they also emphasized the national importance of the issues. In writing the dissent, King stated:

> This case is of exceptional importance to the nation and, in particular, to the states of the Appalachian region. The Appalachian mountains, the oldest mountain chain in the world, are one of the nation's richest, most diverse, and most delicate ecosystems, an ecosystem that the mountaintop coal mining authorized by the Corps' general permit may irrevocably damage or destroy . . . The panel's decision, in authorizing the Corps to skirt the [Clean Water Act–] mandated permitting process, undermines the enactment's primary purpose and poses unnecessary risks to one of this nation's great places.[46]

Had the request been granted, it would have allowed the full thirteen-judge circuit to reconsider the case. So far, the Fourth Circuit Court has overturned all of the MTR environmental decisions that have come to them from West Virginia's District Courts, and the trend is likely to continue.[47]

The 1889–1909 West Virginia Supreme Court adopted a "reasonable use rule" intended to acknowledge the rights of both agriculture and industry in nuisance disputes. At the center of this rule was the "scale of reasonableness" in property use. Rather than one side being preferred, the court concluded that both interested parties had a right to enjoy their property, even if there were competing interests.[48] In its application, however, there was a fundamental departure from traditional court rulings. The old court rested on the foundation of the universal principle of natural rights, centering on the belief that everyone could use their property as they saw fit, so long as it did not infringe on someone else's rights. The new court, however, embraced legal positivism, which assumes that if the benefits of infringing on someone else's property rights outweigh the costs, then that use of the land is in the public's best interest and should be allowed.[49]

It was this concept that the residents of Sylvester used in their lawsuit against Elk Run. In September 2000, residents complained to the DEP regarding the amount of coal dust that permeated their homes and businesses. (Recall that it was at Sylvester Elementary School that cafeteria workers had to wash the coal dust off of their equipment each day before they could use it.) This was one of numerous complaints that had been filed with the DEP from members of the community over a two-year stretch. The DEP issued citations in September and October 1998 and April and July 1999. Elk Run's preparation plant spewed coal dust all over the town and failed to take proper precautions to contain the dust. A DEP inspector noted in his report that Elk Run was not running the coal-dust sprayers on the stockpiles of coal, and that the coal dust was evident throughout the community. In spite of this report, no citations were issued to Elk Run. According to the inspector, his superior told him not to issue citations, stating that the coal company could not be cited unless the inspector himself had actually seen the dust coming from the plant. The superior denied these claims and said that she merely needed some type of proof, such as videotape or "eyewitness accounts from mine inspectors."[50] This diverted from the agency's previous practice of relying on the inspector's professional opinion. Hearings were held through April 2000, and DEP hearing examiner George Warrick concluded that the company had created a "pattern of violations" regarding the coal dust; however, Michael Castle, then-director of the DEP, failed to act on the hearing examiner's recommendations to shut down the facility until the problem ceased, opting instead to vaguely order Elk Run to "make corrections to eliminate complaints about dust from residents."[51] On October 25, 2000, the state Surface Mine Board ordered the plant closed until it fixed the dust problem plaguing the community. While Massey challenged the order, arguing that the DEP "could not prove the company caused dust problems," the company was denied and told that the subsidiary had "[no] right to damage communities."[52]

Still experiencing problems with dust, in February 2001, 154 Sylvester residents, more than three-fourths of the town's citizens, filed a lawsuit in Boone County Circuit Court against Elk Run and Massey. Their lawsuit complained about the coal dust, the light pollution, and the incessant noise that accompanied their mining activities, including the lumbering trucks that paraded through town at all hours. The suit asserted that the company had been unsuccessful in its attempt to control the dust, but that did not preclude the courts from stopping an otherwise unlawful activity.[53] In April 2001, at a shareholders' meeting, Massey's CEO, Don Blankenship, stated that the coal dust came from the trucks, not the preparation plants, and that the company had done more than other companies in similar situations.[54]

In October 2001, Elk Run was once again cited by the DEP for the coal-dust problems that still pervaded Sylvester.[55] A November 21, 2001, *Charleston Gazette* editorial pointed out the long list of violations at the plant, the company's failure to fix the problems, and newly elected Governor Bob Wise's promise to be stronger on environmental issues than his predecessor. The editorial concluded, "If Massey can't keep dust from raining down on the people of Sylvester, it should not be allowed to operate Elk Run."[56] This was exactly the point the citizen's lawsuit was striving to make. A reprieve to the community was granted in late November 2001 when the DEP ordered Elk Run to "eliminate, move or cover the coal stockpile" that was raining coal dust on the community.[57] The company was told that the next result would be to close down the plant entirely.[58] By mid-December 2001, the company proposed a novel approach to the problem as mentioned in chapter three. The company would erect a dome over the stockpile to safely contain the coal dust within it, slating its completion for May 2002.[59]

In March 2002, Elk Run was once again fined by the DEP.[60] In the midst of the problems with coal dust, Elk Run asked for permits to increase the number of trucks going through the town. That request was denied, and the DEP pointed out that increasing the truck traffic would also increase the continuing dust problems the town was experiencing.[61] By the end of June 2002, the dome, which cost $1.5 million and was the largest of its kind, was nearly complete.[62] In July 2002, Massey stated they were moving some of their production to Kentucky for the good of their stockholders. CEO Don Blankenship said that it was becoming too expensive to invest in West Virginia.[63] That same month, Massey faced another public relations disaster when a sediment pond over the town of Lyburn, Logan County, West Virginia, overflowed and flooded the town below, spilling slurry into a stream and onto residents' property. Massey was quick to assist in the cleanup, including putting residents up in hotels and replacing destroyed cars and even homes.[64]

As the Sylvester trial approached, Massey lawyers attempted to have past violations kept out of the court record, a request that was granted on December 10, 2002; a citizens' plea to the West Virginia Supreme Court of Appeals to intervene and permit the jury to hear about the violations was denied.[65] Nearly two years after filing the lawsuit, the trial finally commenced on December 12, 2002.[66] The time spent waiting allowed the residents of the town to collect even more evidence against Elk Run, including videos that clearly showed coal dust from the plant raining down on the town. Along with the dust that came directly from the plant, the plaintiffs showed that the numerous overweight trucks (only 0.1 percent were at or below the legal weight limit) also added to the town's dust frustrations.[67] In January 2003, a Boone County jury was told how the pollution from the plant had led to a decrease of nearly $4 million in property taxes. An appraiser testified that coal dust resulting from the plant had decreased property values in the community by 80 percent. The appraiser also testified that many families had invested their entire life savings into their homes, only to see the property sharply lose its value, rendering them now unable to sell. Far from being soft for the plaintiffs, the appraiser had previously worked for banks, coal companies, and the law firm representing Massey. Her company is the largest appraising company in southern West Virginia.[68]

For its part, Massey admitted the operation had caused some problems and detailed for the jury the steps they had taken to make things better. Steps, the plaintiffs' lawyers pointed out, that did not work.[69] On February 7, 2003, nearly two years after the lawsuit was filed, the plaintiffs won their case. The company was ordered to pay "$473,000 in economic damages caused by coal dust falling on nearby homes, vehicles and other property."[70] The court also ordered the number of coal trucks traveling through the town to be reduced from thirty-five thousand to seven thousand annually.[71] No appeal was made of the decision. While the court decision appears to have brought some reprieve to the residents, the dome continues to experience rips and tears, and while not as prevalent as before the dome was erected, the community continues to experience dust problems.[72]

In November 2000, the West Virginia Highlands Conservancy and Trial Lawyers for Public Justice brought a lawsuit against the Department of the Interior (naming Gale Norton, head of the department), the Office of Surface Mining (particularly Glenda Owens, the director), and Michael

Callaghan (then-director of the West Virginia DEP). Judge Haden would hear the case. At issue was the way in which the DEP handled its regulatory duties under SMCRA, specifically the way it issued reclamation bonds for surface-mined lands. The lawsuit sought to have these deficiencies fixed, or to have federal regulators take over the program.[73]

Under SMCRA, bonds must be sufficient to reclaim a site should it be abandoned. Plaintiffs contended that the West Virginia bonding system received far less in bonding monies than was necessary for adequate reclamation. The Office of Surface Mining had repeatedly found the West Virginia bonding system "incapable of meeting the federal requirements."[74] Furthermore, the Office of Surface Mining had found that the liabilities of West Virginia's bonding system greatly exceeded its assets. Based on June 1994 estimates, those excess liabilities amounted to $22.2 million, a conservative estimate that did not take into account the cost of treating polluted water discharged from bond forfeiture sites. The court noted that West Virginia's system failed to be as strong as the federal law and, therefore, the federal law superseded West Virginia's.[75] While the court dismissed charges against Callaghan in May 2001 (under the Eleventh Amendment), it found that the federal defendants had not been living up to their responsibilities.[76] The court observed that the Office of Surface Mining had been "derelict and dilatory in the extreme" in their duties for better than a decade but were now making attempts to correct those derelictions of duties, "clearly in response" to the lawsuit.[77] In January 2003, while registering a proposal to set aside "federal approval of the state's plan to correct these defects," the court retained jurisdiction to ensure that the plan was enforced.[78]

Although the following case occurred just outside the nine coal counties referred to in this study, it may, nonetheless, prove extremely important in future MTR cases concerning conflicts between companies and private citizens over property rights. In October 2002, a Lincoln County circuit judge ordered the Caudill family home-place to be sold. Ark Land Company (a division of Arch Coal) had bought a majority portion of the land that stands in the way of the expansion of Arch's mammoth Hobet 21 MTR mine from Caudill family heirs. However, Ark was unable to convince six of the heirs to sell. This led to legal action that resulted in the land being sold for $500,000 to Ark at a January 2003 auction. The heirs appealed this judgment to the West Virginia Supreme Court of Appeals, and in May 2004, the court overturned the lower court's ruling on the grounds that the "lower court was wrong to discount the family's 'sentimental or emotional interests' in the property in favor of the economic concerns of a coal operator."[79] Even more striking, Justice Robin Davis, writing on behalf of the court, stated that Ark's argument that theirs was the better use for the land was "self-serving."[80] Justice Davis went on to write:

> In most instances, when a commercial entity purchases property because it believes it can make money from a specific use of the property, that property will increase in value based upon the expectations of the commercial entity. This self-created enhancement in the value of property cannot be the determinative factor in forcing a pre-existing co-owner to give up his/her rights in property. To have such a rule would permit commercial entities to always "evict" pre-existing co-owners, because a commercial entity's interest in property will invariably increase its value.[81]

Ark's lawyers had argued that the company's plans for expansion of an MTR site was "the highest and best use of the property."[82] In response to this, Justice Warren McGraw queried whether "the highest and best use of the land is dumping?"[83] Ark's lawyer replied that "it has become that ... [T]hat's the reality. The use of land changes over time. The value of land changes over time."[84] Ark's lawyer also argued that if the ruling went against his client, his client stood to lose a lot of money since they had already purchased land from other Caudill family heirs. In response to that argument, Justice Larry Starcher stated, "You made a business deal in anticipation of prevailing in this case. And if you don't prevail, you just made a bad business deal."[85] Justice Davis reiterated this opinion in the Court's judgment, writing that:

> Ark Land voluntarily took an economical gamble that it would be able to get all of the Caudill family members to sell their interests in the property. Ark Land's gamble failed. The Caudill heirs refused to sell their interests. The fact that Ark Land miscalculated on its ability to acquire outright all interests in the property cannot form the basis for depriving the Caudill heirs of their

emotional interests in maintaining their ancestral family home. The additional cost to Ark Land that will result from a partitioning in kind simply does not impose the type of injurious inconvenience that would justify stripping the Caudill heirs of the emotional interest they have in preserving their ancestral family home.[86]

The fact that the Caudill heirs triumphed in this lawsuit is a very significant development. It indicates that the rights of private citizens' personal attachment to the land is as valid as the economic, industrial uses of businesses. If the coal company had triumphed, it would have continued a legal legacy of industry enjoying more rights to land than private-property owners had. Moreover, the case indicated that when the two issues come into conflict, emotional ties to the land must not be dismissed for merely monetary considerations. This may also prove helpful in maintaining the land in its original state rather than dismantling it for industrial use. Land still preserved, usable and lush, is more likely to attract outside business interests in the future than barren moonscapes that have no forest covering left to assist in the all-important management of flood waters.

In July 2001, southern West Virginia was hit with one of the most devastating floods ever experienced in the region. More than $150 million dollars in damage occurred as a result of the raging waters that left more than a thousand people displaced and one person dead.[87] The role of timbering and coal mining, particularly MTR, in those floods soon became the focus of no less than seven state lawsuits. Before any of the lawsuits could go to trial, the State Supreme Court, through a special "flood litigation panel," answered specific questions crucial to both plaintiffs and defendants. Companies had to act with reasonable caution to protect the rights of others, so the plaintiffs had to prove that the companies operated with a reckless disregard and caused the damages. To that end, the lawsuits claimed that the timbering and surface mining were done in such a haphazard way that they "caused natural surface waters resulting from the rainfall . . . to be diverted and delivered in an unnatural way and in incomprehensible amounts down the mountains, hills and valleys . . . destroying the lives and property"[88] of the people in the wake of the rushing waters. At issue was how responsible and financially culpable the timber and mining companies were in regard to the flooding. The plaintiffs looked at nuisance and property-damage laws as the basis for their lawsuit. In February 2004, through the "flood litigation panel," the State Supreme Court agreed to address nine complicated legal questions about nuisance law, reasonable use of water and property, and liability in flood-related cases.[89]

In August 2004, both sides were allowed to submit briefs regarding those questions. The plaintiffs asserted that, according to precedence, nuisance is the responsibility—and liability—of the landowner. They further argued that "when an act of nature concurs with an act of man in causing nuisance, the human actor is responsible for the entirety of the harm."[90] In other words, the debris from these sites that came crashing down on the plaintiffs was a direct result of mining and timbering practices and, therefore, the mining and timbering companies were responsible for the damage. The plaintiffs also cited government studies that noted topographical disturbances of the magnitude in southern West Virginia caused a disturbance in the "rate of storm water discharge by as much as 59 percent."[91] They also claimed that historical flood data showed "a direct correlation" between increased flooding and increased coal tonnage and board feet.[92] For their part, the defendants argued that the plaintiffs wanted to discard other legal matters specifically for "nuisance" because they would then have to produce less evidence.[93]

In March 2006, the first case in the flood litigation opened. This trial focused on the two sub-watersheds of the Upper Guyandotte river and the impacted towns of Oceana and Mullens, two of the hardest-hit communities during the 2001 flood. The specific question was, what, if any, impact did MTR and timbering have on the devastating flood? Jurors were asked to determine whether the natural-resource operations materially increased the rate of run-off during the flood; whether run-off from the operations caused or contributed to the streams overflowing their banks; and lastly, whether the company's use of their land was unreasonable as defined by the State Supreme Court in 2004. If the use of the land was reasonable, there could be no liability. The trial was separated into two phases. The first phase determined liability. If the defendants were found liable, and if their actions were deemed the result of negligence or nuisance, then the company would enter the second phase of the trial where damages would be awarded.[94]

The trial began with thirty-one defendants but, through dismissal and settlement, ended with only two. By the last week of the trial, only one MTR operation remained as a defendant. Pioneer Fuel, located just outside Oceana, maintained its innocence throughout the trial; however, right before the decision was handed down, Pioneer Fuel reached a settlement agreement with the plaintiffs' attorneys. In the end, two timber companies, Western Pocahontas Properties Limited Partnership and Western Pocahontas Corporation, remained.[95] In a decision that clearly startled the corporations, the jury ruled in favor of the plaintiffs, finding the remaining two defendants liable. In ruling against the companies, the jury said that the timbering practices of the two companies "did increase water runoff from their land on July 8, 2001, that such an increase in peak runoff did cause the streams below them to overflow, and—perhaps most importantly—that the company's use of land was unreasonable."[96] Coal companies, and in particular Pioneer Fuel, were shrewd in settling the case. Had a coal company been found culpable, a precedent of MTR contributing to flooding would have been set. The coal companies, having settled, avoided this. If such a devastating flood were to occur again, litigation and liability would have to be reestablished. Not so for the timbering industry, whose practices have been found unreasonable. The case involving the Coal River watershed, which was to be heard next, was dismissed in January 2007 because, according to Judge Recht who had been hearing motions to dismiss the case, "the plaintiffs' complaints, amended complaints, and more definite statements fail to state a claim upon which relief can be granted" and he further refused to allow "fishing expeditions."[97] Cases involving the Upper Guyandotte and the Upper Kanawha watershed still remain.

At this writing, the most recent MTR case tried in federal court seeks to force the Army Corps of Engineers to perform more thorough environmental studies before issuing Clean Water Act permits to coal operators. While the suit targets four specific Massey operations, its outcome could have far-reaching consequences for future MTR operations.[98] Plaintiffs in the case allege that the Corps "has failed to thoroughly and properly study mining impacts before approving new permits."[99] In essence, the plaintiffs are asking that the Corps conduct an environmental impact study for each of the four permits in question.[100] A ruling in favor of the plaintiffs, if not overturned by the Fourth Circuit Court, would have an immense impact on MTR, slowing down the permitting process and the execution of the massive operations.

The onslaught of lawsuits over MTR illustrates that the residents of the affected communities are striving to protect their homes and land from what they believe to be an unreasonable infringement upon their rights. Many plaintiffs in these cases had never encountered the legal system before signing on to an anti-MTR lawsuit. While plaintiffs frequently have won in federal court, these decisions have been overturned just as frequently when appealed to the Fourth Circuit Court. The companies have claimed the way they conduct business is necessary in order to maintain the economies of the communities most affected. Participants are vehement on both sides, and there does not appear to be any decline in citizen-initiated lawsuits.

Conclusion

Fed up with the inattentiveness of state regulators and discouraged by lax enforcement of environmental rules and regulations, private citizens and environmental organizations have filed a series of lawsuits against regulators and coal companies. The increase in MTR operations has accompanied an increase in litigation. Since 1998, many lawsuits have challenged the legality of various aspects of mountaintop removal coal mining. As MTR proliferation continues, litigation regarding the practice and the nuisances it generates can be expected to increase in spite of the enormous obstacles presented by a conservative Fourth Circuit Court and a presidential administration firmly aligned with industry interests.

6

"SHOW ME WHERE TO PUT MY FISHING POLE"
The Environmental Impact of MTR

There must be a realization of the fact that to waste, to destroy, our natural resources, to skin and exhaust the land instead of using it so as to increase its usefulness, will result in undermining in the days of our children the very prosperity which we ought by right to hand down to them amplified and developed.
—Theodore Roosevelt, December 1907

At the onset of the nineteenth century, much of Appalachia had yet to be explored, and the forests were thick and dense. From 1880 through 1920, an industrial transition occurred there. This massive industrialization was accompanied by widespread environmental destruction. At the beginning of the twentieth century, two-thirds of West Virginia was covered by virgin forest; by 1920 it was gone, lost to untempered timbering.[1] Particularly harmful was the industrial railroad logging that cleared out thousands of acres of forests. This timber boom lasted less than four decades, but the soil erosion, fires, and flooding that accompanied it persisted for several decades.[2] The changes that came with this economic shift did more damage to the mountains in thirty years than any that had occurred in the past.[3]

The coal industry was just as destructive. The furor to exploit West Virginia's coal resources left little room for concern about the environmental degradation that would follow. All forms of mining produce some environmental impacts, and the acid mine-drainage spewing from both underground and strip mines remains a persistent problem in many mining communities, particularly in the loss of aquatic life and drinkable water. When it became uneconomical for underground coal companies to exploit a seam of coal, they abandoned the site and left coal tipples and machinery to rust, unaware of (or unconcerned about) the environmental repercussions. The strip mining that came later produced massive scars on the land, and early reclamation efforts provided only a window dressing for the nutrient-deficient land left behind. Only after state and federal laws were enacted to enforce regulations did the industry show concern for the environmental costs of their mining practices.[4] This lack of respect for the environment has continued to the present day as massive MTR operations now pervade the mountainous counties of southern West Virginia.

The coal industry in West Virginia began to utilize early forms of MTR in the 1970s, and its use became more widespread in subsequent decades until, by the first decade of the twenty-first century, its magnitude had become a major public concern. Between 1992 and 2002, 90,104 acres had been permitted for MTR in West Virginia, which included 51,382 mining acres and 19,486 valley-fill acres. The remaining permitted 19,236 acres included buildings and other infrastructure.[5] In fact, the granting of one permit could change "thousands of acres of hardwood forests into grasslands."[6] In addition, a 2003 review by the EPA found 150 valley-fill violations in West Virginia, wherein coal companies had been illegally dumping into valleys without the proper Clean Water Act permits.[7] As a result, more than five hundred miles of southern West Virginia streambed have been destroyed.

Even MTR's exploration state is exploitive. Boreholes are drilled or opened using explosives, and trenches and pits are dug. Crude roads are constructed to go to and from the site. This is the most destructive effect of the exploration, and it can lead to erosion, resulting in increased sediment loads in streams.[8] During the extraction, the blasts cause surface disturbances. Immense amounts of coal waste material are created and "the spread of chemically reactive particulate matter to the atmosphere and hydrosphere" takes place, negatively affecting air quality.[9] The many environmental repercussions related to MTR are examined below.

Watershed

The first step in understanding the environmental degradation occurring in the southern coalfields is understanding watersheds. West Virginia Save Our Streams defines a watershed as "an area of land that drains water, and everything in the water, to some sort of outlet."[10] These watersheds are composed of several small streams that feed into larger ones. The question at the forefront of the MTR dilemma is, what role do headwater streams play in the overall water quality? Healthy headwater streams assimilate nutrients and organic matter as well as provide habitats for many distinct and diverse organisms.[11] Headwater streams play a crucial role in the relatively simple concept of "stream ordering." For example, picture a tree: the leaves are connected to twigs, the twigs are connected to small branches, the small branches are connected to large branches, and the large branches are connected to the trunk. In trees, most life-support-

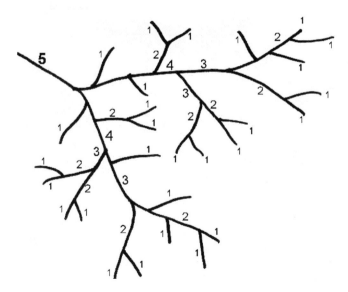

Figure 6.1. Stream ordering sequence.

ing energy is absorbed through the leaves and is then transported to the branches and ultimately to the trunk. Stream ordering follows a similar principle. Headwater streams, like a tree's leaves, are the location where most energy needed for downstream life is acquired before it is transported downstream. These primary headwater streams are called "first-order streams." When two or more first-order streams combine, they form a second-order stream. When two or more second-order streams combine, they form a third-order stream, and so on.[12] (See Figure 6.1.)

Chemical Factors and Sedimentation

To adequately understand the health of a watershed, it is necessary to assess the health of the creatures that live in it and how they respond to human activities.[13] At the base of this assessment, the chemical factors involved must be examined. One of the most prominent factors is dissolved oxygen, the oxygen content present in water.[14] The amount of dissolved oxygen is dependent on water temperature, and the amount of sediment, among other factors. Since aquatic animals depend on dissolved oxygen to live, there is cause for concern in streams that experience elevated amounts of sedimentation and, thus, reduced levels of dissolved oxygen.[15] While sediment is a natural component of a stream, excessive sedimentation occurs by soil erosion in disturbed areas.[16] MTR operations, and in particular, valley fills, contribute to increased sedimentation in surface water runoff.[17]

Sediment moving downstream is classified in two forms: suspended load and bed load.[18] Suspended sediment loads are suspended in the water column. Bed sediment loads are composed of coarser material, such as sand and gravel, and are pushed along the bottom of the channel.[19] The increased sedimentation eliminates vital spawning habitats for many fish species and invertebrates by filling in gravel spaces in the streambed.[20] This sedimentation can also destroy the deep pool habitats that provide vital cooler waters during summer months.[21] Sediment loading in small streams is increased when an area is exposed to mining and logging.[22] The strip mining of higher slopes, like the ones located in the southern coalfields of West Virginia, create a severe sedimentation problem.[23] An

April 2004 report by the National Institute for Chemical Studies included a measurement for water quality using the standards of the Clean Water Act as guidance. The study showed that one of the leading causes of "impairment to West Virginia's streams" was "excessive sediment."[24] Excessive sedimentation leads to a drop in the productivity of the stream (i.e., "the nutrients and organisms produced by a stream").[25] Valley fills can increase sedimentation, mineralization, and acidification of streams, thus altering the water quality and limiting biodiversity, possibly even leading to the extinction of some species.[26] Large sediment loads can also eliminate habitats essential for survival during low-flows associated with normal summertime conditions.[27] The erosion that leads to this increased sedimentation also reduces the streamside vegetation that serves as a habitat and helps moderate temperature fluctuations.[28] Streamside vegetation has also been shown to have a critical role in reducing the flow of excessive nutrients, sediments, and contaminants into small streams.[29]

This loss of vegetation causes a rise in water temperatures and, subsequently, a reduction in the amount of dissolved oxygen in the water.[30] As a result, the metabolic rates of aquatic organisms increase to dangerous levels. When taken together, the impact of sediment loading, loss of vegetation, and increased water temperatures may cause certain organisms to disappear, which would affect animals further up the food chain. A prime example of this is the brook trout, a highly sought-after sport fish, which has experienced a population decline as the lower organisms it feeds upon—the "prey species"—have been reduced by MTR. The shrinking ranks of the prey species could be caused by a decrease in spawning habitats, "lethal levels of chemicals or acidity," changing of the actual habitats, or some combination of the three.[31]

Erosion and Reclamation

In 1972, a symposium was held in Charleston, West Virginia, to discuss the Stanford Report, a report commissioned by the West Virginia legislature to compile information on the effect of surface mining on the environment, the economy, and the legal and social health of the state. It was hoped that the report would gather enough information to conclude whether the West Virginia Surface Mining Reclamation Act of 1967 was effective.[32] In his opening comments, Dr. Ralph Widener, moderator of the symposium, stated that "most surface mining and environmental effects will be concentrated in the southern coalfields."[33] To further this argument, Dr. Robert Leo Smith, a wildlife and biology professor at West Virginia University, pointed to one of the survey areas, Bolt Mountain, Raleigh County, as an example of these problems. Smith testified that infrared photography illustrated that massively strip-mined land did not respond to revegetation, and that the area remained unhealthy. Smith further stated that "revegetation does not stabilize spoils" and that "instabilities are inherent in strip mining."[34]

Revegetation preparation must be precise. Too much regrading will overcompact the spoil and will minimize planting success; insufficient packing will cause the soil to be eroded. Without adequate spoil stabilization controlling runoff and erosion, revegetation cannot be successful.[35] However, revegetating an area does not equal reclamation. Successful reclamation is impossible in the southern coalfields because regulations do not necessitate stringent care of the area after the coal company has satisfied its bond.[36] The study showed that the erosion rate of one acre of a strip mine is equivalent to five acres of timbered forestland or ten acres of farmland.[37] Another study of a partially stripped watershed showed an erosion rate of 5.9 tons/acre per year as opposed to 0.7 tons/acre per year on the unmined watershed. Furthermore, "97 percent of the erosion in the partially stripped watershed was attributed to the strip-mined area" even though the strip-mined area encompassed only 6.4 percent of the entire space.[38]

In a forward-looking statement regarding the Stanford study, Dr. William Miernyk, a West Virginia University economist, declared that if strip mining were allowed to continue, the environmental damage would be so dire that other economic development would not occur, and that this consequence would be irreversible. With the economic and environmental health of the state at stake, Miernyk supported legislation to keep strip mining in check.[39] Since the Stanford study, strip mining has only grown. MTR had—and has—an even greater impact upon the environment than the traditional strip-mining methods discussed in the Stanford Report. The proponents and opponents of strip mining, including MTR, still have more at stake environmentally and economically than ever before.

Reclamation of mine sites is the attempt to return the mined area to a

useful state. Under SMCRA, reclamation is the law. But if it is not implemented properly, it can hurt the environment through soil erosion and "de-
stabilization of mined lands."[40] In 1971, a Mingo County soil conservation
district supervisor commented on the problems with replanting grass and
seedlings on reclaimed strip mines. The success of the planted vegetation
was limited due to the lack of soil, which had been washed away.[41] A West
Virginia University Extension Service study, funded by Arch Coal and
the West Virginia Agricultural and Forestry Experiment Station, asserted
that while the soil on MTR sites is different from the original soil, it shows
signs of development as it ages, particularly on sites where grasses and
other revegetation have occurred.[42] While there is soil formation on these
MTR sites, it is unknown how long it will take the soil to become similar
to what it was before the mining took place, or if such a transformation
will ever occur given the higher pH levels now present in the mine soils.[43]
In addition, planted trees must compete for nutrients with the grasses that
were planted for quick covering, which results in slower regrowth of trees
and woody plants.[44] Vegetation rooting in these soils will have to be the
kind that can withstand a higher pH level; therefore, whatever regrows
will certainly be different from what was originally there.

Opponents to MTR assert that no reclamation can put the land back
to the way it was before the mining took place. While most supporters
of MTR would not necessarily disagree with that claim, some supporters, such as the Mineral Information Institute, go so far as to state that
"reclaimed mine lands are usually more attractive to wildlife and human
uses than before mining started."[45] Others have noted the benefits of increased wetlands and grasslands as well as commercial development. Arch
Coal has also been responsible for more than two hundred acres of newly
created wetlands on reclaimed sites. By contrast, the executive summary
of the EPA's controversial DEIS from 2003 notes that the wetlands created,
intentionally or unintentionally, are typically not of high quality.[46]

Still, the coal industry maintains "successful" reclamation projects are
possible and champions a few selective sites to use as examples. Arch Coal
publicizes three particular reclamation projects. One, in conjunction with
Premium Energy Corporation and Pocahontas Land Corporation, resulted in a premiere golf course, dubbed the Twisted Gun, in Gilbert, Mingo
County. Constructed on top of a reclaimed MTR site, the eighteen-hole

course is the only one of its kind in a three-county region (Mingo, McDowell, and Logan counties).[47] Land also mined by Arch Coal was turned into an Arctic Char fish hatchery, the only such hatchery of its type east of the Mississippi, and is managed by the Mingo County Redevelopment Authority.[48] Arch Coal's Web site touts the use of post-mining land for other economic endeavors as well, including a Wood Products Industrial Park, noting that it had "created 90 new jobs . . . with another 130 jobs anticipated."[49] A *Charleston Gazette* story claimed that as many as one thousand jobs may eventually be created as a result of this endeavor.[50]

Arch Coal has also planted some 1.5 million trees on reclaimed sites, and, according to the Mineral Information Institute, some 80 percent of those survived.[51] However, these statistics are suspect in light of the EPA's first formal DEIS from January 2001, which points out that "historically" such reclamation "has not been particularly successful."[52] It's not that this percentage of tree survival is impossible. If given the proper care, time, and resources, the trees could flourish. But generally, reclaimed MTR land receives only the minimum amount of care, time, and resources required by law. The language in the 2003 DEIS (which would become the final version) had been slightly watered down, mentioning efforts to "eliminate . . . barriers to establishing trees on reclaimed sites."[53]

Some experts assert that the potential for productive forests exists on these sites if the proper measures are taken, such as constructing a soil medium by saving the weathered sandstone overburden materials and mixing in a minor amount of native topsoil in order to provide a source of native seeds.[54] Such efforts require a level of stewardship and attention to detail not typically associated with the beginning stages of MTR, when the order of business is to access the coal as quickly and cheaply as possible. Arch Coal's Raleigh County subsidiary, Catenary Coal Company, has won acclaim for its reclamation of the Samples mine in Logan County. Massey, in conjunction with Mingo County Redevelopment Authority, is creating a dirt track on one of its former MTR sites.[55] Both Arch Coal and Massey contributed money to purchase eight hundred acres of a reclaimed surface-mine site to create the Earl Ray Tomblin Convention Center in Logan County.[56] According to the National Mining Association, other uses of reclaimed MTR sites in West Virginia include shooting ranges, high schools, housing developments, athletic fields, an airport, an

FBI complex, cemeteries, and prisons.[57] While successful reclamation is possible, it is not probable that coal companies will spend millions to do it when current laws only require that they put forth minimal efforts. The sites that industry touts as models of successful reclamation are the exception, not the rule.

Consequences of Valley Fills

By covering hundreds of miles of streams, MTR valley fills alter and destroy stream ecosystems, which undoubtedly destroys countless undiscovered species along the way. This issue has not been lost on the experts. In April 2003, a group of eighty-five aquatic scientists from more than forty states submitted a letter to the EPA regarding proposed rule changes to the Clean Water Act, particularly changes to the act's definition of "waters of the United States." The scientists pointed to the effects of human activities on the watershed and how these resulted in the loss of small streams. They noted how human activities create impervious surfaces. The proposed changes would have altered the rules to allow strip-mining valley fills to cover intermittent streams. It is a continuous cycle: more strip mining leads to more intermittent streams, which lead to more strip mining, leaving no outlet for the replenishment of the water supply.[58] The scientists went on to state that the "elimination of small tributaries from Clean Water Act jurisdiction would lead to further loss and degradation of these [water] systems to the detriment of the physical, chemical, and biotic integrity of ecosystems downstream."[59] The scientists ended their letter with a strong declaration: "The changes discussed in the proposed rulemaking and guidance document will degrade rather than maintain and improve the quality of US waters. If our nation hopes to achieve the goals of the Clean Water Act, ephemeral, intermittent and small headwater streams should remain under its jurisdiction."[60]

One of the biggest effects, however, is that of the valley fills where the coal companies dispose of their excess spoil material. Valley fills can lead to the annihilation of hundreds of miles of streams. Proponents of MTR assert that the streams are not destroyed, just rerouted under the rubble; however, when a stream loses its form and function, it ceases to exist. Although MTR supporters can claim that these streams are still there, they cannot tell anglers where to put their fishing poles in a merely "rerouted" stream.

According to information within the FPEIS, 724 miles of the waterways in the study area have been covered by valley fills from 1985 to 2001, and 1200 miles of headwater streams have been directly impacted by MTR via valley fills, roads, ponds, and coal removal.[61] An environmental impact assessment study of MTR on aquatic resources found that "the covering of headwater perennial and intermittent streams on a large scale with spoil material is the major hydrological impact, and very characteristic of MTR. This is not a case of alteration, but of removal in function and form."[62] Naturally occurring streams are buried in valley-filled areas and replaced with drainage ditches or buried pipes in which to route the water away. These altered drainages flow continuously throughout the year, whereas naturally occurring streams typically dry up during the drought season. Proponents of MTR state that this continuous outflow is beneficial to the environment and that these newly channelized drainages moderate the runoff to a consistent outflow. A study sponsored by the Department of Interior found that storm runoff in streams at valley-fill sites fluctuated less than those located in unmined areas.[63] The 2005 FPEIS included a study, however, that revealed that this minimal fluctuation occurred during smaller storms and actually reversed itself during larger rainfalls.[64] In other words, any benefit of channelization observed during low-intensity rainfalls would be offset by the large amount of runoff that occurred with larger, harder downpours. It is these storms, so typical during summer in southern West Virginia, that often result in flooding. This flooding is only exacerbated by the channelized drainages located on MTR sites and valley fills.

Continuous streamflows may also have negative repercussions on invertebrate communities, which constitute the beginning of the nutrient cycle for downstream ecosystems. Even subtle alterations in streamflow can have a dramatically negative impact. In fact, outflow from valley fills may be detrimental because stream flows originating from valley fills may have higher "specific conductance" rates of dissolved metals in them, which could be harmful to sensitive species and reduce the numbers of tolerant species.[65] Land disturbances and the erosion associated with it typically increase subsequent specific conductivity.[66]

The mountainous topography in West Virginia does not lend itself to the formation of perennial streams, but rather hosts numerous intermittent streams, resulting in small streams in each hollow. The perennial streams impacted by increased MTR have significantly decreased outflows due to the burial of the feeding intermittent streams. This can be compared to cutting off the roots of a plant. The loss of intermittent streams will cause the rivers of Appalachia to die. In 1999 and 2000, the American Rivers Association included Coal River in Boone County on the Nation's Most Endangered Rivers list. In both years, the organization noted the devastation of fish, wildlife, streams, and forests as a result of MTR. The organization further observed that the effects of MTR are far reaching, effecting both environmental and cultural heritage.[67] A 1997 ecological assessment noted that the Coal River watershed is one of the most affected by MTR, and the only one of the thirty-two watersheds studied in West Virginia that "produced no potential reference sites."[68] (Potential reference sites are characterized as "high quality stream[s] with minimal human disturbances" that provide "significant and even irreplaceable wildlife habitat" as well as being a "tremendous recreational resource."[69]) The Coal River watershed was so impaired by coal mining, and by other human activity, that it was virtually impossible to find any area in the watershed that was not harmed.[70]

Loss of Biodiversity

The southeastern United States is home to many rare invertebrate species that are found only in a few fragile locations "with pea-sized gravel or in springbrooks and seepage areas."[71] For instance, sixty species of stoneflies from eastern North America exist only in these first- and second-order streams, or headwaters, and fully half of these sixty are "new to science in the last 25–30 years."[72]

A 2000 study of the environmental impact of MTR on aquatic resources declared that it has a "profound" negative effect "on aquatic resources located within the watersheds of MTR areas."[73] The study noted that the main problems stemmed from the "physical alteration of the aquatic resource, or even its complete removal."[74] Water is removed from the streambed, routed through a culvert, and re-enters the streambed farther down the mountain. These altered drainage outlets do not provide the capacity for the biodiversity that is found in the unaltered channel.[75] The FPEIS stated the following about the importance of headwater streams:

> Even where inaccessible to fish, these small streams provide high levels of
> water quality and quantity, sediment control, nutrients and wood debris for
> downstream reaches of the watershed. Intermittent and ephemeral headwater
> streams are, therefore, often largely responsible for maintaining the quality
> of downstream riverine processes and habitat for considerable distances.[76]

The number of Appalachian streams lost due to MTR does not include
ephemeral streams. Ephemeral streams are those that flow sporadically
throughout the year because of rainfall or melting snow, or intermittent
streams that flow only six months or less per year. Many of the streams in
West Virginia are of this type.[77] According to Dr. Ben Stout, a biology professor at Wheeling Jesuit University, these streams are at least as important as perennial streams.[78] These intermittent streams act as a connection
between the forest and the river. Once they are filled in, that connection
is gone—and not only is the connection gone, but in its place are poisons,
such as aluminum, iron, and manganese, which are present in valley-fill
runoff.[79]

When ephemeral streams are lost due to MTR, all water draining from
these sites is typically routed into channelized drainages or run through
buried pipes. If the headwaters are channelized, piped, or filled, ecosystems downstream can suffer as a result. In their letter to the EPA, the
aquatic scientists stated that "the increased frequency and intensity of
flooding associated with replacement of small streams with impervious
surfaces increases bank erosions, channel widening and incision and other changes in channel form."[80] The scientists emphasized that covering the
streams has increased "fine particles in stream sediments," and has altered
the flow and temperature downstream of the valley fills.[81] This change
can have an impact on downstream populations.[82] Streams remaining in
these watersheds where valley fills exist see an "increase of minerals in the
water" and the macroinvertabrate and fish populations that remain do not
exhibit as much diversity. Only the more "pollutant-tolerant" species can
continue to exist there.[83] Thus, MTR and valley fills change the species
composition of headwater streams.

Loss of Biodiversity: Role of Aquatic Insects

Headwater streams contain a group of aquatic insects—Ephemeroptera, Plecoptera, and Trichoptera (known as "EPT organisms")—that break down nutrients to be absorbed by other organisms downstream. EPT organisms are very useful in determining water quality in headwater streams, and their presence indicates relatively healthy ecological conditions.[84] The greater the number of EPT organisms, the better the quality of the water. The replacement of EPT species with more tolerant species indicates that the water quality is decreasing. Leaf shredders are part of this EPT order.[85] They play an important role in the ecosystem. Ninety percent of the annual energy input for headwater streams is attributed to leaf detritus (decomposed leaves that leaf shredders break down). If these leaf shredders cease to exist and 90 percent of the energy input disappears, how are the downstream organisms going to survive?[86]

In a 1999 workshop held in State College, Pennsylvania, a group of experts discussed the value of headwater streams. Dr. Bruce Wallace, a professor of entomology and ecology, noted the importance of leaf shredders, stating that it takes approximately 275 days for red maple leaves to break down when invertebrates are present. If most of these invertebrates are taken out of the equation, that time can increase to 575 days. He went on to dispel the myth that destroying small portions of headwater streams does not threaten biodiversity. On the contrary, he stated that the waters of Appalachia are rich with biodiversity and any tampering can threaten that biodiversity. He stressed that destroying, or essentially entombing, small headwater streams is a very "dangerous" procedure for "life on this planet."[87] During the same workshop, Dr. Bern Sweeney, director and curator of the Stroud Water Research Center in Avondale, Pennsylvania, noted that disturbing the "continuum of species" through the destruction of the headwaters or lower order of streams "greatly jeopardizes the ability of certain species to maintain local populations and provide propagules [a bud or shoot plants use to spread] for recolonizing disturbed areas," which can affect "60 percent or more of the total food base of a small stream."[88] Samples from downstream of the mining shows a decrease in the number of "sensitive organisms" present.[89]

Due to the channelization of headwater streams, the drainage output of MTR sites and valley fills flows constantly throughout the year, thus changing the outflow from that of an intermittently-flowing stream to a perennially-flowing one. While this may seem inconsequential, headwater streams are actually very fragile ecosystems, and any change can carry devastating repercussions. A 2001 Water Resources Investigation Report by the U.S. Geological Survey, in cooperation with the DEP and the Office of Surface Mining, noted that many aquatic insect taxa[90] have adapted to streams' drying up in the summer; some insect taxa have evolved in such a way that the dry phase is critical to their "life-cycle events"—hatching, emerging, and mating. These insect taxa have also adapted to resist desiccation by entering what is known as the diapause stage where growth or development of eggs, larvae, or pupae is suspended in response to unfavorable conditions.[91] Because of the changes MTR causes in headwater streams, significant portions of these sensitive aquatic insects can no longer survive in their new, artificially created habitat. A study of Arch Coal mining verified this by confirming a decrease in EPT and an increase in pollutant-tolerant organisms in nearby waters.[92]

According to a study sponsored by the Coal and Energy Research Bureau and the West Virginia legislature, and conducted by Dr. Kyle Hartman, a professor of wildlife and fisheries resources at West Virginia University, it is clear that valley fills hurt streams. Due "to the high diversity and faunal similarity to perennial streams, intermittent streams deserve adequate management or regulatory plans to protect species and their habitats."[93] Streams in valley-filled areas exhibited lower numbers of sensitive aquatic insects—typical of an impaired system. This is apparent when comparing non-impacted to impacted sites.[94]

Effects on Wildlife: Bird Populations

Changes of the physical landscape also produce species composition changes in animal populations. MTR transforms mixed mesophytic forest habitats to grassland habitats.[95] Grassland habitats typically occur in dryer areas, whereas mesophytic forests occur in moist environments. There are some spots in southern West Virginia where MTR activities have created grassland and shrub habitats. These changes in the landscape have resulted in a shift of bird-species composition throughout the region.[96] Due to the loss of intact forests, native woodland species are being replaced by non-native species that are typically associated with grasslands. West Virginia is naturally home to an abundance of woodland bird species (such as the red-shouldered hawk and broad-winged hawk); however, since the inception of MTR, the number of open-country species (such as the northern harrier and the American kestrel) have increased.[97] Not surprisingly, a 2003 study showed an increase in grassland bird species (such as grasshopper sparrows, eastern meadowlarks, horned larks, and savannah sparrows). It paid particular attention to the grasshopper sparrow, saying that it outnumbered other species because it colonizes most suitable grassland habitats.[98] Interior forest songbirds are absent from edge created by mining sites because these species require a large amount of intact forest in which to survive.[99]

While populations of grassland birds are declining throughout the United States, reclaimed MTR sites have seen an increase in these species.[100] These birds are "rare" in West Virginia, but they have become more common as intact forests are destroyed. The characteristics of these newly created grasslands are contrary to the native hardwood forests that had once blanketed these areas. While the presence of these grassland birds may be good for their respective populations, any increase in population is temporary. They too will be displaced when their artificial habitat is transformed from grassland to shrub-pole, due to forest succession.[101] In the meantime, native bird species will continue to be displaced as more forests become fragmented as a result of MTR.

Effects on Wildlife: Mammal Populations

A 2002 study of small mammal communities on reclaimed MTR sites indicated that while small mammals continue to thrive, they are largely from the *Peromyscus* family—types of rodents that frequently make their homes in grasslands, among other various kinds of habitats.[102] Studies regarding replanting on surface-mine sites began as early as the 1940s. Early on, it was found that hardwoods failed to grow on the stripped land because of the substantial damage rodents caused to the trees.[103] Another study showed an increase in the rodent population on these mine sites. These areas are of an early successional forest habitat, meaning that they are at the first stage of development. They remain suspended in this stage for a long time because of the competition between the grasses and the trees for the reclaimed soil's nutrients.[104] This is made even more difficult because of the poor-quality, rocky soils present after reclamation.[105] The competition that takes place is the biggest deterrent to regrowth,[106] but the higher number of mice may also play a role due to their damaging effect on seedlings. A study on small-mammal communities also observed that bog lemmings, masked shrews, and house mice have increased on these reclaimed sites, all species that benefit from the creation of grassland habitats. Other species such as white-tailed deer and wild turkey that can thrive in either grassland or wooded areas can be found along with the other primarily grassland species on MTR sites.[107]

Effects on Wildlife: Forest Fragmentation

Species that thrive in the native woodlands do not fair well on reclaimed MTR sites. According to the EPA's FPEIS study, deforestation and forest fragmentation that result from MTR activities interrupt the Appalachian forest and are detrimental to forest-dwelling wildlife species.[108] Eastern chipmunks, woodland jumping mice, woodland voles, and northern short-tailed shrew exhibited a marked decrease in population once their wooded habitat was transformed into grasslands.[109] In addition, the absence of mature trees impedes the natural moderation of temperature fluctuations that a forest buffer normally provides. This means temperatures can rise or fall dramatically according to the weather, and species will not be able to acclimate to the rapidly changing conditions.[110] (Similar temperature fluctuations occur in arid regions where the weather is scorching hot in the daytime and freezing cold after the sun goes down.)

Amphibian and reptilian life is also affected by MTR. The southern Appalachians have one of the richest salamander faunas in the world. When these woodlands are converted to grasslands, however, the salamanders become far less common. Salamanders require loose soil with ample ground cover, and these habitats are generally not found on reclaimed MTR sites. Salamanders are ecologically important to eastern forests, and their recovery in forest-disturbed areas is slow. The soil disturbance caused by MTR is greater than typical forest clearing and may cause the salamander population to take even longer to recover.[111]

MTR has hurt other animals as well—most notably West Virginia's state animal, the black bear. As MTR encroaches on forests, the bears that normally live there—that have, in fact, evolved over the course of millennia to survive there—are displaced. When they are forced from their habitats, they struggle to find another suitable place to live. This often leads to the now-common occurrence of bears wandering around residential neighborhoods and rummaging through garbage cans as they desperately search for food and shelter. This contact often leads to the bears' deaths, not to mention the endangerment of nearby residents.[112]

Another high-profile animal affected by MTR is the wild boar. Although a non-native species, it was introduced into the region by the West Virginia Division of Natural Resources and is regarded as a good choice for a big-game animal.[113] Originally, it only lived in West Virginia's southernmost counties, where MTR occurs most frequently. Consequently, significant portions of the wild-boar habitat have been destroyed.

Tracking studies have shown that, not only are these and other animals losing ground in southern West Virginia, but they are also losing "traditional migration routes, travel corridors, and food sources."[114] Mined land is not as productive as it was before its transformation, and the natural flora—unable to adapt to the new conditions—are rapidly replaced by invasive and non-native species. Once the native forests have been removed, the animal species dependent on those habitats find themselves ill-suited for survival in their new environment.[115] Birds that require forest interior habitats (such as the Acadian flycatcher, American redstart, hooded warbler, ovenbird, and scarlet tanager) are also harmed by the loss or fragmentation of forest due to MTR. An area must contain four major characteristics to be classified as a minimal forest interior habitat: (1) act as a link between headwater and low-order stream networks; (2) maintain an unfragmented habitat for species that are wide-ranging or have a large home range; (3) maintain a habitat for interior or remote species; (4) enhance the habitat with natural disturbance regimes in which most species evolve.[116] As distance from an MTR site increases and forested lands become less fragmented, forest-interior bird species increase.[117]

In addition to the effects mining has on animals and plants, the forest itself is greatly altered by the mining practice of MTR. The FPEIS cited a study that concluded approximately 244,000 acres of the southern coalfields area have been disturbed by past or current mining.[118] Future MTR activities could potentially obliterate an area of Appalachian forest the size of Putnam County, West Virginia.[119] Without more stringent MTR regulations, and adequate reclamation, future MTR will destroy nearly 230,000 acres of West Virginia land.[120]

Slurry Impoundments

The environmental impact of the disposal system associated with MTR is also expansive. Coal-slurry impoundments are filled with highly toxic waste products that can seep into surrounding groundwater if proper precautions are not taken. Before being sent to market, the coal must be processed and cleaned. Each year between 350 and 400 million tons of coal go through processing using water, producing between 70 and 90 million tons of fine refuse slurry, which is, for the most part, stored in impoundments.[121] Impoundments include the embankment, basin, beach, pool, and slurry,[122] but the most important parts are the embankment and the basin.[123] In Appalachia, the most common impoundment type is the cross-valley impoundment, where an embankment is built across a valley. The slurry is discharged in the valley upstream of the embankment and then released into the basin along the embankment by a pipeline system.[124] The slurry must be actively monitored to ensure that it is not discharged into the surrounding areas. The impoundment itself is monitored to ensure its stability. Improper management of these impoundments, breaks in the stability, or lax enforcement of regulations can have devastating effects on the environment. One of the most famous and destructive of these breaks occurred on February 25, 1972, in Buffalo Creek, West Virginia. An unstable dam broke, crashed down on the valley of Buffalo Creek, and brought with it more than 130 million gallons of coal slurry. It flattened the small community in less than three minutes. The break resulted in the death of 125 people, injured more than 1100, and left 4000 people homeless.[125] After Buffalo Creek, it would be logical to assume that such impoundments would be made illegal. They were not. At present, more than one hundred similar impoundments exist all over West Virginia.

Since the Buffalo Creek Disaster, thirty-one other spills have occurred in West Virginia with nineteen (or 61.3 percent) of those occurring from

2000 to 2003.[126] This increase may be attributed to the aging of the impoundments, more accurate reporting of spills, or the increase in the number of stripping operations and waste impoundments. Whatever the reason, since 1972, eighty documented miles of West Virginia streams have been affected by slurry spills, and 169,515,700 gallons of slurry are documented as having been released. Most of the West Virginia spills occurred in the southern West Virginia coalfields.[127] The U.S. Code of Federal Regulations states that an impoundment is only required to have "an elevation of 5 feet or more above the upstream toe of the structure and can have a storage volume of 20 acre feet or more."[128] The West Virginia code increases the height level to twenty-five feet and mandates a storage volume of at least fifteen acre-feet or more.[129] As long as the impoundment is built to code, it can be as large as the company wants it to be. West Virginia codes detail everything from filing paperwork for the construction of an impoundment to emergency planning.[130] Presently, Massey subsidiary Marfork Coal Company, in Raleigh County, has an impoundment that is more than nine hundred feet tall. That is more than two hundred feet higher than the Hoover Dam.[131] Once completely filled, it will contain 8.1 billion gallons of slurry. This is up from the previous 5 billion gallons of slurry that the impoundment had previously been permitted to encase. The Brushy Fork impoundment will be the largest impoundment of its kind; it rests on top of an abandoned underground mine.[132] In addition to the immense size of the impoundment, the slurry it contains is laden with mercury and other coal toxins. As this slurry is periodically discharged into nearby streams, it can contaminate the water. When hydro-geologist Rick Eades surveyed the impoundment, he found that there had already been black water releases from the impoundment and that Massey had been cited for those releases as well as for numerous permit violations. He could find no proof that the "natural fractures in the interburden" (everything between the impoundment and the underground mine that it sits over) had ever been studied for their risk factor.[133] Brushy Fork is classified as a Type C dam, which essentially means that if it breaks, it is expected to exact a high cost: it will interrupt industry and public utilities, ruin homes and commercial buildings, make frequently used roads impassable, and—most significantly—prove fatal.[134] Brushy Fork is but one example of the numerous coal impoundments throughout the state. See appendix 2 for a list of coal impoundments found in the nine southern coalfield counties. Appendix 3 lists coal-spill information for the nine counties.

Flooding

In July 2001, after suffering a devastating flood in May, southern West Virginia was hit with heavy torrents of rainfall and massive flooding. Contemporary accounts of the flooding reported that the rainfall was as heavy as ten inches in Wyoming County, the hardest hit.[135] In actuality, Wyoming County received between 1.53 and 5.32 inches of rainfall. The town of Mullens received the highest amount of rainfall in Wyoming County— 5.32 inches.[136] Earlier accounts had listed Mullens's rainfall as ten inches or more. Like most communities in Wyoming County, Mullens is surrounded by both timbering and strip-mining operations. Having endured a flood not quite two months earlier, the already saturated ground mixed with the rainfall to cause the severe flooding. Of course, receiving more rain in one day than the county typically receives in the entire month of July leaves no question that there would have been flooding regardless; however, how bad would the flooding have been without the effects of strip mining? As the 2002 DEP study concluded, the disturbance of the land by surface mining did have an effect on flooding.[137] However, the same area had endured more rainfall during the flood of 1977 when some areas of southwestern West Virginia experienced 15.5 inches of rainfall.[138] While major flooding did occur in 1977, it did not cause nearly as much damage as the July 2001 flood. The most glaring difference between the two floods is that in 2001 there were more massive timbering and MTR operations affecting the areas than in 1977. This could account for a 5.32-inch rainfall having a more disastrous effect than a 15.5-inch rainfall.

Since MTR disturbs massive amounts of vegetative cover—vegetation that helps to stabilize the soil—the subsequent runoff results in higher levels of flooding for areas affected by surface mining.[139] A 2002 DEP study concluded that surface mining does in fact increase the volume and velocity of runoff in the watershed.[140] Along with runoff, there is an increase in erosion, which fills the water channel. The resulting accumulation of silt at the bottom of the streambed diminishes the draining capacity of streams. Mining on steep slopes may hasten erosion or even block entire stream channels by causing landslides.[141] In turn, the water that would normally run into the channel is now forced to flow out onto the stream bank where it picks up debris and further obstructs the flow of water. This means that even a very small amount of rainfall has the potential to flood low-lying areas. In other words, in strip mined areas, the peak flow rates increase, sometimes by three to five times the usual flow rate amounts. The three to five time peak flow rate increase on surface mined sites means that five inches of rainfall could easily seem like, or have the same destructive effect as, fifteen to twenty-five inches of rain.[142] Thus, the more an area is surface mined, the greater it will be affected by floodwaters.[143] Headwater streams originate at higher elevations. The amount of time these headwater streams retain water is reduced in strip mined areas, thus increasing the amount of floodwaters that move downstream. On flat floodplains, even small increases in flood peak flows can increase the amount of area that are inundated.[144]

Environmental Impact: Proponents and Opponents Views

Despite all the promises of sound reclamation and minimal environmental impact, the reality is often quite different. Originally intended as only a subtype of surface mining, MTR has flourished in the last decade, and numerous opponents have emerged as outspoken critics of the practice. The coal industry has never sat silent when they feel attacked; they have vigorously defended MTR, using an arsenal of tactics. One of their weapons has been a systematic campaign of misinformation through multiple machines. Perhaps not surprisingly, the Internet has come into play. One Web site, for example, is simply called "Mountaintop Mining." The site does not indicate who is responsible for its content, but it is linked to a site called "Mining USA" and then to the site for Mining Internet Services Inc., an organization that was "created solely to provide Internet services tailored to the mining community."[145] The site claims that the amount of stream loss from MTR is minimal and that most hollow fills are placed where there are no streams.[146] Conversely, the FPEIS report announced that more than five hundred miles of West Virginia streams have been impacted as a direct result of MTR and valley fills.[147] Other organizations place that figure higher.[148] Even the streams that are not buried may be compromised through pollution.[149] Perhaps this loss is minimal to industry; however, it can be dire for the ecosystem. In addition, the same FPEIS study reported that if stricter regulations and better reclamation are not implemented, MTR will destroy nearly 230,000 acres of "ecologically diverse hills and hollows." The FPEIS goes on to caution that the changes incurred because of MTR may jeopardize the "biological integrity of the study area"[150] even as it has already significantly altered the area's "landscape and terrestrial wildlife habitats."[151] As the size of these operations increase, one permit may radically alter thousands of acres, leaving grasslands where native hardwood forests once grew.[152] The mining companies use the familiar argument that a reclaimed MTR site leaves "flatter, more useful land" and that the mountains are not actually "flattened."[153]

Some West Virginia politicians also make such claims. In fact, in 2002 the cabinet secretary of the DEP argued before the U.S. Environment and Public Works Committee that the mining created useful flat lands for various recreational and business opportunities.[154] Overall, such arguments do not hold up under close scrutiny. Only minimal economic development has occurred on any of these sites, but industry continues to "spew propaganda about the need for flat land as a panacea [with the] promise [of] a new era of coalfield economic prosperity."[155] Even the oldest MTR site in the state, Bullpush Mountain in Fayette County, has yet to benefit from its flatness. Cannelton Industries began mining Bullpush Mountain in 1970, but the site has never been developed or utilized in its "more useful" metamorphosis.[156] The Mountaintop Mining Web site also implies that MTR was seen as a normal mode of surface mining when the 1977 SMCRA law was enacted. In fact, it was viewed as an occasional variance, and it was not supposed to occur unless the company conducting MTR operations submitted plans to develop the flattened land.[157] At the time of SMCRA's enactment, neither the framers of the act, nor anyone else, could have imagined the large draglines that were on the horizon that would make MTR such a common practice.

Another erroneous argument that Mountaintop Mining and similar Web sites make is that reclaimed MTR sites create more wildlife. While reclaimed sites have the potential to create different artificial habitats that are beneficial to grassland species, the native woodland wildlife must now face survival in these new habitats for which they are ill-adapted. This often leads to starvation and disease. The native species do not have the luxury of waiting for the soil to replenish and the vegetation to take root after massive MTR has occurred. Displaced animals are forced to encroach upon residential areas in search of food and shelter where they face certain death because of the danger they now pose to humans. Pauline Canterberry, of Sylvester, Boone County, produced pictures of emaciated black bears rummaging through her garbage cans; she stated that this has become a more and more frequent occurrence as the MTR site near her home has expanded, forcing animals from their natural habitat.[158] Several years ago, Arch Coal, Inc., produced a commercial that proclaimed, "Mountaintop removal. It's the right thing to do." Likewise, with regards to mountaintop removal, Mountaintop Mining states, "It's simply the right thing to do—both for the environment and for the local economy. A true win-win."[159] That assertion, on both levels, is highly debatable.

Conclusion

The environmental effects of strip mining have been a contentious issue for decades. Visible scars and environmental degradation are inherent effects of strip mining. As a more extreme version of strip mining, MTR disturbs more land at a quicker rate than more traditional methods. Much research has been conducted to explore the issue, including research funded by coal companies and coal-associated organizations. Study after study has concluded that MTR transforms forested woodlands into grasslands. Although these new grasslands support various wildlife species, they enjoy minimal revegetation success and represent an entire change from the native habitats found on the unmined site. Additionally, repercussions of valley fills on the aquatic environment include long-lasting consequences whose effects will continue "until processes occurring at a geologic timescale carve new valleys and transport fill materials downstream."[160] Some of the major problems associated with MTR include soil depletion, sedimentation, low success rate of reforestation, lack of successful revegetation, displacement of native wildlife, and burial of streams. These problems will only worsen as MTR acreage continues to expand.

Epilogue
REQUIEM FOR THE MOUNTAINS?
Central Appalachian Coalfields
at a Crossroad

We shall achieve conservation when and only when the destructive use of land becomes unethical—punishable by social ostracism.

—Aldo Leopold

West Virginia is not alone in its struggles over mountaintop removal. Across central Appalachia, coalfield communities are dealing with the ravages of MTR. In varying degrees, Kentucky, Tennessee, Virginia, and West Virginia, have all witnessed MTR operations flattening mountains and filling in valleys and streams. If the demand for coal continues to increase, these areas can expect MTR activity to intensify as well.

In a sixteen-year period spanning 1985 and 2001, the four states saw a total of 83,797 acres of land covered by 6,697 valley fills.[1] Leading the way was Kentucky with 51,775 acres of land lost to valley fills, followed by West Virginia with 25,178 acres, Virginia with 5,935 acres, and Tennessee with 909 acres. The impact on watersheds also is dramatic. In the four-state region, 438,472 acres of watershed have been impacted by valley fills. Once again, Kentucky has suffered the largest loss with 281,347 acres. West Virginia has lost 111,479 acres; Virginia, 42,629; and Tennessee, 3,017. The majority of these valley fills are connected with surface mining.[2] Slurry-impoundment spills have also affected each of the states. Most notably, the October 2000 spill in Martin County, Kentucky, impacting seventy-five miles of streams from Kentucky to West Virginia.[3] The environmental and cultural cost is astronomical for a process where a "typical operation" requires only eighty-nine employees, mostly heavy-equipment operators, whose average length of operation is a mere ten years.[4]

As in West Virginia, concerned citizens in the three states are fighting back. Kentuckians for the Commonwealth is a vocal champion of the citizens and environment of the state. Since its inception in 1981, the organization's interests have spanned a variety of topics from advocating for welfare recipients to the struggle against MTR. In that vein, the organization joined in lawsuits against MTR. In one case, *Kentuckians for the Commonwealth v. Rivenburgh*, Judge Charles Haden ruled for the plaintiffs whose lawsuit hoped to stop the burying of six miles of Kentucky streams beneath twenty-seven separate valley fills. The permittee in question, Beech Fork Processing, admitted that they could mine the coal without the valley fills. Still, upon appeal, the Fourth Circuit Court overturned Haden, stating that his decision was "overbroad" and overreached the case brought before him.[5] In Tennessee, Save Our Cumberland Mountains confronts everything from logging and strip-mining issues to economic problems. Since 1971, Save Our Cumberland Mountains has participated in efforts to better the quality of life in Tennessee.[6] In North Carolina, which has no MTR activities within its borders, concerned citizens began Appalachian Voices to address the environmental problems facing central and southern Appalachia. Appalachian Voices also has an office in Virginia. Since the 1990s, the organization has remained active in efforts to halt MTR.[7]

The old arguments that pit private citizens against mining companies, environment against employment, and the hopes for tomorrow against the necessities of today show no signs of letting up. When the first MTR mine in West Virginia opened on Bullpush Mountain in Fayette County, it served as a precursor to the massive MTR sites that would pervade the state decades later. The goal of 1990's Clean Air Act may have been to protect the environment by reducing toxic air emissions and acid rain, but when its stricter emission standards gave southern West Virginia's low-sulfur, high-volatility coal a popularity boost, the act had the ironic effect of decimating the region's forests and streams as coal operators there began using MTR in earnest. MTR was a cheap, fast way for them to meet the increased demand. It upped their profits and helped them compete with coal companies in the west, but it triggered catastrophic consequences.

Nearly ninety years ago, the federal government intervened to reforest West Virginia's mountains following industrialization because deforestation and the soil erosion it caused threatened important waterway transport systems. At that time, the government had an overt, vested interest in protecting West Virginia's waterways.[8] Today, the southern West Virginia coalfields need a similar reprieve. The region remains dismally behind the rest of the nation in terms of education, combating poverty, and economic opportunities, despite the fact that the coal mined there helped fuel an industrial revolution, generated modern technological advances, and ultimately propelled America to worldwide influence and power. Even now, when more than 50 percent of the nation's energy comes from coal, West Virginia continues to do its part in keeping America running.

While America has prospered with each ton of coal consumed, little attention has been paid to the region, and its people, that made it possible. The people and land of the coalfields of central Appalachia deserve a simple acknowledgement of their sacrifices made for the comfort and prosperity of the rest of the nation. It's time to pay them back. Citizens must push for reform. Politicians must support policies to diversify the economy of the coalfields. Coal interests must learn to look beyond their bottom line. Unfortunately, West Virginia's history of unresponsive, neglectful politicians unwilling to confront King Coal does not bode well for state intervention on behalf of the coalfield communities. And getting help from a federal administration that has attempted to weaken environmental standards in favor of the coal industry seems like a long shot, too.

In less than two decades, MTR has caused irreparable harm to the environment, the culture, and the people of West Virginia. If coal companies continue to operate outside of the laws, if politicians continue to allow big coal interests to wield ultimate power, and if MTR is allowed to continue unabated, then the coalfield communities will dry up completely. Ghost towns will spring up throughout the region. Grasslands will replace the hardwood forests. Moonscapes will replace the gently rolling mountains. The wilderness will be gone. If MTR is not legally halted or diminished, southern West Virginia coalfield communities, the people and land, will be as gone as the last ton of coal scraped out of the mountains themselves.

NOTES

1   Ronald Lewis, *Transforming the Appalachian Countryside: Railroads, Deforestation, and Social Change in West Virginia, 1880–1920* (Chapel Hill: University of North Carolina Press, 1998), 104–114.

2   Ronald Lewis and John Hennen Jr., eds., *West Virginia: Documents in the History of a Rural-Industrial State* (Dubuque, IA: Kendall/Hunt Publishing Company, 1996), 2nd ed., 168–170.

3   David S. Walls, "Internal Colony or Internal Periphery: A Critique of Current Models and an Alternative Formulation," in *Colonialism in Modern America: The Appalachian Case,* eds. Helen Matthews Lewis, Linda Johnson, and Donald Askins (Boone, NC: Appalachian Consortium Press, 1978), 319–340; see also David S. Walls, "Central Appalachia in Advanced Capitalism" (PhD diss., University of Kentucky, 1978).

4   G. William Domhoff, *Who Rules America: Power and Politics* (Boston: McGraw-Hill Higher Education, 2002), 95.

5   Domhoff, *Who Rules America*, 95–98.

6   David Corbin, *Life, Work, and Rebellion in the Coal Fields: The Southern West Virginia Miners, 1880–1922* (Urbana: University of Illinois Press, 1981), 8; Ronald D. Eller, *Miners, Millhands, and Mountaineers: Industrialization of the Appalachian South, 1880–1930* (Knoxville: University of Tennessee Press, 1982), 162–163.

7   Corbin, *Life, Work, and Rebellion*, 9.

8   See for example, Price Fishback, "Did Coal Miners 'Owe Their Souls to the Company Store?' Theory and Evidence from the Early 1900s," *The Journal of Economic History* 46 (Dec. 1986): 1011–1029; Crandall Shifflett, *Coal Towns: Life, Work, and Culture in Company Towns of Southern Appalachia, 1880–1960* (Knoxville: University of Tennessee Press, 1991); Corbin, *Life, Work, and Rebellion*, 42.

9   Corbin, *Life, Work, and Rebellion*, 9, 42.

10   Corbin, *Life, Work, and Rebellion*, 9.

11   Corbin, *Life, Work, and Rebellion*, 122–123.

12   For more on model company towns, see chapter 2.

13   See for example, Robert Shogan, *The Battle of Blair Mountain: The Story of America's Largest Labor Uprising* (Boulder, CO: Westview Press, 2004); Lon Savage, *Thunder in the Mountains* (Pittsburgh: University of Pittsburgh Press, 1990); Howard B. Lee, *Bloodletting in Appalachia: The Story of West Virginia's Four Major Mine Wars and Other Thrilling Incidents of Its Coal*

Fields (Morgantown: West Virginia University, 1969); Ken Sullivan, ed., *The "Goldenseal" Book of the West Virginia Mine Wars* (Charleston, WV: Pictorial Histories Publishing, 1991).

14 Eller, *Miners, Millhands, and Mountaineers*, 134, 138.

15 Eller, *Miners, Millhands, and Mountaineers*, 222–223.

16 John Gaventa, *Power and Powerlessness: Quiescence and Rebellion in an Appalachian Valley* (Chicago: University of Illinois Press, 1980), 5–20.

17 Shiva Kolli, "Analyses of Coal Extraction and Spoil Handling Techniques in Mountainous Areas" (master's thesis, West Virginia University, 2001), 26–28.

18 Ken Ward Jr., "Clean Air Act May Boost State Coal Sales," *Charleston (WV) Gazette-Mail,* April 12, 1994; "All About Business," *Charleston (WV) Daily Mail,* April 26, 1994.

19 George Hohmann, "No One asked AEP's Opinion: Importance of Coal to its Operation Fuels Support of Mountaintop Removal," *Charleston (WV) Daily Mail,* May 27, 1999.

20 West Virginia Coal Association, *Coal Facts 2003* (Charleston: West Virginia Coal Association, 2003), June 30, 2004, http://friendsofcoal.org/resources/Fact_book.pdf.

21 Numbers derived from adding coal-slurry impoundment statistics found in Appendix 2.

22 Ken Ward Jr., "Mining the Mountains: Industry, Critics Look for Mountaintop Removal Alternative: Is There Another Way?" *Charleston (WV) Gazette,* June 6, 1999.

Chapter 1

The epigraph to this chapter is drawn from the King James Bible.

1 Massey Energy Company, *2005 Annual Report* (Richmond, VA: Massey Energy Company, 2006), 95.

2 Eller, *Miners, Millhands, and Mountaineers*, xix; for more information on the region's transition from a barter economy, see Paul Salstrom, *Appalachia's Path to Dependency: Rethinking a Region's Economic History, 1730–1940* (Lexington: University Press of Kentucky, 1994).

3 Wilma Dunaway, *The First American Frontier: Transition to Capitalism in Southern Appalachia, 1700–1860* (Chapel Hill: University of North Carolina Press, 1996), 54–66, 192–193; Eller, *Miners, Millhands, and Mountaineers*, xxi, 50–52. Identification, mapping, and purchasing of resources occurred as early as the eighteenth century, prior to the intense natural-resource exploitation that

would accompany the industrial transition in the mountains. Still, absentee holdings could not be fully exploited until the railroads entered the treacherous, coal-rich southern West Virginia territories at different times for each county during the late nineteenth and early twentieth centuries.

4 Tom Miller, "Absentees Dominate Land Ownership," *Who Owns West Virginia?* (Huntington, WV, 1974), 1–3.

5 Miller, "Absentees Dominate Land Ownership," 5–6.

6 Robert Munn, "The First Fifty Years of Strip Mining in West Virginia, 1916–1965," *West Virginia History* 35 (October 1973): 66–74.

7 Munn, "The First Fifty Years," 68, 71.

8 Munn, "The First Fifty Years," 68.

9 Munn, "The First Fifty Years," 69.

10 Munn, "The First Fifty Years," 71.

11 *Coal Facts 2003*, 14.

12 Kolli, "Analyses of Coal Extraction," 34.

13 Chad Montrie, "To Save the Land and People: A History of Opposition to Coal Surface Mining in Appalachia" (PhD diss., Ohio State University, 2001), 191; Chad Montrie, *To Save the Land and People: A History of Opposition to Surface Coal Mining in Appalachia* (Chapel Hill: University of North Carolina Press, 2003), 110–111. Montrie's book and the dissertation that preceded it do an excellent job of detailing the struggles of Appalachian citizens to monitor and fight against the strip-mining industry.

14 Munn, "The First Fifty Years," 72–73.

15 Montrie, "To Save the Land and People," 193–194; Montrie, *To Save the Land and People*, 111.

16 Montrie, "To Save the Land and People," 195.

17 Montrie, "To Save the Land and People," 194; Montrie, *To Save the Land and People*, 108.

18 Montrie, "To Save the Land and People," 187–189; Montrie, *To Save the Land and People*, 122–123.

19 Commission on Religion in Appalachia, *Strip Mining in Appalachia: A Social, Economic and Political Issue* (Knoxville, TN: Commission on Religion in Appalachia, 1970).

20 Montrie, "To Save the Land and People," 282, 288–289; Montrie, *To Save the Land and People*, 138, 163–173.

21 Montrie, "To Save the Land and People," 303, 306; Montrie, *To Save the Land and People*, 178.

22 Montrie, "To Save the Land and People," 305; Mark Squillace, *Strip Mining Handbook: A Coalfield Citizens' Guide to Using the Law to Fight Back Against*

the Ravages of Strip Mining and Underground Mining (Washington, DC: Environmental Policy Institute and Friends of the Earth, 1990), 89.

23   Ken Ward Jr., "Flattened: Most Mountaintop Mines Left as Pasture Land in State," *Charleston (WV) Gazette,* August 9, 1998.

24   Ken Ward Jr., "Corps Says it Doesn't Regulate Valley Fills: Stance Could Help Suit Over Mountaintop Removal," *Charleston (WV) Gazette,* July 19, 1998; Ken Ward Jr., "Strip-Mined Acreage Up Again in W.Va.," *Charleston (WV) Gazette,* November 4, 2003.

Chapter 2

The epigraph to this chapter is drawn from Billy Edd Wheeler's "Coal Tattoo," *Ode to the Little Brown Shack Out Back,* Kapp Records KL-1425, 1963.

1   Maier B. Fox, *United We Stand: The United Mine Workers of America, 1890–1990* (Washington, DC: United Mine Workers of America, 1990), 22.

2   Maier, *United We Stand,* iii–iv.

3   Phil Conley, *History of the West Virginia Coal Industry* (Charleston, WV: Education Foundation, Inc., 1960), 43–71; Corbin, *Life, Work, and Rebellion,* 2; Eller, *Miners, Millhands, and Mountaineers,* 65–75; Lewis, *Transforming the Appalachian Countryside,* 7.

4   Corbin, *Life, Work, and Rebellion,* 106–145; Keith Dix, *What's a Coal Miner to Do? The Mechanization of Coal Mining* (Pittsburgh: University of Pittsburgh Press, 1988), 168–173; Eller, *Miners, Millhands, and Mountaineers,* 209–210; Maier, *United We Stand,* 146–147; Shifflett, *Coal Towns,* 55–60; John Alexander Williams, *West Virginia and the Captains of Industry* (Morgantown: West Virginia University Library, 1976), 190–191, 250–251.

5   Jim Woods, *Raleigh County, West Virginia* (Beckley, WV: BJW Printing and Office Supplies, 1994), 367–376; Lois C. McLean, "Warm Receptions and Cordial Invitations for Mother Jones in West Virginia," *The "Goldenseal" Book of the West Virginia Mine Wars,* 3–9. The Battle of Stanaford seems to have been nearly forgotten by scholars of West Virginia's mine wars. Occasionally, it is given a passing mention in a sentence about union-miner struggles or invoked in "remember Stanaford" quotes, but not much detail is ever provided about exactly what we should remember. Aside from Woods, whose book makes use of a myriad of primary sources and is the most thorough history of Raleigh County that I have read, the best telling of what happened at Stanaford is encompassed within a few paragraphs in McLean's *Goldenseal* article about Mother Jones. Mother Jones's autobiography also provides a cursory mention of the encounter.

Yet, as many people lost their lives as a result of Stanaford as did during the far better known "Matewan Massacre." Considering the breadth of scholarship concerning the mine wars and struggle for unionization, the lack of scholarship concerning this early battle is puzzling.

6   Lee, *Bloodletting in Appalachia*, 17-18.

7   Richard D. Lunt, *Law and Order vs. the Miners: West Virginia, 1906–1933* (Charleston, WV: Appalachian Editions, 1992), 23–33.

8   Lunt, *Law and Order*; Corbin, *Life, Work, and Rebellion,* 87–105; Lee, *Bloodletting in Appalachia*, 17–47; Sullivan, *The "Goldenseal" Book of the West Virginia Mine Wars*, 17–32.

9   Rebecca J. Bailey, "Matewan Before the Massacre: Politics, Coal, and the Roots of Conflict in Mingo County, 1793–1920" (PhD diss., West Virginia University, 2001), xiii. For a detailed account of the Blair Mountain battle, please see Shogan, *The Battle of Blair Mountain*. Other sources of interest include Michael Meador, "The Red Neck War of 1921: The Miner's March and the Battle of Blair Mountain," *The "Goldenseal" Book of the West Virginia Mine Wars*, 57–63; Lunt, *Law and Order*, 91–144; Corbin, *Life, Work, and Rebellion*, 195–252; Lee, *Bloodletting in Appalachia*, 51–58; Savage, *Thunder in the Mountains*; and Sullivan, *The "Goldenseal" Book of the West Virginia Mine Wars*, part 3.

10   Meador, "The Red Neck War of 1921," 57–63.

11   Robert Munn, "The Development of Model Towns in the Bituminous Coal Fields," *West Virginia History* 40 (Spring 1979), 243–253.

12   Munn, "The Development of Model Towns," 243–253.

13   Koppers Coal Company was part of the vast natural-resource holdings of the Koppers Company. Eastern Gas and Fuel Associates bought into Koppers Coal holdings to become part of Koppers Coal and Transportation Company. In this capacity, they purchased majority holdings in the Virginian Railway, which was important in getting the coal out of the southern backcounties of West Virginia. The organization now had a direct interest in every aspect of mining—actual mining, transportation, and processing. In 1947, Koppers was ordered to sell its extensive holdings in Eastern Gas and Fuel Associates. The Koppers division of Eastern Gas and Fuel was then renamed Beacon Coal. Eventually, Eastern Gas and Fuel's coal holdings would be under a subsidiary, wholly owned by the company, named Eastern Associated Coal Company. In 1998, the now bankrupted Eastern—the once seemingly union friendly company—sued the UMWA in an attempt to shirk its healthcare and retirement obligations even after they had agreed to provide "cradle to grave" benefits for the company's employees. In a blow for unions and working people, the U.S. Supreme Court ruled in the defunct company's favor, citing that the company had not mined

coal since 1966. However, the company's subsidiaries, including Eastern, had mined coal through the 1980s and signed contracts with the union in 1974, 1978, and 1981. Other companies' attempts to shirk their responsibilities did not meet with such favorable judicial attention. Please see "Eastern Gas Joins in Koppers Merger: Mines, Coal Selling Agencies, Steamships and Dock to Go Under One Company," *New York Times,* February 25, 1933; "Eastern Gas Gets Indirect Interest in Virginian Railway: Acquires Stock of Virginian Corp. Along with Associate, Koppers Co.," *New York Times,* July 2, 1937; "Koppers Coal Becomes 'Beacon,'" *New York Times,* October 3, 1947; and "Court Rejects Companies' Appeal, Businesses Asked to be Relieved of Paying Benefits," *Charleston (WV) Daily Mail,* November 2, 1999.

14 Paul Blankenship, *From Cabins to Coal Mines: More History, Sketches, Anecdotes, Traditional Stories, Culture, and Families of Oceana and the Clear Fork Valley of Wyoming County, West Virginia* (Beckley, WV: Central Printing, 2002), 223.

15 "Miner's Children Play at Own Camp: 750 at a Time Spend Two Weeks in Hill Country of West Virginia," *New York Times,* August 28, 1943.

16 Ann Hughey, "Kopperston . . . Coal Mining Town that's Different," *Charleston (WV) Gazette,* April 20, 1978; Ann Hughey, "Community Pride Evident in Classiest Coal Camp in Appalachia," *Charleston (WV) Gazette,* April 20, 1978; Blankenship, *From Cabins to Coal Mines,* 234–236, 240.

17 James David Kidd, president of UMWA Local Union 7604, telephone conversation with the author, October 27, 2004. Kidd obtained the information from the local union's charter. Through most of the 1970s, Local Union 7604, with more than 1,200 active members, was the largest local union of District 17, which was the largest district of the UMWA. Today, there are only four thousand union members in all of District 17 (now combined with District 29).

18 Around 1977, I clearly remember obtaining my first bicycle at this company store. The store clerk took my father's work information so the payments could be deducted directly from his paycheck.

19 Blankenship, *From Cabins to Coal Mines,* 234–236; Ann Hughey, "Kopperston . . . Coal Mining Town that's Different," *Charleston (WV) Gazette,* April 20, 1978.

20 Blankenship, *From Cabins to Coal Mines,* 240; Ann Hughey, "Community Pride Evident in Classiest Coal Camp in Appalachia," *Charleston (WV) Gazette,* April 20, 1978.

21 Catherine Lucey, "Coal Worker Membership Declines," Associated Press, August 2, 2002; Department of Energy, Energy Information Administration, "Average Number of Employees by State, Mine Type, and Union Type, 2000," *Coal Industry Annual,* 2000. When I got into contact with the UMWA, I learned that the union itself does not keep a record of membership numbers. The

union representative provided me with overall mining employment numbers and suggested that I use percentages to get an estimate. Instead, I continued searching. Special thanks go to Ken Ward Jr., the *Charleston (WV) Gazette*, and Melody Bragg for the UMWA membership information they provided. Also see David Peter, "Earnings, Health, Safety, and Welfare of Bituminous Coal Miners since the Encouragement of Mechanization by the United Mine Workers of America" (PhD diss., West Virginia University, 1972); Joseph Shaplen, "Fullest War Help Pledged by Lewis," *New York Times,* October 7, 1942; Kenneth Noble, "Even in the Mines, There's an Urge to Merge," *New York Times*, October 12, 1986; Jonathan Hicks, "Labor Takes Heart in the Miner Walkout," *New York Times*, June 25, 1989; Department of Energy, Energy Information Administration, *Coal Industry Annual Report Data Table, 1995, 2000* (Washington, DC: Department of Energy, 1995, 2000), http://tonto.eia.doe .gov/FTPROOT/coal/058495.pdf, http://www.eia.doe.gov/cneaf/coal/cia/html/ tbl24p01p1.html.

22 Edward Peeks, "New UMW Chief Has Hard Job," *Charleston (WV) Gazette,* May 21, 2001.

23 Barbara Freese, *Coal: A Human History* (Cambridge: MA: Perseus Books Group, 2003), 180.

24 Dix, *What's a Coal Miner to Do?*, 161.

25 Ken Ward Jr., "Trumka Hails 'Tremendous Victory for UMWA,'" *Charleston (WV) Gazette,* July 1, 1994. For further reading on the Pittston and Massey strikes, please see Richard Couto, "The Memory of Miners and the Conscience of Capital: Coal Miners' Strikes as Free Spaces," in *Fighting Back in Appalachia: Traditions of Resistance and Change,* ed. Stephen Fisher (Philadelphia: Temple University Press, 1993). For further reading on the Pittston strike, see Richard Brisbin Jr., *A Strike Like No Other Strike: Law and Resistance During the Pittston Coal Strike of 1989–1990,* (Baltimore: Johns Hopkins University Press, 2002); Jim Session and Fran Ansley, "Singing Across Dark Spaces: The Union/Community Takeover of Pittston's Moss 3 Plant," in *Fighting Back in Appalachia.*

26 Massey Energy Company, *2003 Annual Report* (Richmond, VA: Massey Energy Company, 2004), 16, 25.

27 Peter M. Slavin, "UMW Battles for Survival Against Old Foe Massey Coal," *Charleston (WV) Gazette,* December 10, 1995.

28 "A New Lease on Life: Achieving Success via the UMWA Career Centers," *United Mine Workers of America Journal,* January–February 2001; Joe Smydo, "Union, State, U.S. Extend a Hand to Coal Town Youth: Goal is to Fortify Communities," *Pittsburgh Post-Gazette,* October 3, 2004.

29 Fox, *United We Stand,* 353–354.

30 Deborah Underwood, "The Ascendancy of Surface Mining over Underground Mining in the United States Coal Industry: Effects on and Issues Relevant to the United Mine Workers of America" (master's thesis, University of Montana, 1987), 27–28, chapter 2.

31 Cecil Roberts, "Responsible Mining: UMWA Wants Communities, Environment Protected," *Charleston (WV) Gazette*, October 12, 1998.

32 Roberts, "Responsible Mining," *Charleston (WV) Gazette, October 12, 1998*.

33 Steve Myers, "Tension Over Mining Could Grow; Those at Rally Say They Need Jobs to Support Families," *Charleston (WV) Daily Mail*, March 13, 1999.

34 Myers, "Tension Over Mining Could Grow," *Charleston (WV) Daily Mail*, March 13, 1999.

35 Steve Myers, "Mountaintop Mining Debate Suggested: Environmental Leader Not Sure if She Will Join," *Charleston (WV) Daily Mail*, May 14, 1999.

36 "No Favors: Why Not Mine Legally?," *Charleston (WV) Gazette,* July 8, 1999.

37 Doug Gibson, United Mine Workers of America spokesperson, telephone message to author, October 29, 2004. Message in response to one letter and one e-mail sent by the author.

38 Randy Sprouse, "Reader's Forum," *Charleston (WV) Gazette*, July 16, 1999. An article in the *Charleston Daily Mail* detailed the media blitz supporting MTR; see Steve Myers, "UMW Launching Ad in Support of Industry; Activist Calls Spot 'Terribly Misleading,'" *Charleston (WV) Daily Mail*, May 22, 1999.

Chapter 3

The epigraph to this chapter is drawn from Pauline Canterberry's interview with the author in Sylvester, West Virginia, on October 9, 2003.

1 Lewis, *Transforming the Appalachian Countryside*, 5, 9.

2 U.S. Census Bureau, *Profile of General Demographic Characteristics: 2000, Sylvester, West Virginia,* generated by the author using American Fact Finder, available from http://factfinder.census.gov, October 14, 2006.

3 Pauline Canterberry, interview by the author, tape recording, Sylvester, West Virginia, October 9, 2003; Mary Miller, interview by the author, tape recording, Sylvester, West Virginia, October 9, 2003; Boone County, West Virginia, "Certificate of Incorporation of the Town of Sylvester," 1952.

4 Mary Miller interview; Pauline Canterberry interview.

5 Massey Energy Company, *2003 Annual Report,* 9–10.

6 Squillace, *Strip Mining Handbook*, 69–70.

7 Squillace, *Strip Mining Handbook*, 70.

8   *All Shaken Up,* interviews with Russell Elkins, Dickie Judy, and Larry Brown (Charleston, WV: Omni Productions, 1998), videocassette.

9   Ken Ward Jr., "State Environmental Officials Limit Blasting at Dal-Tex Mine: Rocks Sailing into Yards Upset Blair Residents," *Charleston (WV) Gazette,* August 23, 1997; Ken Ward Jr., "Strip-mining Battle Resurfaces in State," *Charleston (WV) Gazette,* March 22, 1998; personal conversations between the author and Carlos Gore, various dates.

10   Ken Ward Jr., "Strip-mining Battle Resurfaces in State," *Charleston (WV) Gazette,* March 22, 1998; personal conversations between the author and Carlos Gore, various dates.

11   United States Environmental Protection Agency, Final Programmatic Environmental Impact Statement, Alternatives, Part 2 (Washington, DC: U.S. Environmental Protection Agency, 2005), II.A-6. (Hereinafter, the Final Programmatic Environmental Impact Statement will be referred to as "FPEIS.") According to the FPEIS signature page, the "FPEIS was prepared in accordance with the provision set forth in 40 CFR 1503.4(c) of the regulations implementing NEPA, which allow the agencies to attach an errata sheet to the statement instead of rewriting the draft statement and to circulate the errata, comments, responses, and the changes, rather than the entire document." In essence, much of the FPEIS remains the same document as its precursor, the Draft Environmental Impact Statement (DEIS).

12   Ken Ward Jr., "Mining Study: Blasts not 'Significant,'" *Charleston (WV) Gazette,* August 3, 2003; Ohio Valley Environmental Coalition, January 5, 2004, *Comments on Draft Programmatic Environmental Impact Statement on Mountaintop Removal Mining/Valley Fill Activities in Appalachia: The Social and Cultural Effects of Mountaintop Removal/Valley Fill Coal Mining* (Huntington, WV: Ohio Valley Environmental Association), 6, available from http://www .ohvec.org/issues/mountaintop_removal/articles/EIS_social_cultural.pdf.

13   Ward, "Mining Study," *Charleston (WV) Gazette,* August 3, 2003

14   Ward, "Mining Study," *Charleston (WV) Gazette,* August 3, 2003; Squillace, *Strip Mining Handbook,* 70.

15   Greta Stone, conversation with the author, Oceana-Kopperston, West Virginia, May 10, 2004.

16   Greta Stone, conversation with the author.

17   Greta Stone, conversation with the author.

18   West Virginia Coal Association, Coal Education Development and Resource of Southern West Virginia, Inc., "Welcome to West Virginia Coal," http://www .wvcoal.com/current_issues/index.asp.

19   West Virginia Coal Association, Coal Education Development and Resource of

Southern West Virginia, Inc., "Welcome to West Virginia Coal," http://www
.wvcoal.com/current_issues/index.asp.

20   Sam Tranum, "Coal Haulers See Little Difference," *Charleston (WV) Daily
Mail*, July 29, 2002; Dan Radmacher, "Coal Truck Bill is an Economic Disaster
for West Virginia," *Charleston (WV) Gazette*, February 28, 2003. I have had
numerous close calls with coal trucks in the coalfields of southern West Virginia,
having been both a driver and a passenger in cars that were run off the road
by huge trucks heaped with coal. Longer reaction times could have ended
disastrously. It should be noted that the truck drivers did not appear to be doing
anything malicious. The roads are simply not wide enough to accommodate
the large coal trucks and any other vehicle simultaneously. The coal trucks,
quite simply, must use more than just one lane in order to maneuver the steep,
mountainous terrain.

21   Tara Tuckwiller, "Lighten Up, Haulers Say Coal Truck Owners Hoping
Legislators Ease Weight Limits: Latest State Crackdown Could Close Their
Doors, Company Officials Fear," *Charleston (WV) Gazette*, November 4,
2001; Gavin McCormick, "Wise Names Overweight Truck Panel Members,"
Charleston (WV) Gazette, April 4, 2002.

22   McCormick, "Wise Names Overweight Truck Panel Members," *Charleston (WV)
Gazette*, April 4, 2002.

23   Paul Nyden, "Both Sides Make a Stand on Hauling Bill," *Charleston (WV)
Gazette,* March 2, 2002; Brian Bowling, "Coal Trucks Roll on State Capitol; Both
Sides of Issue Take Message to Lawmakers," *Charleston (WV) Daily Mail*, March
1, 2002.

24   Mary Miller interview. For more on this particular legal case, please see chapter 5.

25   "Replacement Dome Rips at Massey Plant," *Charleston (WV) Gazette,* April 24,
2003.

26   Mary Miller interview; Pauline Canterberry interview.

27   Robert Meyers, *Coal Handbook* (New York: M. Dekker, 1981), chapter 6.

28   Meyers, *Coal Handbook*, chapter 6; Jann Vendetti, "Mining: Storing Coal Slurry,"
Alexandria, VA: American Geological Society, http://www.agiweb.org/geotimes/
dec01/NNcoal.html, September 24, 2006.

29   Robert C. Byrd National Technology Transfer Center (NTTC), Wheeling Jesuit
University, West Virginia University, and the National Energy Technology
Laboratory, "Coal Impoundment Location and Warning System," http://www
.coalimpoundment.com/locate/impoundment.asp?impoundment_id=1211-
WV04-40234-02, September 24, 2006.

30   Rick Eades, *Brushy Fork Slurry Impoundment—A Preliminary Report*
(Huntington, WV: Ohio Valley Environmental Coalition, 2000), 17.

NOTES

31 Mary Miller interview.

32 Eades, *Brushy Fork Slurry Impoundment*, 13; "UMWA Launches Community Education Campaign about Massey's Brushy Fork Impoundment," *United Mine Workers of America Journal,* January–February 2004.

33 Ken Ward Jr., "Criminal Probe Is Ongoing in Coal Mining Dam Failure in Kentucky," *Charleston (WV) Gazette*, May 12, 2004.

34 Jack Spadaro, "Mountaintop Removal Mining Practices Must Change or Ecosystem will be Destroyed," *Charleston (WV) Gazette*, February 21, 2005.

35 Eades, *Brushy Fork Slurry Impoundment*, 11.

36 Eades, *Brushy Fork Slurry Impoundment*, 11; "UMWA launches community education campaign," *United Mine Workers of America Journal,* January–February 2004.

37 Eades, *Brushy Fork Slurry Impoundment*, 11.

38 Mary Miller interview; Pauline Canterberry interview.

39 Mary Miller interview.

40 Pauline Canterberry interview.

41 Judy Bonds, interview by the author, tape recording, Sylvester, West Virginia, October 8, 2003; Patty Sebok, interview by the author, tape recording, Whitesville, West Virginia, October 8, 2003.

42 Boone County Board of Education, *Reasons Supporting Data—Executive Summary of Consolidation of Sylvester Elementary and Whitesville Schools for Boone County Schools* (Madison, WV: Boone County Board of Education, 2002), 37.

43 Pauline Canterberry interview; Mary Miller interview.

44 Ken Ward Jr., "Mine Spill on Tug Underscores Dam Concerns," *Charleston (WV) Gazette,* October 13, 2000; Ward, "Criminal Probe Is Ongoing," *Charleston (WV) Gazette*, May 12, 2004.

45 Consolidation Coal Company, *Monitoring and Emergency Warning Plan and Procedures for the Joe Branch Coal Refuse Dam* (Welch, WV: Department of Environmental Protection, 2003), 12, http://www.coalimpoundment.org/EmergencyPlans/1211-WV4-0709-01.pdf.

46 Consolidation Coal Company, *Monitoring and Emergency Warning Plan and Procedures for the Joe Branch Coal Refuse Dam* (Welch, WV: Department of Environmental Protection, 2003), 12, http://www.coalimpoundment.org/EmergencyPlans/1211-WV4-0709-01.pdf.

47 Consolidation Coal Company, *Monitoring and Emergency Warning Plan*, 12. GIS mapping also illustrates this.

48 Iain McLean and Martin Johnes, *Aberfan: Government and Disasters* (Cardiff, Wales: Welsh Academic Press, 2000), 22.

49 McLean and Johnes, *Aberfan*, 90, 234–235.

50 Ken Ward Jr., "Mining Board Postpones Hearing on Silo Permit," *Charleston (WV) Gazette*, September 10, 2005; "Alternative for Marsh Fork School Site Toured," Associated Press, July 6, 2005; "DEP Denies Massey Permit to Build 2nd Silo Near Elementary," Associated Press, August 15, 2006.

51 Ken Ward Jr., "Work Started Without Permit; Massey Began Construction on Coal Silo Before Approval," *Charleston (WV) Gazette*, July 13, 2005.

52 Ken Ward Jr., "Massey Silo Permit Revoked; DEP Says Silo is Out of Permit Area, Orders Removal," *Charleston (WV) Gazette*, July 27, 2005; Lawrence Messina, "DEP Suspends Disputed Massey Permits," Associated Press, July 16, 2005.

53 Erik Schelzig, "Massey Appeals DEP Silo Ruling," Associated Press, August 2, 2005.

54 Ken Ward Jr., "DEP Right to Block Massey Silo, Board Rules," *Charleston (WV) Gazette*, March 16, 2006.

55 "DEP Denies Massey Permit to Build 2nd Silo Near Elementary School," Associated Press, August 15, 2006.

56 Lawrence Messina, "Marsh Fork Grandfather Conducts Capitol Sit-in," Associated Press, July 5, 2005.

57 Ken Ward Jr., "Manchin Promise Called Bologna," *Charleston (WV) Gazette*, September 2, 2005.

58 Ken Ward Jr., "Marsh Fork Air Quality 'Unknown'; State Never Tested School for Coal Dust, Chemicals," *Charleston (WV) Gazette*, August 27, 2005.

59 Ken Ward Jr., "Manchin Refuses Independent School Review," *Charleston (WV) Gazette*, October 4, 2005.

60 Ken Ward Jr., "Grandfather Plans Walk to Highlight School Concerns," *Charleston (WV) Gazette*, July 27, 2005; "Wiley Arrives in Washington, D.C., Meets with Senator Byrd," Associated Press, September 13, 2006.

61 Marie H. Bias-Jones, "Kayford Mountain Native to Walk the State to Save Mountains," *Charleston (WV) Gazette*, June 24, 1999; Steve Myers, "Activist Finishes Walk Across State: Man's Goal Was to Tell People about Mining Method," *Charleston (WV) Daily Mail*, August 21, 1999.

62 For information on how to visit Kayford Mountain, please see http://www .mountainkeeper.org.

63 Ken Ward Jr., "Miners Pack Hearing to Support Strip Permit: Area Needs the Jobs, UMW Member Says," *Charleston (WV) Gazette*, May 6, 1998.

64 Ward, "Miners Pack Hearing to Support Strip Permit," *Charleston (WV) Gazette*, May 6, 1998.

65 "Miners Outnumber Others at Mountaintop Removal Hearing," *Charleston (WV) Daily Mail*, May 6, 1998.

66 Ward, "Miners Pack Hearing to Support Strip Permit," *Charleston (WV) Gazette*, May 6, 1998.

67 "Miners Outnumber Others at Mountaintop Removal Meeting," *Charleston (WV) Daily Mail*, May 6, 1998.

68 Ken Ward Jr., "EPA Gets Earful on Mountaintop Mining: Supporters of Practice Outnumber Opponents at Hearing in Logan," *Charleston (WV) Gazette*, October 25, 1998.

69 Ward, "EPA Gets Earful on Mountaintop Mining," *Charleston (WV) Gazette*, October 25, 1998.

70 Ward, "EPA Gets Earful on Mountaintop Mining," *Charleston (WV) Gazette*, October 25, 1998.

71 Ward, "EPA Gets Earful on Mountaintop Mining," *Charleston (WV) Gazette*, October 25, 1998.

72 Ward, "EPA Gets Earful on Mountaintop Mining," *Charleston (WV) Gazette*, October 25, 1998.

73 Ward, "EPA Gets Earful on Mountaintop Mining," *Charleston (WV) Gazette*, October 25, 1998.

74 Ken Ward Jr., "UMW Members Protest Mine Ruling," *Charleston (WV) Gazette,* March 6, 1999. While it is true that the lawsuits brought against the coal companies rely largely on arguments that focus on damage afforded the environment, plaintiffs have realized that the most effective arguments are *not* those that deal with the destruction of their personal property but those that deal with the destruction of the environment in general. Any one of a number of federal laws against such damage may be invoked.

75 Ken Ward Jr., "Corp Gives Final OK to Record Strip Mine in Logan," *Charleston (WV) Gazette*, January 30, 2007.

76 Steve Meyers, "Tensions Over Mining Could Grow; Those At Rally Say They Need Jobs to Support Families," *Charleston (WV) Daily Mail*, March 13, 1999.

77 Charles H. Moffat, *Ken Hechler: Maverick Public Servant* (Charleston, WV: Mountain State Press, 1987), 209–231.

78 "Violence Logan, Ravenswood," *Charleston (WV) Gazette,* September 2, 1999; Dan Radmacher, "Union Members Become Blair Thugs," *Charleston (WV) Gazette,* September 3, 1999.

79 Radmacher, "Union Members Become Blair Thugs," *Charleston (WV) Gazette*, September 3, 1999.

80 Greg Stone, "Miners Lament Lost Jobs, Lack of Help," *Charleston (WV) Gazette,* September 7, 1999.

81 Brian Bowling, "Logan Residents Speak Out: People Angry Over Ruling that Would Hobble Mining," *Charleston (WV) Daily Mail*, October 22, 1999.

82 John McFerrin, "Mountaintop Removal is Harmful Tool of Dying Industry," *Charleston (WV) Gazette*, January 18, 1999.

83 Sara Evans and Harry Boyte, *Free Space: The Sources of Dramatic Change in America* (New York: Harper and Row, 1986), 17.

84 Cuoto, "The Memory of Miners and the Conscience of Capital," *Fighting Back in Appalachia*, 165–194.

85 Judy Bonds interview.

86 Judy Bonds interview.

87 Judy Bonds interview.

88 Pauline Canterberry interview; Mary Miller interview.

89 Judy Bonds interview.

90 Judy Bonds interview.

91 Judy Bonds interview.

92 Judy Bonds interview.

93 Judy Bonds interview.

94 Judy Bonds interview.

95 Judy Bonds interview; Pauline Canterberry interview; Mary Miller interview; Greta Stone conversation; Prudence Coleman (pseudonym), conversation with the author, Matheny–Jesse–Glen Fork area, WV, August 10, 2004.

96 Ohio Valley Environmental Coalition, *Comments on Draft Programmatic Environmental Impact Statement*, 4.

97 Ohio Valley Environmental Coalition, letter, 4; Mary Miller interview.

98 Ohio Valley Environmental Coalition, *Comments on Draft Programmatic Environmental Impact Statement*, 53.

99 Mary Miller interview.

100 Christiadi and George Hammond, "How Well Did We Retain and Attract Highly Educated Workers?," *West Virginia Business and Economic Review* 9 (October 2003): 1–6.

101 Numbers derived by adding employment figures for the nine counties found in chapter 1.

102 Christiadi and Hammond, "How Well Did We Retain and Attract," 1–6.

103 West Virginia Coal Association, *West Virginia Coal Facts 2001* (Charleston: West Virginia Coal Association, 2001); West Virginia Bureau of Employment Programs, *West Virginia Nonfarm Employment by Industry, 1939–1999*, http://www.wvbep.org/bep/lmi/e&e/nf_39-99.htm, October 14, 2006.

104 West Virginia Bureau of Employment Programs, *West Virginia Coal Mining Employment, 1950–2004*, http://www.wvbep.org/bep/lmi/e&e/nf_39-99.htm, October 14, 2006.

105 Martha Bryson Hodel, "Residents Praise, Vilify the Coal Industry," *Charleston*

(WV) Gazette, September 23, 1998; "Mine Guts Town, Some Say; Blair Mountain Residents Upset over Shrinking Population," *Charleston (WV) Daily Mail,* August 18, 1997.

106 Hodel, "Residents Praise, Vilify," *Charleston (WV) Gazette,* September 23, 1998.

107 "Buying Blair: Arch Removes Community," *Charleston (WV) Gazette,* November 27, 1998.

108 Patrick McGinley, "From Pick and Shovel to Mountaintop Removal: Environmental Injustice in the Appalachian Coalfields," *Environmental Law* 34, no. 1 (2004): 81.

109 Presentation information in possession of author. During the course of research for this document, I was able to obtain a copy of one of the presentations given in January 2000. I was asked to maintain confidentiality from where the document was originally obtained. In order to do so, no pronouns have been used so the gender of the presenter is not revealed, nor the presenter's employer.

110 During my research for this book, I was able to obtain a copy of one of the presentations the attorney gave in January 2000. I was asked to keep the source of the document confidential.

111 Quote from January 2000 presentation.

112 Please see chapter 6 for more information on how growth of hardwood and softwood trees on reclaimed land is, in fact, usually not successful.

113 Quote from January 2000 presentation.

114 Quote from January 2000 presentation.

Chapter 4

The epigraph to this chapter is drawn from William C. Marland, "Governor William C. Marland Proposes the Severance Tax," *West Virginia: Documents,* ed. Lewis and Hennen, 304.

1 Paul Rakes, "Acceptable Casualties: Power, Culture, and History in the West Virginia Coalfields, 1900-1945" (PhD diss., West Virginia University, 2002), 71.

2 Rakes, "Acceptable Casualties," 70, 71.

3 Rakes, "Acceptable Casualties," 75.

4 John Calhoun Wells Jr., "Poverty Amidst Riches: Why People are Poor in Appalachia" (PhD diss., Rutgers University, 1977), 315.

5 Paul Nyden, "Panel Votes to Drop Big Coal Firms from Lawsuits: Compromise Benefits State, Kiss Says; Critics Say Questions Remain," *Charleston (WV) Gazette,* March 13, 1999; Jennifer Bundy, "Court Says Workers Compensation Cases Can Be Dismissed," Associated Press, July 14, 1999; "Probe? Ugly Allegations," *Charleston (WV) Gazette,* June 14, 2001.

6   Paul Nyden, "Donors Owe Workers Comp Fund: Coal Operators Heavily
     Funded Underwood, Who Called off Suits," *Charleston (WV) Gazette,* December
     31, 1997.

7   Brian Bowling, "Wise Considers Renewing Suits: Governor-Elect is Reviewing
     Status of Workers' Comp Claims," *Charleston (WV) Daily Mail,* November 23,
     2000.

8   Paul Nyden, "Coal Companies to Pay $56.6 Million in Unpaid Workers' Comp
     in West Virginia," *Charleston (WV) Gazette,* April 10, 2002.

9   Lewis, *Transforming the Appalachian Countryside,* 61, 66–67.

10   Miller, *Who Owns West Virginia?,* 3.

11   Barbara Rasmussen, *Absentee Landowning and Exploitation in West Virginia,
     1760–1920* (Lexington: University Press of Kentucky, 1994), 141.

12   Appalachian Land Ownership Task Force, *Land Ownership Patterns and Their
     Impacts on Appalachian Communities: A Survey of 80 Counties* (Washington, DC:
     Appalachian Regional Commission, 1981), 70; Appalachian Land Ownership
     Task Force, *Appalachian Land Ownership Study, Volume VII, West Virginia*
     (Washington, DC: Appalachian Regional Commission, 1981), 6–7.

13   Appalachian Land Ownership Task Force, *Appalachian Land Ownership Study,*
     37.

14   Miller, *Who Owns West Virginia?,* 18.

15   Stephen Singer, "Massey May Move to West Virginia; Underwood Names
     Group to Study Taxes," *Charleston (WV) Daily Mail,* July 26, 1997; Stephen
     Singer, "Reform Measure Would Change Taxes Little, Data Show," Associated
     Press, January 14, 1999; Jennifer Bundy, "Tax Fairness Report Late, but 99%
     Done," *Charleston (WV) Gazette,* December 29, 1998; "State Plans to Shift Tax
     Emphasis," *Charleston (WV) Gazette,* August 9, 1998; Stephen Singer, "Panel
     Urges Revamping of Tax Code," *Charleston (WV) Daily Mail,* February 2, 1998.

16   Karen Fischer, "Study Says 'Lower End' Carries Tax Burden: Labor-Sponsored
     Report Contradicts Governor's Panel," *Charleston (WV) Daily Mail,* March
     24, 1999; Robin Capehart, "Governor's Commission on Fair Taxation Proposes
     Business," *Charleston (WV) Gazette,* March 30, 2000.

17   Jennifer Bundy, "House Leaders Say Tax Plan Will Not Pass As Is," Associated
     Press, July 13, 1999.

18   John C. Musgrave, *Valuation of Active and Reserve Coal Property for Ad Valorem
     Property Tax Purposes* (Charleston: West Virginia State Tax Department, 2004),
     25.

19   Massachusetts Taxpayers Foundation, *Massachusetts' Tax Burden Falls to Bottom
     Tier of States* (Boston: Massachusetts Taxpayers Foundation, 2004.)

20   Mehmet S. Tosun, "A Comparative Assessment of West Virginia's State Tax
     System," *The West Virginia Public Affairs Reporter* 19, no. 3 (Summer 2002): 2–7.

21 John Alexander Williams, *West Virginia: A History* (Morgantown: West Virginia University Press, 2001), 153.

22 Williams, *West Virginia: A History*, 153–154.

23 Paul Lutz, *From Governor to Cabby: The Political Career and Tragic Death of West Virginia's William Casey Marland, 1950–1965* (Huntington, WV: Marshall University Library Associates, 1996), 41–61. Also see Thomas F. Stafford, *Afflicting the Comfortable: Journalism and Politics in West Virginia*, chapter 5 (Morgantown: West Virginia University Press, 2005), 45–55.

24 Lutz, *From Governor to Cabby*, 220.

25 Lutz, *From Governor to Cabby*, xi, 220–242.

26 Jean Harris, "Severance, Telecommunications, Business Franchise Taxes Examined," *Charleston (WV) Gazette*, September 30, 1985. Enacted in 1985, the severance tax became effective July 1, 1987.

27 Otis Rice and Stephen Brown, *West Virginia: A History* (Lexington: University Press of Kentucky, 1993), 282.

28 Bennett Judkins, "The People's Respirator: Coalition Building and the Black Lung Association," *Fighting Back in Appalachia*, 225–241; Barbara Ellen Smith, *Digging Our Own Graves: Coal Miners and the Struggle over Black Lung Disease* (Philadelphia: Temple University Press, 1987), 83–85; Rice and Brown, *West Virginia: A History*, 284.

29 Rice and Brown, *West Virginia: A History*, 284–285.

30 Rice and Brown, *West Virginia: A History*, 287–289.

31 Rice and Brown, *West Virginia: A History*, 288–289.

32 West Virginia Department of Tax and Revenue and West Virginia Development Office, *Analysis and Recommendations for West Virginia Tax Incentives* (Charleston, WV: Department of Tax and Revenue, 2002), 10–12.

33 Center for Business and Economic Research, Gatton College of Business and Economics, *A Study on the Current Economic Impacts of the Appalachian Coal Industry and its Future in the Region: Final Report* (Louisville: University of Kentucky, March 27, 2001), 3.

34 Center for Business and Economic Research, *A Study on the Current Economic Impacts of the Appalachian Coal Industry*, 3.

35 George Bockosh, Barbara Fotta, and William McKewan, "Employment, Production, and Fatality Trends in the U.S. Coal Mining Industry," *Coal Age* 107 (October 28, 2002): 18–20.

36 Steve Fiscor, "Top Ten Mines of Appalachia," *Coal Age* 107 (March 1, 2002): 21–22; Bill Meister, "Top Ten Mines of Appalachia," *Coal Age* 107 (March 1, 2001): 40–43.

37 Bockosh et al., "Employment, Production, and Fatality Trends," *Coal Age*; Meister, "Top Ten Mines," *Coal Age*.

38 Bockosh et al., "Employment, Production, and Fatality Trends," *Coal Age;* Meister, "Top Ten Mines," *Coal Age.*

39 Edward Peeks, "Coal Industry Sees Better Times Ahead," *Charleston (WV) Gazette,* May 11, 2004.

40 United States Department of Energy, Energy Information Administration, *Monthly Mined Coal Statistics* (2003–2005), http://tonto.eia.doe/gov/FTPROOT/coal/weekly/monthprod2003tot.xls, http://tonto.eia.doe.gov/FTPROOT/coal/weekly/monthprod2004tot.xls, http://tonto.eia.doe.gov/FTPROOT/coal /weekly/monthprod2005tot.xls.

41 Ken Ward Jr., "Coal Industry Competition Made Mines Bigger," *Charleston (WV) Gazette,* June 6, 1999.

42 Josh Hafenbrack, "State Welfare Rolls Rise: Officials Cite Poor Economy Efforts to Assist Families," *Charleston (WV) Daily Mail,* September 25, 2003.

43 Hafenbrack, "State Welfare Rolls Rise," *Charleston (WV) Daily Mail*, September 25, 2003.

44 Hafenbrack, "State Welfare Rolls Rise," *Charleston (WV) Daily Mail,* September 25, 2003.

45 Chris Condon, Randy Childs, and Leah Bogdan, *County Data Profile: Kanawha County* (Morgantown: Bureau of Business and Economics, West Virginia University, 2000), 15.

46 Percentages are taken from page 15 of each of the following respective publications: *County Data Profile: Boone County; County Data Profile: Fayette County; County Data Profile: Logan County; County Data Profile: McDowell County; County Data Profile: Mingo County; County Data Profile: Nicholas County; County Data Profile: Raleigh County; County Data Profile: Wyoming County.* All data profiles were prepared by Chris Condon, Randy Childs, and Leah Bogdan, and all were published in 2000 by West Virginia University's Bureau of Business and Economics in Morgantown, WV.

47 Center for Business and Economic Research, *A Study on the Current Economic Impacts of the Appalachian Coal Industry,* 87.

48 Center for Business and Economic Research, *A Study on the Current Economic Impacts of the Appalachian Coal Industry,* 140–141.

49 For further discussion of *Bragg v. Robertson*, please see chapter 5.

50 Ken Ward Jr., "Mountaintop Removal Could Devastate Region: Federal Study Paints Ugly Picture for Much of State," *Charleston (WV) Gazette,* May 5, 2002.

51 Coal Operators and Associates, the Kentucky Coal Association, the National Mining Association, the Ohio Coal Association, and the West Virginia Coal Association to John Forren, US EPA, January 6, 2004, letter, *Joint Coal Industry Comments on the Mountaintop Mining/Valley Fill Draft Environmental Impact*

Statement (Charleston, WV: West Virginia Coal Association), 118, http://www
.wvcoal.com/resources/pdfs/FinalEIS.pdf.

52 Coal Operators and Associates et al., letter, 118.

53 United States Department of Energy, Energy Information Administration, *West
Virginia Coal Statistics, 1991, 1996–2000,* http://www.eia.doe.gov/cnAeaf/coal/cia/
a15p01.txt.

54 United States Department of Energy, Energy Information Administration,
Average Open Market Sales Price of Coal by State and Mine Type, http://www.eia
.doe.gov/cneaf/coal/page/acr/table28.html.

55 Coal Operators and Associates et al., letter, 124.

56 FPEIS, chapter 3, "Affected Environment and Consequences," III.K-15, 191.

57 Coal Operators and Associates et al., letter, 116.

58 Coal Operators and Associates et al., letter, 116.

59 "Engineer: No Harm in Haden's Ruling—Valley Fills Prohibited," *Coal Age* 107
(July 1, 2002): 11–12.

60 "Coal Truck Weight Fight Heading North," *Charleston (WV) Gazette-Mail,*
September 21, 2003.

61 "Coal's Victims: Just the Cost of Doing Business?," *Huntington (WV) Herald-
Dispatch,* July 19, 2003.

62 "Coal's Victims: Just the Cost of Doing Business?," *Huntington (WV) Herald-
Dispatch,* July 19, 2003.

63 "Coal Truck Bill Leaves DOH with Tough Road to Hoe," *(Morgantown, WV)
Dominion Post,* March 17, 2003.

64 Dan Radmacher, "Coal Truck Bill is an Economic Disaster for West Virginia,"
Charleston (WV) Gazette, February 28, 2003.

65 "Coal Truck Weight Fight Heading North," *Charleston (WV) Gazette-Mail,*
September 21, 2003.

66 "Coal Truck Weight Fight Heading North," *Charleston (WV) Gazette-Mail,*
September 21, 2003.

67 Flood Advisory Technical Task Force, *Runoff Analyses of Seng, Scrabble, and
Sycamore Creeks,* part 1 (Charleston, WV: Division of Environmental Protection,
2002), 2, 75.

68 Jim Wallace, "Officials Seek Renewal Funding: State Hopes Firm Can Find Money
for Demolitions," *Charleston (WV) Daily Mail,* July 5, 2002.

69 Jim Wallace, "Plan Would Redraw Lines of Towns in Flood Areas," *Charleston
(WV) Daily Mail,* August 28, 2002.

70 Jim Wallace, "Plan Would Redraw Lines," *Charleston (WV) Daily Mail,* August 28,
2002.

71 Martha Bryson Hodel, "Flood Recovery Looking at Long-Term Solutions,"

Associated Press, August 27, 2002; Jim Wallace, "Plan Would Redraw Lines," *Charleston (WV) Daily Mail,* August 28, 2002.

72 Jim Wallace, "Mayors Oppose Moving to New Developments; Mountaintop Spots Aren't the Answer, Two Officials Say," *Charleston (WV) Gazette,* August 30, 2002.

73 Jim Wallace, "Mayors Oppose Moving to New Developments," *Charleston (WV) Gazette,* August 30, 2002.

74 Wallace, "Mayors Oppose Moving to New Developments," *Charleston (WV) Gazette,* August 30, 2002.

75 "Flooding: Taxpayers Should Decide on Bonds," *Raleigh Register-Herald,* March 4, 2004.

76 Mary Catherine Brooks, "Three Inches of Rain Cause Millions in Destruction," *Raleigh Register-Herald,* January 5, 2004.

77 I learned about these floods from conversations with numerous personal acquaintances, family members, and friends affected by them.

78 Ken Ward Jr., "Mountaintop Mining Ban Would Cut Coal Production 10 Percent," *Charleston (WV) Gazette,* July 23, 1999.

79 Ward, "Mountaintop Mining Ban," *Charleston (WV) Gazette,* July 23, 1999.

80 Robert Bays, "Mountaintop Removal Foes Have Broader Agenda," *Charleston (WV) Gazette,* April 12, 1999.

81 Bays, "Mountaintop Removal Foes," *Charleston (WV) Gazette,* April 12, 1999.

82 Paul Wilson, "Marmet Landowner Hopes to Lure Wal-Mart by Removing the Mountaintop on His Property," *Charleston (WV) Gazette,* November 22, 2003.

83 "New Mayor Proposes Mountaintop Removal," *(Morgantown, WV) Dominion Post,* January 12, 2003.

84 FPEIS, chapter 3, "Affected Environment and Consequences," III.T-4, 299.

85 FPEIS, chapter 3, "Affected Environment and Consequences," III.T-4, 300.

86 Jim Balow, "Don't Leave Coal Out of Future, Consultant Says," *Charleston (WV) Gazette,* January 13, 2004.

87 "Economic Diversity Key to Region's Future," *Raleigh Register-Herald,* June 29, 1998.

88 Mary Catherine Brooks, "Next Coalfields Expressway Design Due Soon," November 22, 2006.

89 Mannix Porterfield, "Lawmakers Still Miffed Over Road Strategy," October 16, 2006.

90 Mannix Porterfield, "Lawmakers Still Miffed," October 16, 2006.

91 Mannix Porterfield, "Lawmakers Still Miffed," October 16, 2006.

92 Mannix Porterfield, "Lawmakers Still Miffed," October 16, 2006.

93 West Virginia Department of Transportation, Division of Highways, "Memorandum: Six Year Highway Improvement Plan," State of West Virginia,

June 15, 2005, rev. June 2006, http://www.wvdot.com/6-year-plan/Content%20 Files/Letter.pdf, October 15, 2006.

94   Phil Kabler, "Official Walks 134 Miles for Better Roads," *Charleston (WV) Gazette*, September 26, 2006; Mary Catherine Brooks, "Stover Walks from Welch to Charleston," *Raleigh Register-Herald*, September 22, 2006; Fred Pace, "Circuit Clerk Walking to Charleston," *Raleigh Register-Herald*, September 16, 2006.

95   "Hatfield-McCoy Trail System Revives Coalfield Economies," *Charleston (WV) Gazette,* April 29, 2003.

96   "Hatfield-McCoy Trail System," *Charleston (WV) Gazette,* April 29, 2003.

97   "Hatfield-McCoy Trail System," *Charleston (WV) Gazette,* April 29, 2003.

98   Si Galperin, "Testimony at the Edmondson Hearing; Part Two from Appalachian Strip Mining Information Service," strip-mining collection, A&M 2618, Box 1, ff1, West Virginia and Regional History Collection, West Virginia University.

99   Karin Fischer, "Senate Suspends Rules, Passes Mining Measures," *Charleston (WV) Daily Mail*, March 5, 1999; Ken Ward Jr., "EPA Urges Veto of Bill Making Valley Fills Easier," *Charleston (WV) Gazette*, March 28, 1998; Steve Myers, "Governor Now Favors Tighter Mining Rules; Underwood Urges State DEP Officials to Apply Old Laws," *Charleston (WV) Daily Mail*, August 6, 1998.

100 George Hohmann, "Economic Panel Eyes Mining Bill-Policy Setters Must Prepare for Coalfield Development Office," *Charleston (WV) Daily Mail*, March 31, 1999.

101 Ken Ward Jr., "Strip-mined Acreage Up Again in W.Va.," *Charleston (WV) Gazette*, November 4, 2003.

102 Sam Truman, "Mining and Money: Supporter, Opponents Clash on Effects of Surface Mining, Reclamation," *Charleston (WV) Daily Mail,* June 14, 2002.

103 Paul J. Nyden, "Perpetrator or Victim? Man at Center of Supreme Court Controversy Speaks," *Charleston (WV) Gazette*, September 23, 2004.

104 Nyden, "Perpetrator or Victim?," *Charleston (WV) Gazette*, September 23, 2004; Chris Wetterich, "Court Rules Abuse Reporting Law Not Applicable in Pendleton Case," *Charleston (WV) Gazette*, December 4, 2003; "School Sex Abuse Lawsuit May Settle for $500,000," Associated Press, September 22, 2004; "Former Students Sue Pendleton Board; Suit Alleges School Officials Knew Teacher Was a Sexual Predator," *Charleston (WV) Daily Mail*, May 19, 2005.

105 Toby Coleman, "Court Race Focus Stays on Case, McGraw Defends Decision; Benjamin Says He is Qualified," *Charleston (WV) Gazette*, October 7, 2004.

106 "Potshots Continue in High Court Race; On Both Sides, Backers Have a Little History," *Charleston (WV) Daily Mail*, October 18, 2004.

107 Vicki Smith, "Massey Chief Now Taking Aim at Starcher; Justice, Who Has Not Decided about 2008 Run, Says Blankenship Interested Only in Profit," *Charleston (WV) Daily Mail*, October 27, 2005.

108 Smith, "Massey Chief Now Taking Aim at Starcher," *Charleston (WV) Daily Mail*, October 27, 2005; Christian Giggenbach, "Democrats Unified Against Blankenship," *Raleigh Register-Herald*, July 30, 2006.

109 Christian Giggenbach, "Democrats Unified Against Blankenship," *Raleigh Register-Herald*, July 30, 2006.

110 Lawrence Messina, "Democrats to Target Blankenship," *Charleston (WV) Daily Mail*, September 4, 2006.

111 "Blankenship Effort for GOP Largely Fails," *Charleston (WV) Gazette*, November 8, 2006; "The Blankenship Factor," *Raleigh Register-Herald*, November 8, 2006; Justin Anderson, "No Love for Blankenship at Polls," *Charleston (WV) Daily Mail*, November 8, 2006.

112 Scott Finn, "Blankenship Hurt GOP, Chairman Says," *Charleston (WV) Gazette*, November 9, 2006.

113 McFerrin, "Mountaintop Removal is Harmful Tool of Dying Industry," *Charleston (WV) Gazette*, January 18, 1999.

114 West Virginia People's Election Reform Coalition: Common Cause West Virginia, Ohio Valley Environmental Coalition, West Virginia Citizen Research Group, and West Virginia Citizen Action Group, *2004 Election Cycle Report*, http://www.wvcag.org/issues/clean_elections/perc2004.pdf, October 1, 2006.

115 West Virginia People's Election Reform Coalition: Mountain State Education and Research Foundation, Ohio Valley Environmental Coalition, and West Virginia Citizen Action Group, *2002 Election Cycle Report*, http://www.wvcag.org/issues/clean_elections/perc2004.pdf, October 1, 2006.

116 Lake, Snell, Perry, and Associates, *New Poll Findings On Mountaintop Removal in West Virginia. Opposition to Mountaintop Removal is Broad and Deep* (Washington, DC: Lake, Snell, Perry, and Associates, 2004), http://www.appalachian-center.org/poll_results/index.html, conducted for the Appalachian Center for the Economy and the Environment, July 14, 2004.

117 Squillace, *Strip Mining Handbook,* 137.

118 Ken Ward Jr., "Wise, Rahall Blast Coal Permit Process," *Charleston (WV) Gazette*, May 5, 1998.

119 Ken Ward Jr., "Congressman Criticizes OSM: Agency Must Improve Mountaintop Removal Efforts, Rahall Says," *Charleston (WV) Gazette*, February 28, 1999.

120 Ward, "Wise, Rahall Blasts Coal Permit Process," *Charleston (WV) Gazette*, May 5, 1998.

121 Ken Ward, Jr., "Rahall Blasts OSM; Wise Wants Permit Moratorium," *Charleston (WV) Gazette*, August 11, 1998.

122 Ward, "Rahall Blasts OSM; Wise Wants Permit Moratorium," *Charleston (WV) Gazette*, August 11, 1998.

123 Mannix Porterfield, "Rahall Stands by Mountaintop Mining," *Raleigh Register-Herald*, December 21, 2002.

124 Mannix Porterfield, "Rahall Stands by Mountaintop Mining," *Raleigh Register-Herald*, December 21, 2002.

125 "West Virginia Congressman Lends Perspective on Mining Issues," *Coal Age* 107 (March 2002): 40.

126 "West Virginia Congressman Lends Perspective on Mining Issues," *Coal Age* 107 (March 2002): 40.

127 "West Virginia Congressman Lends Perspective on Mining Issues," *Coal Age* 107 (March 2002): 40; for further discussion of *Bragg v. Robertson,* please see chapter 5.

128 The Wilderness Society, press release, "Rahall Wins Ansel Adams Award for Efforts to Protect Nation's Lands" (Washington, DC: Wilderness Society, June 2, 2004).

129 Ken Ward Jr., "Congressmen Want Windmill Study," *Charleston (WV) Gazette*, June 27, 2004.

130 Ward, "Congressmen Want Windmill Study," *Charleston (WV) Gazette*, June 27, 2004.

131 Ward, "Congressmen Want Windmill Study," *Charleston (WV) Gazette*, June 27, 2004.

132 Jim Zoia for Congressman Nick J. Rahall to the author, September 28, 2004, e-mail, *Congressman Rahall General Position Paper on Southern West Virginia Coal.*

133 Montrie, "To Save the Land and People," 194.

134 Montrie, "To Save the Land and People," 199; Strip Mining Collection, box 1, ff1, WVRH.

135 "Excerpts from a Speech at Morris Harvey College," January 15, 1972, Strip Mining Collection, box 1, ff1, WVRH.

136 Montrie, "To Save the Land and People," 200, 206.

137 Montrie, "To Save the Land and People," 215–216.

138 United States Senator John D. Rockefeller to the author, personal letter, January 21, 2005.

139 United States Senator John D. Rockefeller to the author, personal letter, January 21, 2005.

140 Robert Byrd, Jay Rockefeller, Nick Rahall, Bob Wise, and Alan Mollohan, "Balance Needed in Mining Issue," *Charleston (WV) Gazette*, November 7, 1999.

141 Francis X. Clines, "With 500 Miners as a Chorus, Byrd Attacks Court Ruling," *New York Times*, November 10, 1999.

142 Francis X. Clines, "With 500 Miners as a Chorus, Byrd Attacks Court Ruling," *New York Times*, November 10, 1999.

143 Tom Kenworthy and Juliet Eilperin, "White House Backs W.Va. on Mine Dumping; Conservationists Say Action Undermines Vetoes, Conflicts with Environmental Stance," *Washington Post*, October 30, 1999.

144 Senate, Senator Robert Byrd speaking to the Senate on mountaintop mining, *Congressional Record* (November 18, 1999), S14783.

145 Senate, Senator Robert Byrd speaking to the Senate on mountaintop mining, *Congressional Record* (November 18, 1999), S14783.

146 "Lord of the 'Fies' Defeat Gives Everyone Time," *Charleston (WV) Gazette*, November 24, 1999.

147 "Lord of the 'Fies' Defeat Gives Everyone Time," *Charleston (WV) Gazette*, November 24, 1999; Senate, Byrd, S14784.

148 Senate, Byrd, S14781.

149 Ken Ward Jr., "Clinton Backs off Mining Rider: Byrd Legislation Unnecessary in Light of Stay, White House Says," *Charleston (WV) Gazette*, October 31, 1999.

150 Ken Ward Jr., "Clinton Backs off Mining Rider," *Charleston (WV) Gazette*, October 31, 1999.

151 Senate, Byrd, S14784.

152 United States Senator Robert C. Byrd to the author, personal letter, September 17, 2004.

153 "Slicing Peaks, Burying Streams," *Washington Post*, April 13, 2000.

154 Ken Ward Jr., "Valley Fill Rule Rewrite Due by April," *Charleston (WV) Gazette*, February 26, 2002; Ken Ward Jr., "Senate Panel to Hold Hearings on Fill Rule: Toilets, Junk Cars Could Go Into Fills," *Charleston (WV) Gazette*, February 27, 2002.

155 "Slicing Peaks, Burying Streams," *Washington Post*, April 13, 2000.

156 Christopher Shays, press release, February 12, 2003, http://www.house.gov/shays/news/2003/february/febpallone.htm.

157 Christopher Shays, press release, February 12, 2003, http://www.house.gov/shays/ncws/2003/february/febpallone.htm.

158 Ken Ward Jr., "Bill Would Make Haden Ruling Law," *Charleston (WV) Gazette*, February 17, 2003.

159 Congress, House, *Federal Water Pollution Control Act Amendment to Clarify that Fill Material Cannot be Comprised of Waste*, 109th Cong., 2d sess., 2005 H.R. 2719, *Bill Summary and Status for the 108th Cong.* (May 26, 2005).

160 Shays, press release, February 12, 2003.

161 Congress, House, *Federal Water Pollution Control Act*.

162 In particular, *Kentuckians for the Commonwealth v. Rivenburgh*. Please see *Kentuckians for the Commonwealth v. Rivenburgh*, U.S.D.C. for the Southern District of West Virginia (May 2002). See chapter 5, fn 33.

163 Ken Ward Jr., "Valley Fill Rule Rewrite Due by April," *Charleston (WV) Gazette*, February 26, 2002.

164 Ken Ward Jr., "Bush Administration Plan Broadens Valley Fill Rule Changes: Cars, Toilets Could Be Dumped into Streams," *Charleston (WV) Gazette*, April 26, 2002.

165 *Kentuckians for the Commonwealth v. Rivenburgh*, 5.

166 *Kentuckians for the Commonwealth v. Rivenburgh*, 37.

167 *Kentuckians for the Commonwealth v. Rivenburgh*, 40, 41; Ken Ward Jr., "Judge Blocks New Valley Fills: Corps of Engineers' Practice Illegal, Violates Clean Water Act, Haden Rules," *Charleston (WV) Gazette, May 9, 2002.*

168 Ken Ward Jr., "U.S. Asks Haden to Suspend Fill Ruling," *Charleston (WV) Gazette*, May 14, 2002.

169 *Kentuckians for the Commonwealth v. Rivenburgh*, Memorandum Opinion and Understanding, U.S.D.C. for the Southern District of West Virginia (July 2002), 41.

170 Ken Ward Jr., "Haden Won't Suspend Valley Fill Ruling," *Charleston (WV) Gazette,* June 18, 2002.

171 Ken Ward Jr., "Mine Ruling Tossed: Haden's Valley Fills Ruling Overturned Again," *Charleston (WV) Gazette*, January 30, 2003.

172 Ted Williams, "Sludge Slinging," *Audubon* (May 2004), http://magazine .audubon.org/incite/incite0405.html; Ken Ward Jr., "Mine Inspector Settles Fight with MSHA, Retires," *Charleston (WV) Gazette*, October 9, 2004.

173 Ken Ward Jr., "Fill Rule Removes Stream Protections," *Charleston (WV) Gazette*, January 8, 2004.

174 John Raby, "Buffer Proposal 'Absurd'; Mountaintop Mine Rules Changes Gain Opposition," *Charleston (WV) Gazette*, August 27, 2005.

175 McGinley, "From Pick and Shovel to Mountaintop Removal," 77.

Chapter 5

The epigraph to this chapter is drawn from *Kentuckians for the Commonwealth v Rivenburgh,* denial of stay, 43.

1 *Federal Water Pollution Control Act*, U.S. Code, title 33, chapter 26, sec. 1251 (2005); Corps of Engineers, Department of the Army, Nationwide Permit Program. Code of Federal Regulations, title 33, parts 330.1(b) and 330, appendix A (2003).

2   *Federal Water Pollution Control Act*, U.S. Code, title 33, chapter 26, sec. 1251 (2005); Corps of Engineers, Department of the Army, Nationwide Permit Program. Code of Federal Regulations, title 33, parts 330.1(b) and 330, appendix A (2003).

3   For further information on the long political trip to obtain passage of SMCRA, please see chapter 1.

4   Surface Mining Control and Reclamation Act of 1977, U.S. Code, title 30, sec. 1201(c) (1995).

5   Surface Mining Control and Reclamation Act of 1977, U.S. Code, title 30, sec. 1201(j) (1995).

6   Michael G. Crotty, "Bragg v. West Virginia Mining Association: The Eleventh Amendment Challenge to Mountaintop Coal Mining," *Villanova Environmental Law Journal* 13 (2002): 287–311; *SMCRA*, 30 U.S.C. 1254(b)–(c).

7   Ken Ward Jr., "Corps Says It Doesn't Regulate Valley Fills: Stance Could Help Suit Over Mountaintop Removal," *Charleston (WV) Gazette,* July 19, 1998; *Bragg v. Robertson*, 1998 U.S. Dist. Lexis 22077 (S.D. W.Va. 1998); Jack McCarthy, "Judge Upholds EPA's Authority," *Charleston (WV) Gazette*, December 29, 1989; *West Virginia Coal Association v. Reilly*, 1989 U.S. Dist. Lexis 15881 (S.D. W.Va. 1989).

8   *Bragg v. Robertson*, October 9, 1998.

9   Ward, "Corps Says It Doesn't Regulate Valley Fills," *Charleston (WV) Gazette*, July 19, 1998.

10 Ward, "Corps Says It Doesn't Regulate Valley Fills," *Charleston (WV) Gazette*, July 19, 1998.

11 Ward, "Corps Says It Doesn't Regulate Valley Fills," *Charleston (WV) Gazette*, July 19, 1998.

12 Paul Nyden, "Legal Agreement May Save Mountaintops: New Limits Placed on Strip Operations," *Charleston (WV) Gazette*, December 24, 1998.

13 Ken Ward Jr., "Controversial Mining Permit Issued: Mountaintop Project to Face Challenges on Several Fronts," *Charleston (WV) Gazette*, November 4, 1998.

14 Ken Ward Jr., "Ruling Sets Up Next Mining Battle: Judge Refuses to Revoke Mountaintop Removal Permit in Prelude to Long Legal Fight," *Charleston (WV) Gazette*, November 10, 1998.

15 *Bragg v. Robertson*, Memorandum Opinion and Order granting preliminary injunction, March 3, 1999.

16 *Bragg v. Robertson*, Memorandum Opinion and Order granting preliminary injunction, March 3, 1999.

17 Ken Ward Jr., "Corps Withdraws Arch Coal Permit: 'New Material Facts' Send Federal Agency in Opposite Direction," *Charleston (WV) Gazette*, June 25, 1999.

18 Ward, "Corps Withdraws Arch Coal Permit," *Charleston (WV) Gazette*, June 25, 1999.

19 Ken Ward Jr., "Dal-Tex Mining to Cease Friday: Shutdown to Put 210 Out of Work," *Charleston (WV) Gazette*, July 22, 1999.

20 Ken Ward Jr., "Mountaintop Removal Settlement Filed," *Charleston (WV) Gazette*, July 27, 1999; Ken Ward Jr., "Haden Schedules Friday Hearing on Mining Settlement," *Charleston (WV) Gazette*, July 28, 1999.

21 Ken Ward Jr., "Valley Fill Mining Outlawed: Landmark Ruling Prohibits Mountaintop Coal Operators from Burying State Streams," *Charleston (WV) Gazette*, October 21, 1999.

22 *Bragg v. Robertson*, Memorandum Opinion and Order, 18.

23 *Bragg v. Robertson*, Memorandum Opinion and Order, 24.

24 *Bragg v. Robertson*, Memorandum Opinion and Order, 43.

25 *Bragg v. Robertson*, Memorandum Opinion and Order, 44.

26 *Bragg v. Robertson*, Memorandum Opinion and Order. Also, see the *Charleston Gazette* on any day from October 21 through October 29, 1999, when stories appear regarding the "consequences" of Haden's decisions. A perusal of local papers in southern West Virginia coal counties reveals the same thing. In particular, the *Logan Banner* in Logan County was especially vocal, going so far as to call the decision a declaration of war (see the March 9, 1999 edition, "This is War"); across the country, the Associated Press released a story headlined "Mountaintop Removal Ban May Kill Coal, Critics Say."

27 For further information on this political struggle, please see chapter 4.

28 *Bragg v. West Virginia Coal Association*, 248 F.3d 275 (4th Cir. 2001). Note that while the case is still the same exact case as *Bragg v. Robertson*, the name of the case changed once the case went to the Fourth Circuit.

29 Ken Ward Jr., "Lawsuit Challenges Coal Mining Permit," *Charleston (WV) Gazette*, October 24, 2003.

30 Ken Ward Jr., "Judge Blocks Massey Permit: Full Hearing is Scheduled for Stream Fill," *Charleston (WV) Gazette*, April 6, 2004.

31 Ken Ward Jr., "Judge Blocks Massey Fill Plan," *Charleston (WV) Gazette*, April 8, 2004.

32 Ward, "Judge Blocks Massey Fill Plan," *Charleston (WV) Gazette*, April 8, 2004.

33 Please see chapter 6 for further discussion of this topic.

34 Ken Ward Jr., "Judge Adds 10 Days to Order Blocking Massey Stream Fill," *Charleston (WV) Gazette*, April 13, 2004.

35 Ken Ward Jr., "Massey Fill Started Before Permit Plan Complete, Judge Told," *Charleston (WV) Gazette*, April 23, 2004.

36 Ken Ward Jr., "Environmental Group Seeks Quick Ruling in Mining Case,"

Charleston (WV) Gazette, May 12, 2004.

37 *Ohio Valley Environmental Coalition et al. v. William Bulen*, 315 F. Supp. 2d 821
(S.D. W.Va. 2004); Ken Ward Jr., "Environmental Group Seeks Quick Ruling in
Mining Case," *Charleston (WV) Gazette*, May 12, 2004.

38 *Ohio Valley Environmental Coalition et al. v. William Bulen*, 315 F. Supp. 2d 821
(S.D. W.Va. 2004); Ken Ward Jr., "Environmental Group Seeks Quick Ruling in
Mining Case," *Charleston (WV) Gazette*, May 12, 2004.

39 *Ohio Valley Environmental Coalition et al. v. William Bulen*, 315 F. Supp. 2d 821
(S.D. W.Va. 2004); Ken Ward Jr., "Environmental Group Seeks Quick Ruling in
Mining Case," *Charleston (WV) Gazette*, May 12, 2004.

40 Ken Ward Jr., "Goodwin Mine Ruling 'Whole New Ballgame,'" *Charleston (WV)
Gazette*, July 18, 2004.

41 Chris Wetterich, "U.S. Judge Curtails Valley Fills. Environmentalists See Big
Win in Fight Against Mountaintop Removal," *Charleston (WV) Gazette*, July 9,
2004; *Ohio Valley Environmental Coalition et al. v. William Bulen*, Memorandum
Opinion and Injunctive Order, Civil Action Number 3:03-2281 (S.D. W.Va. July
8, 2004).

42 Martha Bryson Hodel, "Judge Asked to Expand Ruling on Valley Fills:
Environmentalists Cite Six Other Mines," *Charleston (WV) Gazette*, July 23,
2004; Ken Ward Jr., "Judge Expands Ruling Blocking Coal Mines from Getting
Simplified Fill Permits," *Charleston (WV) Gazette*, August 14, 2004.

43 Ken Ward Jr., "Goodwin Declines to Clarify Mountaintop Removal Ruling,"
Charleston (WV) Gazette, September 1, 2004.

44 Lawrence Messina, "Corps to Appeal Federal Mining Ruling," Associated Press,
September 2, 2004.

45 Larry O'Dell, "Appeals Court Reinstates Mountaintop Removal Permits,"
Associated Press, November 23, 2005; *Ohio Valley Environmental Coalition v.
Bulen*, 429 F.3d 493 (4th Cir. 2005).

46 Ken Ward Jr., "Mountaintop Mining Rehearing Denied, 5-3; Two W.Va. Appeals
Court Judges Dissent," *Charleston Gazette*, February 16, 2006; *Ohio Valley
Environmental Coalition v. Bulen*, 437 F.3d 421 (4th Cir. 2006).

47 While not dealing specifically with MTR in West Virginia, the Fourth Circuit
Court also reversed another Judge Charles Haden decision in a case called
Kentuckians for the Commonwealth v. Rivenburgh. The lawsuit hoped to stop
the burying of six miles of Kentucky streams beneath twenty-seven separate
valley fills. Again, Haden ruled for the plaintiffs, and the permittee in question,
Beech Fork Processing, even admitted that they could mine the coal without the
valley fills. Upon appeal, the Fourth Circuit again overturned Haden, this time
noting that Haden's decision was "overbroad" and overreached the case brought

before him. For further information on this case, please see various articles from August 2001 through January 2003 in the *Charleston Gazette* and the *Charleston Daily Mail*. See also Haden's original decision of May 8, 2002, where he once again noted the illegality of valley fills under the Clean Water Act: *Kentuckians for the Commonwealth v. Rivenburgh*, 2002 U.S. Dist. Lexis 12048 (S.D. W.Va. 2002), and the Fourth Circuit Court's overturning of Haden's decision: *Kentuckians for the Commonwealth v. Rivenburgh*, 317 F.3d 425 (4th Cir. 2003).

48 Lewis, *Transforming the Appalachian Countryside,* 115, 117.

49 Lewis, *Transforming the Appalachian Countryside,* 118.

50 Ken Ward Jr., "DEP Backs off Massey Dust Problems; Surface Mine Board to Hear Arguments This Week over Problems in Sylvester," *Charleston (WV) Gazette*, October 22, 2000.

51 Ken Ward Jr., "DEP Backs off Massey Dust Problems," *Charleston (WV) Gazette*, October 22, 2000.

52 Ken Ward Jr., "Massey Told to Fix Dust Problems," *Charleston (WV) Gazette*, October 26, 2004.

53 Ken Ward Jr., "Sylvester Residents Sue Massey Coal Subsidiary: Dust and Noise," *Charleston (WV) Gazette*, February 4, 2001; Ken Ward Jr., "Massey Coal Dust Trial Opens in Boone County," *Charleston (WV) Gazette*, December 13, 2002; Mary Miller interview; Pauline Canterberry interview. For further information on the dust's effects on the school, please see chapter 3.

54 Brian Bowling, "Massey President Blames Dust on Trucks, Not Plant," *Charleston (WV) Daily Mail*, April 18, 2001.

55 Ken Ward Jr., "Massey Cited Again for Dust in Sylvester," *Charleston (WV) Gazette*, November 18, 2001.

56 "Sylvester Rain of Dust Continues," *Charleston (WV) Gazette*, November 21, 2001.

57 Brian Bowling, "Elk Run Ordered to Fix Dust Problem," *Charleston (WV) Daily Mail*, November 29, 2001.

58 Ken Ward Jr., "Massey Dust Order Repeated," *Charleston (WV) Gazette*, November 30, 2001.

59 Ken Ward Jr., "State Wants Dome Details; Massey Proposal Has Friday Deadline," *Charleston (WV) Gazette*, December 18, 2001; Ken Ward Jr., "Coal 'Dome' Finished by May, Massey Says," *Charleston (WV) Gazette*, December 22, 2001.

60 "DEP Issues Citation Against Massey Subsidiary Elk Run Coal," Associated Press, March 3, 2002.

61 "Boone County Mine Denied Permit for Increased Truck Traffic," Associated Press, April 23, 2002; Paul Nyden, "DEP Denies Massey's Permit Request," *Charleston (WV) Gazette*, April 29, 2002.

62 Brian Bowling, "Sylvester's Dust Getting Covered: $1.5 million Dome Latest Effort to Comply with State," *Charleston (WV) Daily Mail*, June 25, 2002.

63 Paul Nyden, "Massey CEO Says Company Looking to Ky," *Charleston (WV) Gazette*, July 20, 2002.

64 Gavin McCormick, "Massey Pays Flood Bill: Logan Residents Receive Cars, New Homes," *Charleston (WV) Gazette*, August 13, 2002.

65 Ken Ward Jr., "Massey Wants Violations Kept Out of Trial," *Charleston (WV) Gazette*, November 23, 2002; Ken Ward Jr., "Jury Won't See Massey Violations; Judge Rules on Evidence in Sylvester Dust Suit," *Charleston (WV) Gazette*, December 11, 2002; Brian Bowling, "Fines Don't Point to Fault, Lawyer Says; Attorney Claims Overeager Officials are to Blame," *Charleston (WV) Daily Mail*, December 11, 2002; "Supreme Court Won't Intervene in Coal Pollution Trial," Associated Press, December 19, 2002.

66 Ken Ward Jr., "Massey Coal Dust Trial Opens in Boone County," *Charleston (WV) Gazette*, December 13, 2002.

67 Ken Ward Jr., "Most Elk Run Trucks Overweight, Jury Told," *Charleston (WV) Gazette*, December 19, 2002.

68 Ken Ward Jr., "Massey Costs Town $4 Million in Property Value, Jury Hears," *Charleston (WV) Gazette*, January 25, 2003.

69 Brian Bowling, "Massey Subsidiary Begins Defense in Coal Dust Case," *Charleston (WV) Daily Mail*, January 31, 2003; Ken Ward Jr., "Massey Energy Starts Defense in Sylvester Dust Court Case," *Charleston (WV) Gazette*, January 31, 2003.

70 Martha Bryson Hodel, "Jury Finds Massey Subsidiary Liable in Coal Dust Case," Associated Press, February 7, 2003.

71 Hodel, "Jury Finds Massey Subsidiary Liable in Coal Dust Case," Associated Press, February 7, 2003; also see *Ralph Anderson et al. v. Elk Run Coal Company, Inc.*, 2003 Cir. Ct of Boone County, West Virginia (April 8, 2003).

72 Please see chapter 3 for further discussion of the continuing dust problems in Sylvester.

73 Trial Lawyers for Public Justice, press release, "Citizens' Group and TLPJ Sue Federal and State Regulators to Fix West Virginia's Coal Mining Program," November 14, 2000, http://www.tlpj.org/pr/wv_coal.htm, October 21, 2006; *West Virginia Highlands Conservancy v. Norton*, 2001 U.S. Dist. Lexis 4441 (S.D. W.Va. 2001).

74 *West Virginia Highlands Conservancy v. Norton*, 2001 U.S. Dist. Lexis 4441 (S.D. W.Va. 2001).

75 *West Virginia Highlands Conservancy v. Norton*, 2001 U.S. Dist. Lexis 4441 (S.D. W.Va. 2001).

76 *West Virginia Highlands Conservancy v. Norton*, 2001 U.S. Dist. Lexis 4441 (S.D.

W.Va. 2001); *West Virginia Highlands Conservancy v. Norton*, 2001 U.S. Dist. Lexis 7038 (S.D. W.Va. 2001); *West Virginia Highlands Conservancy v. Norton*, 2001 U.S. Dist. Lexis 13574 (S.D. W.Va. 2001).

77 *West Virginia Highlands Conservancy v. Norton*, 2002 U.S. Dist. Lexis 4597 (S.D. W.Va. 2002). Note that by this time, Owens had stepped down in her role as director of the Office of Surface Mining and was replaced by Jeffrey Jarrett, whose name now appeared in the court case in place of Owens'.

78 *West Virginia Highlands Conservancy v. Norton*, 2003 U.S. Dist. Lexis 292 (S.D. W.Va. 2003); Trial Lawyers for Public Justice, press release.

79 *Ark Land Company v. Rhonda Gail Harper, Edward A. Caudill, Rose M. Thompson, Edith D. Kitchen, Therman R. Caudill, John A. Caudill, Jr., Tammy Willis, and Lucille M. Miller*, 2004 W.Va. Lexis 24 (W.Va. Sup. Ct. 2004); Ken Ward Jr., "Court Blocks Forced Sale of Lincoln Family's Land," *Charleston (WV) Gazette*, May 8, 2004.

80 *Ark Land Company v. Rhonda Gail Harper*, 2004.

81 *Ark Land Company v. Rhonda Gail Harper*, 2004.

82 Ken Ward Jr., "Forced Land Sale for Mine Debated in Supreme Court," *Charleston (WV) Gazette,* April 1, 2004.

83 Ward, "Forced Land Sale for Mine Debated in Supreme Court," *Charleston (WV) Gazette,* April 1, 2004.

84 Ward, "Forced Land Sale for Mine Debated in Supreme Court," *Charleston (WV) Gazette,* April 1, 2004.

85 Ward, "Forced Land Sale for Mine Debated in Supreme Court," *Charleston (WV) Gazette,* April 1, 2004.

86 *Ark Land Company v. Rhonda Gail Harper*, 2004.

87 Randy Coleman, "State's $43 Million May Not Be Enough for Flood Recovery," *Charleston (WV) Gazette*, August 10, 2001; Shirley Stewart, "What Caused the Flood to Be So Devastating?," *(Pineville, WV) Independent Herald*, July 18, 2001. While more than $150 million in damages occurred, the state was responsible for a fraction of that, a little more than $43 million—which was still, of course, a significant amount of money for a cash-strapped state.

88 Ken Ward Jr., "State Court to Hear Flood Case that Blames Mines, Timbering," *Charleston (WV) Gazette*, June 8, 2004.

89 Ward, "State Court to Hear Flood Case that Blames Mines, Timbering," *Charleston (WV) Gazette*, June 8, 2004.

90 *Flood Litigation, No. 31688, Plaintiff's Supplemental Brief*, 2004 (W.Va. Sup. Ct. August 3, 2004), http://www.state.wv.us/wvsca/clerk/cases/FloodLitigation/3168 8PlaintiffSupp.pdf.

91 *Flood Litigation, No. 31688, Plaintiff's Supplemental Brief*, 2004 (W.Va. Sup. Ct.

August 3, 2004), http://www.state.wv.us/wvsca/clerk/cases/FloodLitigation/3168
8PlaintiffSupp.pdf.

92 *Flood Litigation, No. 31688, Plaintiff's Supplemental Brief*, 2004 (W.Va. Sup. Ct.
August 3, 2004), http://www.state.wv.us/wvsca/clerk/cases/FloodLitigation/3168
8PlaintiffSupp.pdf.

93 *Flood Litigation, No. 31688, Defendant's Supplemental Brief*, 2004 (W.Va. Sup. Ct.
August 2, 2004), http://www.state.wv.us/wvsca/clerk/cases/FloodLitigation/3168
8DefendantSupp.pdf.

94 Ken Ward Jr., "Flood Case to Open; Mining, Logging Runoff at Issue," *Charleston
(WV) Gazette*, March 10, 2006.

95 Audrey Stanton, "Defense Rests in Flood Trial," *Raleigh Register-Herald*, April 26,
2006.

96 Audrey Stanton, "Jury Finds for Plaintiffs in Flood Case," *Raleigh Register-Herald*,
May 2, 2006.

97 Audrey Stanton, "Coal River Watershed Claims Dismissed," *Raleigh Register-
Herald*, January 22, 2007.

98 Ken Ward Jr., "Trial Set in Latest Mountaintop Removal Case," *Charleston (WV)
Gazette*, October 3, 2006.

99 Ken Ward Jr., "Experts Testify on Damage from Mining; Lawsuit Targets Corps
of Engineers' Mountaintop Removal Permit Process," *Charleston (WV) Gazette*,
October 4, 2006.

100 Ken Ward Jr., "Fills Burying Valuable Streams, Judge Told; Georgia Ecologist
Testifies in 2nd Day of Trial over Restricting Mountaintop Removal," *Charleston
(WV) Gazette*, October 5, 2006; Ken Ward Jr., "Mining Case Ruling Not
Expected Soon," *Charleston (WV) Gazette*, October 17, 2006.

Chapter 6

The epigraph to this chapter is drawn from Theodore Roosevelt, *Seventh Annual
Message to the Senate and House of Representatives*, from John Woolley and
Gerhard Peters, The American Presidency Project [online]. Santa Barbara, CA:
University of California (hosted), Gerhard Peters (database), http://www
.presidency.ucsb.edu/ws/?pid=29548.

1 Lewis, *Transforming the Appalachian Countryside*, 5.

2 Davis, *Where There Are Mountains: An Environmental History of the Southern
Appalachians* (Athens: University of Georgia Press, 2000), 166–169.

3 Davis, *Where There Are Mountains*, 212

4 The Appalachian Land Ownership Task Force, *Who Owns Appalachia?*

Landownership and Its Impact (Lexington, KY: University of Kentucky Press, 1983), 124.

5   FPEIS, "Cumulative Impact Study," Appendix I, 45–46.

6   Ken Ward Jr., "Mountaintop Removal Could Devastate Region: Federal Study Paints Ugly Picture for Much of State," *Charleston (WV) Gazette*, May 5, 2002; FPEIS, chapter 3, "Affected Environment and Consequences," III-F.12, 102.

7   Ken Ward Jr., "EPA Review Finds 274 Valley Fill Violations," *Charleston (WV) Gazette*, September 5, 2003.

8   Jeff Hansbarger, "Mountaintop Removal Mining: An Environmental Impact Assessment (EIA) Scoping Exercise and Impact Assessment of Mining Activities on Aquatic Resources" (master's thesis, West Virginia University, 2000), 45.

9   Hansbarger, "Mountaintop Removal Mining," 45. For more information on the effects of blasting, see chapter 3.

10 West Virginia Department of Environmental Protection, *West Virginia Save Our Streams Advanced Stream Assessment Manual* (Charleston: West Virginia Department of Environmental Protection, Division of Water and Waste Management, 2004), 3.

11 Kentucky Department for Environmental Protection, *A Macroinvertebrate Bioassessment Index for Headwater Streams of the Eastern Coalfield Region, KY*, (Frankfort, KY: Kentucky Department for Environmental Protection, Division of Water, Water Quality Branch, 2002), 1.

12 West Virginia Department of Environmental Protection, *West Virginia Save Our Streams*, 3.

13 West Virginia Department of Environmental Protection, *West Virginia Save Our Streams*, 3.

14 West Virginia Department of Environmental Protection, *West Virginia Save Our Streams*, 16.

15 West Virginia Department of Environmental Protection, *West Virginia Save Our Streams*, 16.

16 West Virginia Department of Environmental Protection, *West Virginia Save Our Streams*, 18.

17 Kentucky Department for Environmental Protection, *Macroinvertebrate Bioassessment*, 25.

18 West Virginia Department of Environmental Protection, *West Virginia Save Our Streams*, 18.

19 West Virginia Department of Environmental Protection, *West Virginia Save Our Streams*, 18.

20 West Virginia Department of Environmental Protection, *West Virginia Save Our Streams*, 18.

21 Jeffrey B. Wiley, Ronald D. Evaldi, James H. Eychaner, and Douglas B. Chambers, *Reconnaissance of Stream Geomorphology, Low Streamflow, and Stream Temperature in the Mountaintop Coal-Mining Region, Southern West Virginia, 1999–2000* (Charleston, WV: U.S. Department of the Interior, U.S. Geological Survey, in cooperation with the West Virginia Department of Environmental Protection, Office of Mining and Reclamation, Water-Resources Investigations Report 01-4092, 2001), 3.

22 Kentucky Department for Environmental Protection, *Macroinvertebrate Bioassessment*, 26.

23 John Stacks, *Stripping* (San Francisco: Sierra Club, 1972), 39.

24 Martha Bryson Hodel, "West Virginia Report Focuses on Environment," *Washington Post*, April 22, 2004.

25 Hansbarger, "Mountaintop Removal Mining: EIA," 50.

26 Hansbarger, "Mountaintop Removal Mining: EIA," 49.

27 West Virginia Department of Environmental Protection, *West Virginia Save Our Streams*, 18.

28 West Virginia Department of Environmental Protection, *West Virginia Save Our Streams*, 19.

29 Kentucky Department for Environmental Protection, *Macroinvertebrate Bioassessment*, 26.

30 Kentucky Department for Environmental Protection, *Macroinvertebrate Bioassessment*, 18-19.

31 Hansbarger, "Mountaintop Removal Mining," 51; Wiley et al., *Reconnaissance of Stream Geomorphology*, 2.

32 *Surface Mining in West Virginia: The Stanford Report in Perspective, Proceedings of a Symposium held February 26, 1972, Charleston Civic Center, Charleston, W.Va.* (Charleston, WV: Mid-Appalachian Environmental Service, 1973), 1.

33 *Surface Mining in West Virginia*, 3.

34 *Surface Mining in West Virginia*, 7.

35 *Surface Mining in West Virginia*, 8; Congress, House of Representatives, Committee on Government Operations, Environment, Energy, and Natural Resources Subcommittee, *Strip Mining and the Flooding in Appalachia: Hearing Before a Subcommittee of the Committee on Government Operations, House of Representatives*, 95th Cong., 1st sess., July 26, 1977, 146.

36 *Surface Mining in West Virginia*, 8.

37 *Surface Mining in West Virginia*, 10.

38 Congress, House of Representatives, Committee on Government Operations, Environment, Energy, and Natural Resources Subcommittee, *Strip Mining and the Flooding in Appalachia*, 147.

39 *Surface Mining in West Virginia,* 25.

40 Hansbarger, "Mountaintop Removal Mining," 46.

41 Montrie, "To Save the Land and People," 204.

42 K. A. Thomas, Jeffrey Skousen, John Sencindiver, and Jim Gorman, *Soil Horizon Development on a Mountaintop Surface Mine in Southern West Virginia* (Morgantown: West Virginia University, Agriculture Extension, 2000), http://www.wvu.edu/~agexten/landrec/soilhori.htm.

43 Mineral Information Institute, "Mine Reclamation: Coal and Energy," http://www.mii.org/reclcoal.html, November 10, 2006.

44 FPEIS, "Executive Summary," 3.

45 Mineral Information Institute, "Mine Reclamation."

46 FPEIS, "Executive Summary," 4.

47 Further information on Twisted Gun can be found at http://www.thegolfcourses.net/golfcourses/WV/38273.htm.

48 Arch Coal, Inc., "Environment: Today's Energy is a Brighter Future," http://www.archcoal.com/environment, October 14, 2006; Carl Hoffman, "Mining Fresh Water for Aquaculture," *Appalachia Magazine,* May–August 2000, http://www.arc.gov/index.do?nodeId=918, October 14, 2006.

49 Arch Coal, Inc., "Today's Energy is Building a Brighter Future."

50 Michelle Saxton, "West Virginia Needs Balance, Governor Underwood says," *Charleston (WV) Gazette,* October 6, 2000.

51 Mineral Information Institute, "Reclamation Success: Arch Coal, Inc.," http://www.mii.org/ArchTree/ArchTree.html, October 14, 2006.

52 Ward, "Mountaintop Removal Could Devastate Region," *Charleston (WV) Gazette*, May 5, 2002; First DEIS, chapter 5, "Environmental Consequences," sections 5–15, January 2001 (Washington, DC: United States Environmental Protection Agency), 34.

53 FPEIS, chapter 3, "Affected Environment and Consequences," III.B-12, 19.

54 Ken Ward Jr., "Arch Coal Strikes at Researcher," *Charleston (WV) Gazette*, May 30, 2004.

55 More information about Massey's restoration activities can be found in the "Environment" section of their Web site, http://www.masseyenergyco.com.

56 Logan County Chamber of Commerce, "Earl Ray Tomblin Convention Center," http://logancountychamberofcommerce.com/conventcenter.htm, October 14, 2006.

57 National Mining Association, "Post-Mining Land Use," http://www.nma.org/policy/reclamation/land_use_article.asp, October 14, 2006.

58 *Aquatic Scientists* to the U.S. Environmental Protection Agency, comments, on Docket ID OW-2002-0050, April 10, 2003, 3. Comments concerned the

Advanced Notice of Proposed Rulemaking (ANPRM) on the Clean Water Act Regulatory Definition of "Waters of the United States." Document in the author's possession.

59 *Aquatic Scientists*, 4.

60 *Aquatic Scientists*, 9.

61 FPEIS, "Summary," 4.

62 Hansbarger, "Mountaintop Removal Mining," 49.

63 Wiley et al. *Reconnaissance of Stream Geomorphology*, 3, 17.

64 FPEIS, "Executive Summary," 4, noted in "Errata," 79.

65 Wiley et al., *Reconnaissance of Stream Geomorphology*, 3.

66 Kentucky Department for Environmental Protection, *Macroinvertebrate Bioassessment*, 25.

67 Ken Ward Jr., "Threat to Coal River Called Worse," *Charleston (WV) Gazette*, October 20, 2000.

68 Watershed Assessment Program, Division of Water Resources, West Virginia Department of Environmental Protection, *An Ecological Assessment of the Coal River Watershed* (Charleston, WV: West Virginia Department of Environmental Protection, Report number 05050009—1997, 1997), 55.

69 Watershed Assessment Program, *An Ecological Assessment of the Coal River Watershed*, 55.

70 Watershed Assessment Program, *An Ecological Assessment of the Coal River Watershed*, 55.

71 FPEIS, chapter 3, "Affected Environment and Consequences," III.D-3, 57.

72 FPEIS, chapter 3, "Affected Environment and Consequences," III.D-3, 57.

73 Hansbarger, "Mountaintop Removal Mining," 49.

74 Hansbarger, "Mountaintop Removal Mining," 1.

75 *Aquatic Scientists*, 3–4.

76 FPEIS study, chapter 3, "Affected Environment and Consequences," III.C-1, 33.

77 Ken Ward Jr., "Mining Fills Are 'Dumps' Biologist Says," *Charleston (WV) Gazette*, June 22, 2002.

78 Ted Williams, "Mountain Madness," *Audubon*, May–June 2001, http://magazine.audubon.org/incite/incite0105.html.

79 Williams, "Mountain Madness."

80 *Aquatic Scientists*, 4.

81 *Aquatic Scientists*, 4.

82 FPEIS, chapter 3, "Affected Environment and Consequences," III.D-14, 68.

83 FPEIS, "Executive Summary," 4.

84 Kentucky Department for Environmental Protection, *Macroinvertebrate Bioassessment*, 26

85 Environmental Monitoring and Assessment Program, National Health and Environmental Effects Research Laboratory, Western Ecology Division, Office of Research and Development, *EPA Mid-Atlantic Highlands Streams Assessment, Aquatic Insect Assemblages, EPA-903-R-00-015* (Corvalis, OR, Philadelphia, PA, Washington, DC: U.S. Environmental Protection Agency, August 2000), 12.

86 FPEIS, part 3, "Affected Environment and Consequences," III.C-4, 36.

87 U.S. Fish and Wildlife Service, *The Value of Headwater Streams: Results of a Workshop, State College, Pennsylvania, April 13, 1999* (Washington, DC: U.S. Fish and Wildlife Service, April 2000), 16, 22–23.

88 U.S. Fish and Wildlife Service, *The Value of Headwater Streams*, 36–37.

89 FPEIS, "Affected Environment and Consequences," III.D-9, 63.

90 In general, taxa refers to broad groups of organisms.

91 Kentucky Department for Environmental Protection, *Macroinvertebrate Bioassessment*, 26.

92 Kentucky Department for Environmental Protection, *Macroinvertebrate Bioassessment*, 26; FPEIS, III.D-14, 68.

93 Kentucky Department for Environmental Protection, *Macroinvertebrate Bioassessment*, 26.

94 Kyle Hartman, Michael Kaller, John Howell, and John A. Sweka, "How Much Do Valley Fills Influence Headwater Streams?" *Hydrobiologia* 532 (2005): 91–102; Kentucky Department for Environmental Protection, *Macroinvertebrate Bioassessment*, 29.

95 Frank Ammer, "Population Level Dynamics of Grasshopper Sparrow Populations Breeding on Reclaimed Mountaintop Mines in West Virginia" (PhD diss., West Virginia University, 2003), 32.

96 FPEIS, chapter 3, "Affected Environment and Consequences," III.F-7, 97.

97 Melissa Balcerzak, "Raptor Abundance and Diversity and Red-shouldered Hawk (*Buteo lineatus*) Habitat Characteristics on Reclaimed Mountaintop Mines in Southern West Virginia," (master's thesis, West Virginia University, 2001), 28.

98 Ammer, "Population Level Dynamics," 43.

99 FPEIS, "Executive Summary," 3.

100 FPEIS, chapter 3, "Affected Environment and Consequences," III.F-8, 98.

101 Ammer, "Population Level Dynamics," 48. Forest succession is, generically, the evolution of forests through various stages of development. This is a very simply stated definition. For further information on forest succession, please see the text Wildlife Habitat Relationships in Forested Ecosystems by David R. Patton, particularly pages 28-33, 365.

102 Douglas Chamblin, "Small Mammal Communities on a Reclaimed Mountaintop Mine/Valley Fill Landscape in Southern West Virginia" (master's thesis, West Virginia University, 2002), 40, 43.

103 Jeff Skousen, Paul Ziemkiewicz, Christina Venable, *Evaluation of Tree Growth on Surface Mined Lands in Southern West Virginia* (Morgantown, WV: Agricultural and Natural Resources Development, Extension Service, 1998), 1. Originally in *Green Lands*, Winter 1998.

104 Skousen et al., *Evaluation of Tree Growth,* 12–13.

105 Ammer, "Population Level Dynamics," 5.

106 Skousen et al., *Evaluation of Tree Growth,* 12–13.

107 Chamblin, "Small Mammal Communities," 50.

108 Ward, "Mountaintop Removal Could Devastate Region," *Charleston (WV) Gazette*, May 5, 2002; FPEIS, part 3, "Affected Environment and Consequences," III-F.11, 101.

109 Chamblin, "Small Mammal Communities," 50–51.

110 Chamblin, "Small Mammal Communities," 51.

111 FPEIS, part 3, "Affected Environment and Consequences," III-F.9, 99.

112 Hansbarger, "Mountaintop Removal Mining," 52; Pauline Canterberry interview.

113 Hansbarger, "Mountaintop Removal Mining," 51.

114 Hansbarger, "Mountaintop Removal Mining," 52.

115 Hansbarger, "Mountaintop Removal Mining," 52–53.

116 Neil F. Payne and Fred C. Bryant, *Techniques for Wildlife Habitat Management of Uplands* (New York: McGraw-Hill, 1994), 26.

117 FPEIS, part 3, "Affected Environment and Consequences," III-F.8, 98.

118 FPEIS, part 3, "Affected Environment and Consequences," III-F.12, 102.

119 Ward, "Mountaintop Removal Could Devastate Region," *Charleston (WV) Gazette*, May 5, 2002.

120 Ward, "Mountaintop Removal Could Devastate Region," *Charleston (WV) Gazette*, May 5, 2002.

121 National Academy of Sciences, National Research Council, Committee on Coal Waste Impoundments, Committee on Earth Resources, Board on Earth Sciences and Resources, Division on Earth and Life Studies, *Coal Waste Impoundments: Risks, Responses, and Alternatives* (Washington, DC: National Academy Press, 2002), 24.

122 National Academy of Sciences, *Coal Waste Impoundments,* 215.

123 National Academy of Sciences, *Coal Waste Impoundments,* 59.

124 National Academy of Sciences, *Coal Waste Impoundments,* 67.

125 Jack McCarthy, "A Man-made Disaster: Twenty-five Years Ago, a Dam Washed Away the Lives of 125 People," *Charleston (WV) Gazette*, February 23, 1997.

126 Mine Impoundment Project, *Mine Impoundment Location and Warning System* (Wheeling, WV: Robert C. Byrd National Technology Transfer Center [NTTC], Wheeling Jesuit Center, 2006), http://www.coalimpoundment.com/aboutimpoundments/spillList.asp, October 14, 2006. It should be noted that

since the time I began conducting my research for this book, the Web site has reported a smaller number of stream miles affected by slurry release, thus changing the statistics. The Web site gives no reason for this change in the figures it reports.

127 Mine Impoundment Project, *Mine Impoundment Location and Warning System*. Number derived from adding up all of the stream-miles-affected aspects of information from 1972 through 2004 as well as the spill information available at http://www.coalimpoundment.com/aboutimpoundments/spillList.asp?InfoNam e=state&identifier=WV, June 14, 2004 and October 14, 2006.

128 Department of Labor, 2003, "Water, Sediment, or Slurry Impoundments and Impounding Structures," *Code of Federal Regulations*, title 30, part 77.216.

129 Department of Environmental Protection, Division of Mining and Reclamation, "Series 4, Coal Related Dam Safety Rule," *West Virginia Code of State Rules*, title 4, sec. 38, especially §38-4-2.7.

130 Department of Environmental Protection, Division of Mining and Reclamation, "Series 4, Coal Related Dam Safety Rule," *West Virginia Code of State Rules*, title 4, sec. 38, especially §38-4-2.7.

131 Martha Bryson Hodel, "Massey Stockholders Reject Executive Bonus Proposal," *Charlotte (NC) Observer*, May 18, 2004.

132 Phillip Babich, "Dirty Business," November 13, 2003, http://www.salon.com/ tech/feature/2003/11/13/slurry_coverup/index_np.html; "UMWA Launches Community Education Campaign about Massey's Brushy Fork Impoundment," *United Mine Workers of America Journal*, January–February 2004.

133 Eades, *Brushy Fork Slurry Impoundment*, 3–4; *United Mine Workers of America Journal*, January–February 2004.

134 Department of Environmental Protection, Division of Mining and Reclamation, "Series 4, Coal Related Dam Safety Rule," *West Virginia Code of State Rules*, title 4, sec. 38, especially §3.4.b.3.

135 Ken Ward Jr., "Devastating Flood Could Have Been Much Worse," *Charleston (WV) Gazette-Mail*, August 5, 2001.

136 Flood Advisory Technical Task Force, *Runoff Analyses of Seng, Scrabble, and Sycamore Creeks*, part 1 (Charleston, WV: Division of Environmental Protection, 2002), 75.

137 Flood Advisory Technical Task Force, *Runoff Analyses of Seng, Scrabble, and Sycamore Creeks*, 2, 75.

138 U.S. Geological Survey, "Summary of Significant Floods in the United States, Puerto Rico, and the Virgin Islands, 1970 through 1989," http://ks.water.usgs. gov/Kansas/pubs/reports/wsp.2502.sum77.html, October 14, 2006.

139 Alan Randall, *Estimating Environmental Damages from Surface Mining of Coal*

in Appalachia: A Case Study (Cincinnati: Industrial Environmental Research Laboratory, Office of Research and Development, U.S. Environmental Protection Agency, 1978), 67.

140 Flood Advisory Technical Task Force, *Runoff Analyses of Seng, Scrabble, and Sycamore Creeks*, 2.

141 Randall, *Estimating Environmental Damages*, 67.

142 Randall, *Estimating Environmental Damages*, 67.

143 Randall, *Estimating Environmental Damages*, 67.

144 Randall, *Estimating Environmental Damages*, 67.

145 Mining Internet Services, Inc., "Who is MISI?," http://www.miningusa.com/misi/who_is_misi.htm, October 14, 2006.

146 Mining Internet Services, Inc., "Mountaintop Mining," http://www.mountaintopmining.com, October 14, 2006.

147 FPEIS, "Cumulative Impact Study," appendix I, 49.

148 Ohio Valley Environmental Coalition, flyer, "Mountaintop Removal Mining Fact Sheet," http://www.ohvec.org/issues/mountaintop_removal/articles/mtr_fact_sheet.pdf, October 14, 2006.

149 Ward, "Mountaintop Removal Could Devastate Region," *Charleston (WV) Gazette*, May 5, 2002.

150 Ward, "Mountaintop Removal Could Devastate Region," *Charleston (WV) Gazette*, May 5, 2002.

151 FPEIS, chapter 3, "Affected Environment and Consequences," III.F-12, 102.

152 Ward, "Mountaintop Removal Could Devastate Region," *Charleston (WV) Gazette*, May 5, 2002; FPEIS, chapter 3, "Affected Environment and Consequences," III.F-12, 102.

153 Mining Internet Services, Inc., "Mountaintop Mining," http://www.mountaintopmining.com, October 14, 2006.

154 U.S. Senate Committee on Environment and Public Works, Senate Subcommittee on Clean Air, hearing to review proposed revisions to the wetlands program of the Clean Water Act with respect to "fill material" and "discharge of fill material," statement of Michael Callaghan, Secretary, West Virginia Department of Environmental Protection, 107th Cong., 2nd sess., June 6, 2002, http://cpw.senate.gov/107th/Callaghan_060602.htm, June 20, 2004.

155 McGinley, "From Pick and Shovel to Mountaintop Removal," 75.

156 Ken Ward Jr., "Flattened: Most Mountaintop Mines Left as Pasture Land in State," *Charleston (WV) Gazette*, August 9, 1998.

157 Surface Mining Control and Reclamation Act of 1977, U.S. Code, title 30, sec. 1265 (e)(2); Ward, "Mountaintop Removal Could Devastate Region," *Charleston (WV) Gazette*, May 5, 2002.

158 Pauline Canterberry interview.

159 Mining Internet Services, Inc., "Mountaintop Mining," http://www
.mountaintopmining.com, October 14, 2006.

160 Hartman et al., *How Much Do Valley Fills Influence Headwater Streams?*, 10.

Epilogue

The epigraph to this chapter is drawn from Aldo Leopold, "Wildlife in American
Culture," *Journal of Wildlife Management* 7, no. 1: 1–6.

1 FPEIS, chapter 3, "Affected Environment and Consequences," III.K-32, 208.

2 FPEIS, chapter 3, "Affected Environment and Consequences," III.K-21–III.K-47,
197–223.

3 Robert C. Byrd National Technology Transfer Center (NTTC), Wheeling Jesuit
University, West Virginia University and the National Energy Technology
Laboratory, "Coal Impoundment Location and Warning System," http://www
.coalimpoundment.com/aboutimpoundments/spills.asp, November 10, 2006.

4 FPEIS, chapter 3, "Affected Environment and Consequences," III.L-8–III.L-14,
235–241.

5 Please see http://www.kftc.org for more information on Kentuckians for the
Commonwealth. For further information on this case, please see various articles
from August 2001 through January 2003 in the *Charleston* (WV) *Gazette* and
the *Charleston Daily Mail*. Also see Haden's original decision of May 8, 2002,
where he once again noted the illegality of valley fills under the Clean Water
Act (*Kentuckians for the Commonwealth v. Rivenburgh*, 2002 U.S. Dist. Lexis
12048 [S.D. W.Va. 2002]) and the Fourth Circuit Court's overturning of Haden's
decision (*Kentuckians for the Commonwealth v. Rivenburgh*, 317 F.3d 425 [4th
Cir. 2003]).

6 For more information on Save Our Cumberland Mountains, please see http://
www.socm.org.

7 For more information on Appalachian Voices, see http://www.appvoices.org.

8 Lewis, *Transforming the Appalachian Countryside*, 278.

BIBLIOGRAPHY

Archival Records

Strip-mining collection. Papers. West Virginia and Regional History Collection, A&M 2618. West Virginia University, Morgantown, WV.

West Virginia Government Documents

Consolidation Coal Company. Monitoring and Emergency Warning Plan and Procedures for the Joe Branch Coal Refuse Dam. Welch, WV: Department of Environmental Protection, Permit Section, Region IV, 2003.

"Department of Environmental Protection Division of Mining and Reclamation Series 4 Coal Related Dam Safety Rule." *West Virginia Code of State Rules*. Title 4, Sec. 38.

Flood Advisory Technical Task Force. *Runoff Analyses of Seng, Scrabble, and Sycamore Creeks*. Charleston, WV: Division of Environmental Protection, 2002.

Musgrave, John C. *Valuation of active and reserve coal property for Ad Valorem property tax purposes*. Charleston, WV: West Virginia State Tax Department, 2004.

Tosun, Mehmet S. "A Comparative Assessment of West Virginia's State Tax System." *The West Virginia Public Affairs Reporter*, vol. 19, no. 3, summer 2002.

West Virginia Bureau of Employment Programs. *Employment and Unemployment Data*. Charleston, WV: Bureau of Employment Programs, Research, Information and Analysis, 2004.

West Virginia Department of Environmental Protection, Division of Water and Waste Management. *West Virginia Save Our Streams Advanced Stream Assessment Manual*. Charleston, WV: West Virginia Department of Environmental Protection, 2004.

West Virginia Department of Environmental Protection, Watershed Assessment Program, Division of Water Resources. *An Ecological Assessment of the Coal River Watershed*. Report #OS-OS0009. Charleston, WV: West Virginia Department of Environmental Protection, 1997.

West Virginia Department of Tax and Revenue and West Virginia Development Office. *Analysis and Recommendations for West Virginia Tax Incentives*. Charleston, WV: Department of Tax and Revenue, 2002.

BIBLIOGRAPHY

U.S. Government Documents

Appalachian Land Ownership Task Force. *Land Ownership Patterns and Their Impacts on Appalachian Communities: A Survey of 80 Counties*. Washington, DC: Appalachian Regional Commission, 1981.

Aquatic Scientists. Comments to the U.S. Environmental Protection Agency on Docket ID OW-2002-0050 reg. the Advanced Notice of Proposed Rulemaking (ANPRM) on the Clean Water Act Regulatory Definition of "Waters of the United States." Washington, DC: U.S. Environmental Protection Agency, 2003.

Byrd, Robert C., Senate, Senator Robert Byrd of West Virginia speaking to the Senate on mountaintop mining. *Congressional Record*, November 18, 1999.

Department of Energy, Energy Information Administration. *Coal Industry Annual Report Data Table, 1995*. Washington, DC: Department of Energy, 1995.

Department of Energy, Energy Information Administration. *Coal Industry Annual Report Data Table, 2000*. Washington, DC: Department of Energy, 2000.

Environmental Monitoring and Assessment Program, National Health and Environmental Effects Research Laboratory, Western Ecology Division, Office of Research and Development. *EPA Mid-Atlantic Highlands Streams Assessment, Aquatic Insect Assemblages, EPA-903-R-00-015*. Corvalis, OR, Philadelphia, PA, Washington, DC: U.S. Environmental Protection Agency, 2000.

Hoffman, Carl. "Mining Fresh Water for Aquaculture." *Appalachia Magazine*, May–August 2000, http://www.arc.gov/index.do?nodeId=918.

National Academy of Sciences et al. *Coal Waste Impoundments: Risks, Responses, and Alternatives*. Washington DC: National Academy Press, 2002.

Randall, Alan. *Estimating Environmental Damages from Surface Mining of Coal in Appalachia: A Case Study*. Cincinnati: Industrial Environmental Research Laboratory, Office of Research and Development, U.S. Environmental Protection Agency, 1978.

Shays, Christopher. Press release. Washington, DC: United States Congress, 2003, http://www.house.gov/shays/news/2003/february/febpallone.htm.

United States Department of Energy. Energy Information Administration. *West Virginia Coal Statistics*, 1991, 1996–2000, http://www.eia.doe.gov/cnAeaf/coal/cia/a15p01.txt

United States Department of Energy. Energy Information Administration. *Monthly Mined Coal Statistics, 2003*, http://tonto.eia.doe.gov/FTPROOT/coal/weekly/monthprod2003tot.xls.

United States Department of Energy. Energy Information Administration. *Monthly Mined Coal Statistics, 2004*, http://tonto.eia.doe.gov/FTPROOT/coal/weekly/monthprod2004tot.xls.

United States Department of Energy. Energy Information Administration. *Average Open Market*

Sales Price of Coal by State and Mine Type, 2003, 2002, http://www.eia.doe.gov/cneaf/coal/page/acr/table28.html.

U.S. Congress. House. *Federal Water Pollution Control Act amendment to clarify that fill material cannot be comprised of waste.* 108th Cong., H.R. 738. *Bill Summary and Status for the 108th Congress.* Washington, DC: United States Congress, 2003.

U.S. Congress. House. Committee on Government Operations. Environment, Energy, and Natural Resources Subcommittee. *Strip Mining and the Flooding in Appalachia: Hearing Before a Subcommittee of the Committee on Government Operations, House of Representatives, ninety-fifth Congress, first session, July 26, 1977.* Washington, DC: U.S. Government Printing Office, 1977.

U.S. Environmental Protection Agency, Mid-Atlantic Region, Environmental Assessment and Innovation Division of the Mid-Atlantic Region. *Draft Environmental Impact Statement on Mountaintop Mining.* Washington, DC: United States Environmental Protection Agency, 2003.

U.S. Fish and Wildlife Service. *The Value of Headwater Streams: Results of a Workshop.* State College, PA: U.S. Fish and Wildlife Service, 2000.

U.S. Geological Survey Water Resources in Kansas. *Summary of Significant Floods, 1970 through 1989, by Year,* http://ks.water.usgs.gov/Kansas/pubs/reports/wsp.2502.sum77.html.

U.S. Senate Committee on Environment and Public Works, Senate Subcommittee on Clean Air. *Hearing to review proposed revisions to the wetlands program of the Clean Water Act with respect to "fill material" and "discharge of fill material," statement of Michael Calaghan, Secretary, West Virginia Department of Environmental Protection,* 107th Cong., 2d sess., June 6, 2002, http://epw.senate.gov/107th/Callaghan_060602.htm.

"Water, sediment, or slurry impoundments and impounding structures." *Code of Federal Regulations* Title 30, Pt. 77.216, 2003.

Wiley, Jeffrey B., Ronald D. Evaldi, James H. Eychaner, and Douglas B. Chambers. *Reconnaissance of Stream Geomorphology, Low Streamflow, and Stream Temperature in the Mountaintop Coal-Mining Region, Southern West Virginia, 1999–2000.* Report 01-4092. Charleston, WV: U.S. Department of the Interior, U.S. Geological Survey, in cooperation with the West Virginia Department of Environmental Protection, Office of Mining and Reclamation, Water-Resources Investigations, 2001.

Court Cases

Ark Land Company v. Rhonda Gail Harper, Edward A. Caudill, Rose M. Thompson, Edith D. Kitchen, Therman R. Caudill, John A. Caudill, Jr., Tammy Willis, and Lucille M. Miller. West Virginia Supreme Court, 2004.

Bragg v. Robertson. U.S.D.C. for the Southern District of West Virginia, Charleston Division, 1998.

Bragg v. West Virginia Coal Association. Fourth Circuit Court of Appeals, 2001.

Flood Litigation, No. 31688, Defendant's Supplemental Brief, Supreme Court of Appeals of West Virginia (August 2, 2004),

http://www.state.wv.us/wvsca/clerk/cases/FloodLitigation/31688DefendantSupp.pdf.

Flood Litigation, No. 31688, Plaintiff's Supplemental Brief, Supreme Court of Appeals of West Virginia (August 3, 2004), http://www.state.wv.us/wvsca/clerk/cases/FloodLitigation/31688 PlaintiffSupp.pdf

Kentuckians for the Commonwealth v. Rivenburgh. Fourth Circuit Court of Appeals, 2003.

Kentuckians for the Commonwealth v. Rivenburgh. U.S.D.C. for the Southern District of West Virginia, 2002.

Ohio Valley Environmental Coalition et al. v. William Bulen. Fourth Circuit Court of Appeals, 2003.

Ohio Valley Environmental Coalition et al. v. William Bulen. U.S.D.C. for the Southern District of West Virginia, 2004.

Ralph Anderson et al. v. Elk Run Coal Company, Inc. Circuit Court of Boone County, West Virginia, 2003.

West Virginia Coal Association v. Reilly. U.S.D.C. for the Southern District of West Virginia, 1989.

West Virginia Highlands Conservancy v. Norton. U.S.D.C. for the Southern District of West Virginia, Charleston Division, 2001.

Miscellaneous

Logan County Chamber of Commerce. Earl Ray Tomblin Convention Center. Logan, WV: Logan County Chamber of Commerce, http://logancountychamberofcommerce.com/convent-center.htm.

Mine Impoundment Project. Mine Impoundment Location and Warning System. Wheeling, WV: Robert C. Byrd National Technology Transfer Center and Wheeling Jesuit Center, 2006, http://www.coalimpoundment.com.

Mineral Information Institute. Golden, CO: Mineral Information Institute, http://www.mii.org/reclcoal.html.

Mining Internet Services, Inc. Lexington, KY: Mining Internet Services, Inc., http://www.miningusa.com/misi/who_is_misi.htm.

National Mining Association. *Post-Mining Land Use.* Washington, DC: National Mining Association, http://www.nma.org/policy/reclamation/land_use_article.asp.

Ohio Valley Environmental Coalition. Flyer. *Mountaintop Removal Mining Fact Sheet*. Hunting-ton, WV: Ohio Valley Environmental Coalition, http://www.ohvec.org/issues/mountaintop_removal/articles/mtr_fact_sheet.pdf.

Reports

Center for Business and Economic Research, Gatton College of Business and Economics. *A Study on the Current Economic Impacts of the Appalachian Coal Industry and its Future in the Region: Final Report*. Louisville: University of Kentucky, March 27, 2001.

Commission on Religion in Appalachia. Social, Economic, and Political Issues Task Force. *Strip Mining in Appalachia: a Social, Economic and Political Issue: a Dialogue-focuser*. Knoxville, TN: Commission on Religion in Appalachia, 1970.

Eades, Rick. *Brushy Fork Slurry Impoundment—A Preliminary Report*. Huntington, WV: Ohio Valley Environmental Coalition, 2000.

Massey Energy. *2005 Annual Report*. Richmond, VA: Massey Energy Company, 2006.

Massey Energy. *2003 Annual Report*. Richmond, VA: Massey Energy Company, 2004.

A Study on the Current Economic Impacts of the Appalachian Coal Industry and its Future in the Region: Final Report. Louisville: Center for Business and Economic Research, Gatton College of Business and Economics, University of Kentucky, March 27, 2001.

Surface Mining in West Virginia: The Stanford Report in Perspective, Proceedings of a Symposium Held February 26, 1972, Charleston Civic Center, Charleston, W. Va. Charleston, WV: Mid-Appalachian Environmental Service, 1973.

West Virginia People's Election Reform Coalition: Common Cause West Virginia, Ohio Valley Environmental Coalition, West Virginia Citizen Research Group, West Virginia Citizen Action Group. *2000 Election Cycle Report*, http://www.wvcag.org/issues/clean_elections/perc2000.pdf.

West Virginia People's Election Reform Coalition: Mountain State Education and Research Foundation, Ohio Valley Environmental Coalition, West Virginia Citizen Action Group. *2002 Election Cycle Report*, http://www.wvcag.org/issues/clean_elections/perc2002.pdf.

Books

Baratz, Morton. *The Union and the Coal Industry*. Westport, CT: Greenwood Press, 1955.

Battlo, Jean. *McDowell County in West Virginia and American History*. Parsons, WV: McClain Printing Company, 1998.

Blankenship, Paul. *From Cabins to Coal Mines: More History, Sketches, Anecdotes, Traditional*

Stories, Culture, and Families of Oceana and the Clear Fork Valley of Wyoming County, West Virginia. Beckley, WV: Central Printing, 2002.

Boone County Genealogical Society. *Boone County, West Virginia, History, 1990.* Madison, WV: Boone County Genealogical Society, 1990.

Bowman, Mary Keller. *Reference Book of Wyoming County History.* Parsons, WV: McClain Printing Co., 1965.

Brisbin, Jr., Richard. *A Strike Like No Other Strike: Law and Resistance During the Pittston Coal Strike of 1989–1990.* Baltimore: Johns Hopkins University Press, 2002

Brown, William G. *History of Nicholas County, West Virginia.* Richwood, WV: The News Leader, 1981.

Conley, Phil. *History of the West Virginia Coal Industry.* Charleston, WV: Education Foundation, 1960.

Cook, Samuel R. *Monacans and Miners: Native American and Coal Mining Communities in Appalachia.* Lincoln: University of Nebraska Press, 2000.

Corbin, David. *Life, Work, and Rebellion in the Coal Fields: The Southern West Virginia Miners, 1880–1922.* Urbana: University of Illinois Press, 1981.

Cuoto, Richard. "The Memory of Miners and the Conscience of Capital: Coal Miners' Strikes as Free Spaces." *Fighting Back in Appalachia: Traditions of Resistance and Change.* Philadelphia: Temple University Press, 1993.

Davis, Donald. *Where There Are Mountains: An Environmental History of the Southern Appalachians.* Athens: University of Georgia Press, 2000.

Dix, Keith. *What's a Coal Miner to Do? The Mechanization of Coal Mining.* Pittsburgh: University of Pittsburgh Press, 1988.

Domhoff, William. *Who Rules America: Power and Politics.* Boston: McGraw-Hill Higher Education, 2002.

Dunaway, Wilma. *The First American Frontier: Transition to Capitalism in Southern Appalachia, 1700–1860.* Chapel Hill: University of North Carolina Press, 1996.

Eller, Ronald. *Miners, Millhands, and Mountaineers: Industrialization of the Appalachian South, 1880–1930.* Knoxville: University of Tennessee Press, 1982.

Evans, Sara and Harry Boyte. *Free Space: The Sources of Dramatic Change in America.* New York: Harper and Row, 1986.

Fayette County Chamber of Commerce. *History of Fayette County, West Virginia.* Oak Hill, WV: Fayette County Chamber of Commerce, 1993.

Fox, Maier B. *United We Stand: The United Mine Workers of America, 1890–1990.* Washington, DC: United Mine Workers of America, 1990.

Freese, Barbara. *Coal: A Human History.* Cambridge: MA: Perseus Books Group, 2003.

Gaventa, John. *Power and Powerlessness: Quiescence and Rebellion in an Appalachian Valley.* Urbana: University of Illinois Press, 1980.

Harris, V. B. *Great Kanawha: An Historical Outline.* Charleston, WV: Kanawha County Court, 1976.

Hatcher, Thomas, Geneva Steele, Sandra Long, and Christine Carr McGuire, eds. *The Heritage of McDowell County, West Virginia, 1858-1995.* War, WV: McDowell County Historical Society, 1995.

Judkins, Bennett. "The People's Respirator: Coalition Building and the Black Lung Association." *Fighting Back in Appalachia: Traditions of Resistance and Change.* Philadelphia: Temple University Press, 1993.

Kephart, Horace. *Our Southern Highlanders: A Narrative of Adventure in the Southern Appalachians and a Study of Life among the Mountaineers.* Knoxville: University of Tennessee Press, 1976.

Lee, Howard B. *Bloodletting in Appalachia: The Story of West Virginia's Four Major Mine Wars and Other Thrilling Incidents of Its Coal Fields.* Morgantown: West Virginia University, 1969.

Lewis, Ronald L. *Transforming the Appalachian Countryside: Railroads, Deforestation, and Social Change in West Virginia, 1880-1920.* Chapel Hill: University of North Carolina Press, 1998.

Lewis, Ronald L. and John Hennen. *West Virginia: Documents in the History of a Rural-Industrial State.* Dubuque, IA: Kendall/Hunt Publishing Company, 1991.

Lewis, Virgil. *History of West Virginia. In Two Parts.* Philadelphia: Hubbard Brothers Publishers, 1889.

Lunt, Richard D. *Law and Order vs. the Miners: WV 1906-1933.* Charleston, WV: Appalachian Editions, 1992.

Lutz, Paul. *From Governor to Cabby: The Political Career and Tragic Death of West Virginia's William Casey Marland, 1950-1965.* Huntington, WV: Marshall University Library Associates, 1996.

Marland, William C. "Governor William C. Marland Proposes The Severance Tax." *West Virginia: Documents in the History of a Rural-Industrial State,* eds. Ronald Lewis and John Hennen. Dubuque, IA: Kendall/Hunt Publishing Company, 1991.

McLean, Iain and Martin Johnes. *Aberfan: Government & Disasters.* Cardiff, Wales: Welsh Academic Press, 2000.

Meyers, Robert A., ed. *Coal Handbook.* New York: M. Dekker, 1981.

Miller, Tom. *Who Owns West Virginia?* Huntington, WV: *Herald Adviser* and the *Herald-Dispatch,* 1974.

Moffat, Charles H. *Ken Hechler: Maverick Public Servant.* Charleston, WV: Mountain State Press, 1987.

Montrie, Chad. *To Save the Land and People: A History of Opposition to Surface Coal Mining in Appalachia*. Chapel Hill: University of North Carolina Press, 2003.

Morris, Homer. *The Plight of the Bituminous Coal Miner*. Philadelphia: University of Pennsylvania Press; London: H. Milford, Oxford University Press, 1934.

Patton, David R. *Wildlife Habitat Relationships in Forested Ecosystems*. Portland, OR: Timber Press, 1992.

Payne, Neil F. and Fred C. Bryant. *Techniques for Wildlife Habitat Management of Uplands*. New York: McGraw-Hill, 1994.

Rasmussen, Barbara. *Absentee Landowning and Exploitation in West Virginia, 1760–1920*. Lexington: University Press of Kentucky, 1994.

Rice, Otis. *West Virginia: The State and Its People*. Parsons, WV: McClain Printing Company, 1972.

Rice, Otis and Stephen Brown. *West Virginia: A History*. Lexington: University Press of Kentucky, 1993.

Salstrom, Paul. *Appalachia's Path to Dependency: Rethinking a Region's Economic History, 1730–1940*. Lexington: University Press of Kentucky, 1994.

Session, Jim and Fran Ansley. "Singing Across Dark Spaces: the Union/Community Takeover of Pittston's Moss 3 Plant." *Fighting Back in Appalachia: Traditions of Resistance and Change*. Philadelphia: Temple University Press, 1993.

Shifflett, Crandall. *Coal Towns: Life, Work, and Culture in Company Towns of Southern Appalachia, 1880–1960*. Knoxville: University of Tennessee Press, 1991.

Shogan, Robert. *The Battle of Blair Mountain: The Story of America's Largest Labor Uprising*. Boulder, CO: Westview Press, 2004.

Smith, Barbara Ellen. *Digging Our Own Graves: Coal Miners and the Struggle over Black Lung Disease*. Philadelphia: Temple University Press, 1987.

Squillace, Mark. *Strip Mining Handbook: A Coalfield Citizens' Guide to Using the Law to Fight Back Against the Ravages of Strip Mining and Underground Mining*. Washington, DC: Environmental Policy Institute and Friends of the Earth, 1990.

Stacks, John F. *Stripping*. San Francisco: Sierra Club, 1972.

Stafford, Thomas F. *Afflicting the Comfortable: Journalism and Politics in West Virginia*. Morgantown: West Virginia University Press, 2005.

Stealey, III, John E. *The Antebellum Kanawha Salt Business and Western Markets*. Lexington: University Press of Kentucky, 1993.

Sullivan, Ken, ed. *The "Goldenseal" Book of the West Virginia Mine Wars*. Charleston, WV: Pictorial Histories Publishing, 1991.

The Land Ownership Task Force. *Who Owns Appalachia? Landownership and Its Impact*. Lexington, KY: University of Kentucky Press, 1983.

Thurmond, Walter R. *Logan Coal Field of West Virginia: A Brief History*. Morgantown: West Virginia University Library, 1964.

Walls, David S. "Internal Colony or Internal Periphery: A Critique of Current Models and an Alternative Formulation." *Colonialism in Modern America: The Appalachian Case*. Boone, NC: Appalachian Consortium Press, 1978.

Williams, John Alexander. *West Virginia and the Captains of Industry*. Morgantown: West Virginia University Library, 1997, reprint edition.

Williams, John Alexander. *West Virginia: A History*. Morgantown: West Virginia University Press, 2001.

Woods, Jim. *Raleigh County, West Virginia*. Beckley, WV: BJW Printing and Office Supplies, 1994.

Dissertations and Theses

Ammer, Frank. "Population Level Dynamics of Grasshopper Sparrow Populations Breeding on Reclaimed Mountaintop Mines in West Virginia." PhD diss., West Virginia University, 2003.

Bailey, Rebecca J. "Matewan Before the Massacre: Politics, Coal, and the Roots of Conflict in Mingo County, 1793–1920." PhD diss., West Virginia University, 2001.

Balcerzak, Melissa. "Raptor Abundance and Diversity and Red-shouldered Hawk (Buteo lineatus) Habitat Characteristics on Reclaimed Mountaintop Mines in Southern West Virginia." M.A. thesis, West Virginia University, 2001.

Chamblin, Douglass. "Small Mammal Communities on a Reclaimed Mountaintop Mine/Valley Fill Landscape in Southern West Virginia." Master's thesis, West Virginia University, 2002.

Hansbarger, Jeff. "Mountaintop Removal Mining: An Environmental Impact Assessment (EIA) Scoping Exercise and Impact Assessment of Mining Activities on Aquatic Resources." Master's thesis, West Virginia University, 2000.

Kolli, Shiva. "Analyses of Coal Extraction and Spoil Handling Techniques in Mountainous Areas." Master's thesis, West Virginia University, 2001.

Montrie, Chad. "To Save the Land and People: A History of Opposition to Coal Surface Mining in Appalachia." PhD diss., Ohio State University, 2001.

Peter, David. "Earnings, Health, Safety, and Welfare of Bituminous Coal Miners Since the Encouragement of Mechanization by the United Mine Workers of America." PhD diss., West Virginia University, 1972.

Rakes, Paul. "Acceptable Casualties: Power, Culture, and History in the West Virginia Coalfields, 1900–1945." PhD diss., West Virginia University, 2002.

Underwood, Deborah. "The Ascendancy of Surface Mining over Underground Mining in the

United States Coal Industy: Effects on and Issues Relevant to the United Mine Workers of America." Master's thesis, University of Montana, 1987.

Walls, David S. "Central Appalachia in Advanced Capitalism." PhD diss., University of Kentucky, 1978.

Wells, Jr., John Calhoun. "Poverty Amidst Riches: Why People are Poor in Appalachia." PhD diss., Rutgers University, 1977.

Journal Articles

Crotty, Michael G. "Bragg v. West Virginia Mining Association: The Eleventh Amendment Challenge to Mountaintop Coal Mining." *Villanova Environmental Law Journal* 13 (2002): 287–311.

Fishback, Price. "Did Coal Miners 'Owe Their Souls to the Company Store'? Theory and Evidence from the Early 1900s," *The Journal of Economic History* 46 (December 1986), 1011–1029.

Hammond, Christiadi and George Hammond. "How well did we retain and attract highly educated workers?" *West Virginia Business and Economic Review* 9 (2003): 1–6.

Hartman, Michael Kaller, John Howell, and John A. Sweka, "How Much Do Valley Fills Influence Headwater Streams?" *Hydrobiologia* 532 (2005): 91–102.

Munn, Robert . "The First Fifty Years of Strip Mining in West Virginia, 1916–1965." *West Virginia History* 35 (October 1973): 66–74.

Munn, Robert. "The Development of Model Towns in the Bituminous Coal Fields." *West Virginia History* 40 (Spring 1979): 243–253.

Rasmussen, Barbara. "The Politics of the Property Tax in West Virginia." *Journal of Appalachian Studies* 2, no. 1: 141–147.

Rice, Otis. "Coal Mining in the Kanawha Valley to 1861: A View of Industrialization in the Old South." *The Journal of Southern History* 31 (November 1965): 393–416.

Skousen, Jeff, Paul Ziemkiewicz, and Christina Venable. "Evaluation of Tree Growth on Surface Mined Lands in Southern West Virginia." Morgantown, WV: Agricultural and Natural Resources Development, Extension Service, 1998, http://www.wvu.edu/~agexten/landrec/evaltree.htm. First published in *Green Lands*, Winter 1998.

Williams, Ted. "Mountain Madness." *Audubon*, May/June 2001.

Studies, Public Correspondences, and Organized Press Releases

American Rivers. Press release. *Coal River Listed Among Nation's Most Endangered Rivers*. Washington, DC: American Rivers, 2000.

Center for Economic Research. *Boone County, WV, County Data*. Morgantown: West Virginia University, 1991.

Center for Economic Research. *Fayette County, WV, County Data*. Morgantown: West Virginia University, 1991.

Center for Economic Research. *Kanawha County, WV, County Data*. Morgantown: West Virginia University, 1991.

Center for Economic Research. *Logan County, WV, County Data*. Morgantown, WV: West Virginia University, 1991.

Center for Economic Research. *McDowell County, WV, County Data*. Morgantown: West Virginia University, 1991.

Center for Economic Research. *Mingo County, WV, County Data*. Morgantown: West Virginia University, 1991.

Center for Economic Research. *Nicholas County, WV, County Data*. Morgantown: West Virginia University, 1991.

Coal Operators and Associates, the Kentucky Coal Association, the National Mining Association, the Ohio Coal Association, and the West Virginia Coal Association to John Forren, U.S. Environmental Protection Agency. Letter, *Joint Coal Industry Comments on the Mountaintop Mining/Valley Fill Draft Environmental Impact Statement*. Charleston: West Virginia Coal Association, January 6, 2004, http://www.wvcoal.com/resources/pdfs/FinalEIS.pdf.

Condon, Chris, Randy Childs, and Leah Bogdan. *County Data Profile: Boone County*. Morgantown: Bureau of Business and Economic Research, West Virginia University, September 2000.

Condon, Chris, Randy Childs, and Leah Bogdan. *County Data Profile: Fayette County*. Morgantown: Bureau of Business and Economics, West Virginia University, September 2000.

Condon, Chris, Randy Childs, and Leah Bogdan. *County Data Profile: Kanawha County*. Morgantown: Bureau of Business and Economics, West Virginia University, September 2000.

Condon, Chris, Randy Childs, and Leah Bogdan. *County Data Profile: Logan County*. Morgantown: Bureau of Business and Economics, West Virginia University, September 2000.

Condon, Chris, Randy Childs, and Leah Bogdan. *County Data Profile: McDowell County*. Morgantown: Bureau of Business and Economics, West Virginia University, September 2000.

Condon, Chris, Randy Childs, and Leah Bogdan. *County Data Profile: Mingo County*. Morgantown: Bureau of Business and Economics, West Virginia University, September 2000.

Condon, Chris, Randy Childs, and Leah Bogdan. *County Data Profile: Nicholas County*. Morgantown: Bureau of Business and Economics, West Virginia University, September 2000.

Condon, Chris, Randy Childs, and Leah Bogdan. *County Data Profile: Raleigh County*. Morgantown: Bureau of Business and Economics, West Virginia University, September 2000.

Condon, Chris, Randy Childs, and Leah Bogdan. *County Data Profile: Wyoming County*. Morgantown: Bureau of Business and Economics, West Virginia University, September 2000.

Kentucky Department for Environmental Protection, Division of Water, Water Quality Branch. *A Macroinvertebrate Bioassessment Index for Headwater Streams of the Eastern Coalfield Region, KY.* Frankfort: Kentucky Department for Environmental Protection, 2002.

Lake, Snell, Perry, and Associates. "New Poll Findings On Mountaintop Removal in West Virginia: Opposition to Mountaintop Removal is Broad and Deep." Conducted for Appalachian Center for the Economy and the Environment, http://www.appalachian-center.org/poll_results/index.html.

Massachusetts Taxpayers Foundation. *Massachusetts' Tax Burden Falls to Bottom Tier of States.* Boston: Massachusetts Taxpayers Foundation, 2004.

Ohio Valley Environmental Coalition. *Comments on Draft Programmatic Environmental Impact Statement on Mountaintop Removal Mining/Valley Fill Activities in Appalachia: The Social and Cultural Effects of Mountaintop Removal/Valley Fill Coal Mining.* Huntington, WV: Ohio Valley Environmental Association, 2004.

Thomas, K. A., Jeffrey Skousen, John Sencindiver, and Jim Gorman. *Soil Horizon Development on a Mountaintop Surface Mine in Southern West Virginia.* Morgantown: West Virginia University, Agriculture Extension, 2000, http://www.wvu.edu/~agexten/landrec/soilhori.htm.

Trial Lawyers for Public Justice. Press Release. *Citizens' Group and TLPJ Sue Federal and State Regulators to Fix West Virginia's Coal Mining Program.* Washington, DC: Trial Lawyers for Public Justice, 2000, http://www.tlpj.org/pr/wv_coal.htm.

Vendetti, Jann. *Mining: Storing Coal Slurry.* American Geological Institute. Alexandria, VA: American Geological Institute, 2004.

Ward, Ken. Mining the Mountains series. *Charleston (WV) Gazette.*

West Virginia Coal Association. *Coal Education Development and Resource of Southern West Virginia, Inc. (CEDAR).* Charleston: West Virginia Coal Association, 2004.

West Virginia Coal Association. *West Virginia Coal Facts 2001.* Charleston: West Virginia Coal Association, 2001.

West Virginia Coal Association. *West Virginia Coal Facts 2003.* Charleston: West Virginia Coal Association, 2003.

The Wilderness Society. Press Release. *Rahall Wins Ansel Adams Award for Efforts to Protect Nation's Lands.* Washington, DC: Wilderness Society, 2004.

Media

All Shaken Up, prod. and dir. Bob Gate, Penny Loeb. 32 min., Omni Productions, 1998, videocassette.

Other Sources of Interest

Books

Johansen, Kristin, Bobbie Ann Mason, and Mary Ann Taylor-Hall, eds. *Missing Mountains: We Went to the Mountaintop but It Wasn't There.* Nicholasville, KY: Wind, 2005.

Reece, Erik. *Lost Mountain: A Year in the Vanishing Wilderness.* New York: Riverhead Books, 2006.

Articles

Abramson, Rudy. "New Coal Isn't Old Coal." *The Alicia Patterson Foundation Reporter*, 2001, http://www.aliciapatterson.org/APF2001/Abramson/Abramson.html.

Abramson, Rudy. "A Judge in Coal Country." *The Alicia Patterson Foundation Reporter*, 2003, http://www.aliciapatterson.org/APF2003/Abramson/Abramson.html.

Anderson, George M. "*Of Many Things.*" *America*, February 3, 2003.

Babich, Phillip. "Dirty Business." *Salon*, November 13, 2003, http://www.salon.com/tech/feature/2003/11/13/slurry_coverup/index_np.html.

Bingham, Clara. "Under Mined." *Washington Monthly*, January/February 2005.

Bowe, Rebecca. "In Defense of Mountains." *E: The Environmental Magazine*, January/February 2006.

Chamblin, H. Douglas, Petra Wood, and John Edwards. "Allegheny Woodrat (Neotoma magister) Use of Rock Drainage Channels on Reclaimed Mines in Southern West Virginia." *American Midland Naturalist*, April 2004.

Clarke, Kevin. "And every mountain brought low." *U.S. Catholic*, September 1999.

Gabriel, Margaret. "Appalachian Catholics Tackle Divisive Mining Issue." *National Catholic Reporter*, July 30, 2004.

Galuszka, Peter. "Strip-mining on Steroids." *Business Week*, Novebmer 17, 1997.

Goodell, Jeff. "You fight for what you've got, even if it it's only worth a dime." *O*, July 2006.

Hattam, Jennifer. "Dethroning King Coal." *Sierra*, November/December 2003.

Kiger, Patrick J. "Unnatural Wonders." *Mother Jones*, July/August 2006.

Loeb, Penny. "Shear Madness." *U.S. News and World Report*, August 11, 1997.

Loeb, Penny. "Coal activists stir up dust in West Virginia." *U.S. News and World Report*, October 13, 1997.

Mitchell, John G. "When Mountains Move." *National Geographic*, March 2006.

Nichols, John. "A Novelist Runs for Governor." *Progressive*, November 2000.

Paulson, Amanda. "In Coal Country, Heat Rises Over Latest Method of Mining." *Christian Science Monitor*, January 3, 2006.

Reece, Erik. "Death of a Mountain." *Harper's*, April 2005.

Reece, Erik. "Moving Mountains: The Battle for Justice Comes to the Coalfields of Appalachia." *Orion*, January/February 2006.

Shnayerson, Michael. "The Rape of Appalachia," *Vanity Fair*, May 2006.

Sleight-Brennan, Sandra. "Appalachia's Vanishing Mountains." *Contemporary Review*, October 2002.

Vollers, Maryanne. "Razing Appalachia." *Mother Jones*, July/August 1999.

Ward, Ken. "Mountaintop Removal." *IRE Journal*, July/August 2001.

Ward, Jr., Ken. "Using Documents to Report on Mountaintop Mining." *Nieman Reports*, summer 2004.

Warren, Carol E. "Power Down in Solidarity With All Creation." *National Catholic Reporter*, February 12, 1999.

Williams, Scott. "Mine Wars." *Christian Century*, May 31, 2005.

Wood, Petra, Scott Bosworth, and Randy Dettmers. "Cerulean Warbler Abundance and Occurrence Relative to Large-Scale Edge and Habitat Characteristics." *Condor*, February 2006.

Movies

Black Diamonds, prod. and dir. Catherine Pancake, 90 min, Bullfrog Films, 2005.

Buffalo Creek Revisited, dir. Mimi Pickering, 31 min., Appalshop, 1984.

Coal Bucket Outlaw, dir. Tom Hansell, 26.40 min., Appalshop, 2002.

Razing Appalachia, dir. Sasha Waters, 54 min., Bullfrog Films, 2003.

Sludge, dir. Robert Salyers, Appalshop, 2005.

The Buffalo Creek Flood: An Act of Man, dir. Mimi Pickering, 40 min., Appalshop, 1975.

The Mountain Mourning Collection, http://www.christiansforthemountains.org/Titles_MountainMourning.htm.

Web sites

Appalachian Voices, http://www.appvoices.org, http://www.ilovemountains.org.

Christians for the Mountains, http://www.christiansforthemountains.org.

Coal River Mountain Watch, http://webpages.charter.net/crmw/.

Kentuckians for the Commonwealth, http://www.kftc.org.

Ohio Valley Environmental Coalition, http://www.ohvec.org.

Save Our Cumberland Mountains, http://www.socm.org.

Sierra Club, http://www.sierraclub.org.

SouthWings, http://www.southwings.org.

Tending the Commons: Folklife and Landscape in Southern West Virginia, http://memory.loc.gov/ammem/collections/tending/.

West Virginia Coalfield Communities, http://www.wvcoalfield.com.

West Virginia Highlands Conservancy, http://www.wvhighlands.org.

West Virginia Rivers Coalition, http://www.wvrivers.org.

APPENDIX ONE

An excerpt from John D. Rockefeller's
"Citizens to Abolish Surface Mining" Speech

(Text drawn from "Excerpts from a speech at Morris Harvey College, January 15, 1972," Strip-mining collection, A&M 2618, Box 1, ff1, West Virginia Collection, West Virginia University.)

Government has turned its back on the many West Virginians who have borne out of their own property and out of their own pocketbooks the destructive impact of stripping.

We hear that our Governor once claimed to have wept as he flew over the strip mine devastation of this state.

Now it's the people who weep.

They weep because of the devastation of our mountains, because of the disaster of giant high walls, acid-laden benches, and bare, precipitous outslopes which support no vegetation at all but erode thousands of tons of mud and rocks into the streams and rivers below.

Strip-mining must be abolished because of its effect on those who have given most to the cause—the many West Virginians who have suffered actual destruction of their homes; those who have put up with flooding, mud slides, cracked foundations, destruction of neighborhoods, decreases in property values, the loss of fishing and hunting, and the beauty of the hills.

And we are not alone in our feeling.

West Virginians love their hills. We identify ourselves with our hills, and are not about to let our hills be torn aside and demolished so that a small fraction of the coal beneath them can be taken away.

And we can make a difference.

But if we are to communicate as an abolition movement, we have to stretch ourselves further.

It's not enough just to be against strip-mining. In the emotion of seeing a newly-clobbered hill, it's easy to forget the largest justification for abolition. The strongest arguments, other than environmental ones, can be made for abolition on economic terms. And we have to manifest concern for new industries and jobs in West Virginia.

We are trying to affect the overall economic development of West Virginia, and we can show the linkage between abolition and long-term economic development.

The overwhelming percentage of our coal can only be obtained by deep mining. We know that. And we know that when the industry is cured of its binge of exploitation stripping, and returns to real mining, there will be more jobs for West Virginians—jobs that contribute to our prosperity without destroying the communities and counties in which they are located.

We can be a powerful force toward both halting the destruction of our state and also toward coming up with economically sound alternatives that will demonstrate best to all people that we have the long-term economic interests of the state at heart.

APPENDIX TWO

Coal Impoundments Found in the Nine
Southern Coalfield Counties of West Virginia

(Note: During the time that research was being done for this book, the coal-impoundment Web site listed slurry impoundments as low, medium, or high risk. At the time of this present study, that information had been omitted; no explanation was given for the omission. The original statements of low-, medium-, or high-risk level have been retained here, as they appeared during the original research.)

COUNTY	COAL COMPANY	DAM NAME	HEIGHT in feet	CAPACITY in gallons	DEP Class-ification	MSHA RISK LEVEL (Hazard Potential)
Boone	Elk Run Coal Company	Chess Processing Refuse Disposal Area No. 1	410	769 million	Class C	High
Boone	Jupiter Coal Company, Inc.	Pond Fork Slurry Impoundment	290	267.85 million	Class C	High
Boone	Eastern Associated Coal Corp	Rocklick Branch Refuse Impoundment	390	3.0174 billion	Class C	Moderate
Boone	Eastern Associated Coal Corp	Jarrells Branch Refuse Impoundment	385	2.2810 billion	Class C	Moderate
Boone	Pine Ridge Coal Company	Spruce Lick Refuse Impoundment	420	1.5618 billion	Class C	High

COUNTY	COAL COMPANY	DAM NAME	HEIGHT in feet	CAPACITY in gallons	DEP Class-ification	MSHA RISK LEVEL (Hazard Potential)
Boone	Omar Mining Company	Chesterfield Preparation Plant	500	2.9594 billion	Class C	High
Boone	Independence Coal Company	Elisa Fork Slurry Impoundment	800	769.01 million	Class C	Low
Boone	Eagle Energy, Inc.	Brown's Branch Slurry Impoundment	183	619,157,484	Class C	Low
Boone	Catenary Coal Company	Moccasin Hollow Slurry Impoundment	310	837,764,019	Class C	High
Boone	Hobet Mining, Inc.	Slippery Gut Slurry Impoundment	280	1,717,964,697	Class C	N/A
Boone	Jacks Branch Coal Company	Crooked Run Impoundment	350	2,769,334,331	Class C	N/A
Boone	Independence Coal Company	Jake Gore Slurry Impoundment	650	4.3664 billion	Class C	N/A
Boone	Wind River Resources Corp	Plant One Coal Refuse Disposal	270	670,971,189	N/A	Low
Boone	Pine Ridge Coal Company	Lotts Fork Refuse Impoundment	354	985,763,889	Class C	Low
Kanawha	Jacks Branch Coal Company	Dunn Hollow Coal Refuse Dam	400	1.2806 billion	Class C	High
Kanawha	Catenary Coal Company	Campbell's Creek Slurry Impoundment	360	545.5 million	Class C	Moderate
Kanawha	Kanawha Eagle, LLC	New West Hollow Impoundment	190	609.67 million	Class C	High
Logan	Hobet Mining, Inc.	Monclo Refuse Dam/ Impoundment	450	1.4119 billion	Class C	High

COUNTY	COAL COMPANY	DAM NAME	HEIGHT in feet	CAPACITY in gallons	DEP Class-ification	MSHA RISK LEVEL (Hazard Potential)
Logan	Coal-Mac, Inc Dba Phoenix Coal -Mac Mining, Inc.	Holden No. 22 Slurry Impoundment	330	912,251,308	Class C	Low
Logan	Island Creek Coal Company	Elk Creek No. 10 Slurry Impoundment	280	944,831,712	Class C	Low
Logan	Trace Creek Coal Company	Holden No. 29 Slurry Impoundment	320	793.12 million	Class C	High
Logan	Apogee Coal Company d/b/a Arch of WV	Little White Oak Slurry Impoundment	360	185,409,462	Class C	Low
Logan	Hobet Mining, Inc.	Pine Creek Slurry Impoundment	285	1.0264 billion	Class C	High
Logan	Stirrat Coal Company	Rockhouse Mitigation Pond	50	66,138,219	Class A	N/A
McDowell	Mid-Vol Leasing,Inc.	Harmon Branch Coal Refuse Disposal Facility	281	186.71 million	N/A	High
McDowell	Virginia Crews Coal Company	Lick Branch Slurry Impoundment	N/A	N/A	Class C	High
McDowell	Consolidation Coal Company	Amonate Slurry Dam	375	1.6130 billion	Class C	N/A
McDowell	Deepgreen West Virginia, Inc.	Pageton Preparation Plant	298	1,029,690,510	Class C	N/A
McDowell	Mineral Development Corporation	Grapevine Branch Impoundment Pond 1	430	490.08 million	Class C	Moderate

COUNTY	COAL COMPANY	DAM NAME	HEIGHT in feet	CAPACITY in gallons	DEP Class-ification	MSHA RISK LEVEL (Hazard Potential)
McDowell	West Virginia Properties, Inc.	Barrenshe Branch Fine Coal Refue Disposal Area	90	228,062,827	Class C	Low
McDowell	Mineral Development Corporation	Grapevine Branch Impoundment Pond 2	510	2.2441 billion	Class C	Moderate
McDowell	Cannelton Industries, Inc.	Elkhorn Creek Coal Refuse Dam	157	76.2 million	Class C	N/A
McDowell	Consolidation Coal Company	Dalton's Branch Coal Refuse Dam	305	20,062,162	Class C	N/A
McDowell	Second Sterling Corp.	Clark Branch Coal Refuse Dam	63	1,009,878,443	Class C	Moderate
Mingo	Mingo Logan Coal Company	Ben Creek Slurry Impoundment	390	5.2038 billion	Class C	High
Mingo	Coal-Mac, Inc Dba Phoenix Coal -Mac Mining, Inc.	Ragland Coal Refuse Impoundment	345	4.7411 billion	Class C	Moderate
Mingo	LCC West Virginia, LLC	Millseat Refuse	215	N/A	Class C	N/A
Mingo	Southern West Virginia Resources, LLC	Aldrich Branch Coal Refuse Impoundment	270	4,294,097,233	N/A	Low
Mingo	None Listed	Delbarton Impoundment	1520	3,250,689,576	Class C	N/A
Mingo	None Listed	Left Fork Impoundment	Not listed	N/A	N/A	N/A
Mingo	Mingo Logan Coal Company	Ben Creek #1 Freshwater Impoundment	41	29,326,628	Class C	N/A

COUNTY	COAL COMPANY	DAM NAME	HEIGHT in feet	CAPACITY in gallons	DEP Class- ification	MSHA RISK LEVEL (Hazard Potential)
Mingo	Greyeagle Coal Comp (Kermit Coal Comp)	Left Fork Coal Refuse Impoundment	121	336,278,673	N/A	N/A
Mingo	Rawl Sales and Processing, Co.	Sprouse Creek Slurry Impoundment	625	4.0080 billion	Class C	Low
Mingo	Laurel Creek Company, Inc.	Twelvepole Refuse Impoundment	211	716.87 million	N/A	N/A
Mingo	Southern West Virginia Resources, LLC	Spruce Fork Coal Refuse Impoundment	145	14.7 million	N/A	N/A
Nicholas	Gauley Eagle Holdings, Inc.	Crooked Run Coal Refuse Dam	100	848.51 million	Class C	High
Nicholas	Peerless Eagle Coal Comp.	Rockcamp Branch #2 Refuse Dam	Not listed	N/A	N/A	N/A
Raleigh	Marfork Coal Company	Brushy Fork Coal Impoundment	900	8,178,870,823	Class C	High
Raleigh	Left Fork Processing, LLC	Killarney Refuse Area Impoundment	645	1.3353 billion	Class C	High
Raleigh	Performance Coal Company	Shumate Coal Refuse Disposal Facility	385	2.8316 billion	Class C	N/A
Raleigh	Performance Coal Company	Lower Big Branch	Not listed	19,551,086	N/A	Moderate
Raleigh	Clear Fork Coal Company	Performance Coal Company	380	1,055,758,624	Class C	N/A
Raleigh	Clear Fork Coal Company	McGraw Fork Coal Refuse Dam	155	1.63 million	Class C	N/A

COUNTY	COAL COMPANY	DAM NAME	HEIGHT in feet	CAPACITY in gallons	DEP Class- ification	MSHA RISK LEVEL (Hazard Potential)
Wyoming	Kepler Processing Company, Inc.	Wallace Cabin Branch	388	995.15 million	Class C	Moderate
Wyoming	Dynamic Energy	Coal Mountain No. 9-B Slurry Impoundment	400	925,283,470	Class C	N/A
Wyoming	Eastern Associated Coal Corp	Upper Mill Branch Impoundment	810	1,724,079,901	Class C	Low
Wyoming	Pinnacle Mining Comp, LLC	Smith Branch Refuse Facility	485	4.4808 billion	Class C	Low
Wyoming	Consolidation Coal Company	Itmann Preparation Plant	344	2.0887 billion	Class C	High

APPENDIX THREE

Coal-slurry Spill Information for the Nine

Southern Coalfield Counties of West Virginia

COUNTY	COAL COMPANY	YEAR OF SPILL	SPILL VOLUME (gallons)	TOWN
Boone	Island Creek Coal Company	1977	2,200,000	Bob White
Boone	Ashland Coal	1997	1,000	Julian
Boone	Ashland Coal	1997	1,000,000	Julian
Boone	Massey Energy Coal Company	1999	1,500	Sylvester
Boone	Massey Energy Coal Company	1999	2,200	Sylvester
Boone	Massey Energy Coal Company	2001	30,000	Uneeda
Boone	Massey Energy Coal Company	2001	not listed	Quinland
Boone	Massey Energy Coal Company	2001	15,000	Madison
Boone	Massey Energy Coal Company	2001	not listed	Quinland
Boone	Massey Energy Coal Company	2002	not listed	Quinland
Boone	Arch Coal	2002	25,000	Julian
Boone	Massey Energy Coal Company	2003	not listed	Uneeda
Boone	Massey Energy Coal Company	2003	250,000	Prenter
Boone	Massey Energy Coal Company	2003	250,000	Uneeda
Logan	Pittston Coal Company	1972	132,000,000	Lorado
Logan	Belva Coal Company	1981	not listed	Earling
Logan	Massey Energy Coal Company	2001	50,000	Dehue

COUNTY	COAL COMPANY	YEAR OF SPILL	SPILL VOLUME (gallons)	TOWN
Logan	Massey Energy Coal Company	2002	100,000	Dehue
Logan	Massey Energy Coal Company	2003	27,000	Dehue
Logan	Falcon Land Co.	2003	not listed	Omar
Logan	Falcon Land Co.	2003	not listed	Omar
McDowell	Abandoned Mine Land	2002	10,000,000	Wilcoe
Mingo	Massey Energy Coal Company	2002	20,000	Delbarton
Mingo	Abandoned Mine Land	2003	not listed	Sprattsville
Nicholas	Lady H. Coal Company	1995	not listed	Green Valley
Nicholas	Massey Energy Coal Company	2003	1,000	Summersville
Raleigh	Philpot Coal Corp.	1980	168,000	not listed
Raleigh	Peabody Coal Company	1987	23,000,000	Montcoal
Raleigh	Massey Energy Coal Company	1999	not listed	Sundial
Raleigh	White Mountain Mining Co., LLC	2003	not listed	Rhodell

INDEX

SHIRLEY STEWART BURNS holds a B.S. in news-editorial journalism, a master's degree in social work, and a Ph.D. in history with an Appalachian focus, from West Virginia University. A native of Wyoming County in the southern West Virginia coalfields and the daughter of an underground coal miner, she has a passionate interest in the communities, environment, and histories of the southern West Virginia coalfields. Shirley Stewart Burns lives in Charleston, West Virginia.